IMAGES
of America

CLARKE COUNTY

IMAGES
of America

CLARKE COUNTY

Joyce White Burrage

ARCADIA
PUBLISHING

Copyright © 1998 by Joyce White Burrage
ISBN 978-0-7385-6871-3

Published by Arcadia Publishing
Charleston, South Carolina

Printed in the United States of America

Library of Congress Catalog Card Number: 98-88055

For all general information contact Arcadia Publishing at:
Telephone 843-853-2070
Fax 843-853-0044
E-mail sales@arcadiapublishing.com
For customer service and orders:
Toll-Free 1-888-313-2665

Visit us on the Internet at www.arcadiapublishing.com

Contents

Acknowledgments

A project like Clarke County would have been impossible to complete without the cooperation of the people of Clarke County who were so generous and helpful in sharing their collections of photographs which appear within these pages.

The author's sincere appreciation is extended to every person who was willing to lend materials and share their knowledge of Clarke County's history. It would be impossible to name all the individuals who contributed to this project, since most of the photographs came from the private sector.

Much appreciation is extended to the Clarke County Historical Museum for lending photographs from the Mary Tucker Collection and the Minnie Mae Pugh Collection.

To Elizabeth Jackson, Laverne Mott, and Jim Cox, a special thanks for the guidance and expertise to ensure a successful project.

INTRODUCTION

Nestled between the Alabama and the Tombigbee Rivers, in a quaint, rural section of south Alabama lies the county of Clarke. Its history is told through struggles, triumphs, and the eventual settling of pioneers, mostly from the Carolinas, Georgia, Tennessee, and Virginia. The Scotch-Irish influence is still felt in the county's temperament, its language, and its lifestyle. A sense of place, where one lives side by side with nature, finding a peace uncommon and unfamiliar to the rest of the world, can be felt in Clarke County. A proud people live, even as our forefathers lived, the kind of life that is an offspring of the rich, historical tapestry of events, which has unfolded over the last 200 years, beginning even before the county of Clarke was formed on December 10, 1812, by the legislature of the Mississippi Territory.

Clarke County was one of seven counties in existence before Alabama was even a territory. The county, named for General John Clarke of North Carolina and Georgia, had a troubled and violent early history due to the Native American uprisings, which were an indirect result of the War of 1812. According to Pickett, an early Alabama historian, "Everything foreboded the extermination of the Americans in Alabama, who were the most isolated and defenseless people imaginable." The Native American tribes were encouraged by the British and the Spanish to perform acts of hostility against the settlers. The bloodshed during the year of 1813 came to an end when Andrew Jackson defeated the Red Sticks on March 27, 1814, and brought to a close the Native American strife in South Alabama, in the Battle of Horseshoe Bend on the Tallapoosa River.

Following the Creek War, the Native American lands were opened to settlers who flooded what would become Alabama. In Clarke County, the larger settlements were "on Bassetts' Creek, around Magoffin's Store, south of Suggsville, near Pine Level, on Jackson's Creek, and at West Bend and Coffeeville," between 1812 and 1817.

Greenlee had the first store at the mouth of Cedar Creek. Other firsts included a gristmill, near Suggsville, built by John Slater, probably in 1812. Jonathan Emmons had the first cotton gin, on Smith's Creek, south of Suggsville. Robert Hayden had one of the first tanneries and the first shoe factory, about 3 miles south of Suggsville, in 1815. Robert Caller had a mill and a gin where "an iron screw for packing cotton by hand or by horsepower, was used as early as 1816," according to T.H. Ball's account, in *Clarke County, Alabama*, a history of Clarke County published in 1879.

The town of Jackson was incorporated in 1816, Coffeeville in 1819, and Claiborne in 1820. The Alabama Territory was organized in 1817, consisting of seven counties, which included

Clarke. Then on December 14, 1819, Alabama became a state. In 1818, Clarkesville was designated as the county seat. The first courthouse and jail were located here. Due to lack of a good water supply, the county seat was moved to Grove Hill, then called Macon (or Smithville) in 1832. The first courthouse was built in Macon that same year. In the 1850s, the name Grove Hill was chosen for the county seat. By 1824, three areas were becoming principal neighborhoods. In the upper part of the county, Loftin or Bashi; in the central portion, Magoffin (near Grove Hill); and in the lower part of the county, Fort Madison.

According to tradition, no village existed where Grove Hill is now until about 1830, when a trading post and a blacksmith shop were reported to have been located there. Magoffin's Store was located about 2 miles north of this area. By 1850, the Native Americans, Mexicans, and British were quiet. The United States had respect all over the world. Clarke County enjoyed many years of peace and plenty. Educational needs were being met for the affluent. Churches were growing and new ones being organized. In 1853, a yellow fever epidemic caused all business to cease in and around Grove Hill, due to the deaths of so many. Choctaw Corner was flourishing, and Carlton and Slade and Lycurgus Poole had houses of business, ordering clothing apparel from New York. The principal centers for education were Choctaw Corner, Suggsville, and Grove Hill.

Isaac Grant began the publication called the *Clarke County Democrat*, a weekly newspaper, in 1856. By 1857, free public schools were open. To round out the decade, by 1860, "Cotton was King." The motto, "no cotton, no credit," became the cry from the world of mercantilism. The farmers planted cotton to have credit and receive cash for the crop. In turn, the money was paid to the merchant for goods received on credit during the year, a flawed system, which spelled doom for many farmers. Trouble on the national front was brewing. Talk of war loomed heavy over Clarke County. In 1861, Alabama seceded from the Union, and Clarke began to unite for the Cause. Taking Southerners by surprise, the war lasted five years or more, and the aftermath of this great civil strife was almost worse than the war itself in many respects.

Surviving the loss of men to the Civil War and pulling through Reconstruction left the county to once again unite and continue with their way of life by farming and raising cotton. By the end of the 1890s, Thomasville was well underway as a growing town on the railroad, just recently completed from Birmingham to Mobile. The railroad brought progress, communication, and transportation. The railroad systems, used by Scotch Lumber Company and Zimmerman Manufacturing Company, opened up the county to jobs where men earned cash money for a day's work. The agrarian way of life for everyone would never return to Clarke County again. The timber industry, the heart of Clarke County's economy today, was here to stay. Rural areas were afforded a large array of goods which they had never had access to before, when the lumber companies set up commissaries near the lumber camps. The railroad network, which stretched for miles from the lumber mills in Fulton and Jackson, served the communities and the mills as well. The empty trains, returning to the woods, brought large objects such as furniture, caskets, etc. to the families in the country. A telephone system was even in place from the camps to the mill sites, where these large commissaries were located. The Great Depression stopped the lumber industry briefly. But, gradually, the timber business began again.

Over the next decades transportation improved, and cars were becoming more plentiful and private trips in one's own vehicle became a reality. The gap between country and town was closing rapidly. Schools in the country were consolidated and country children were taken to the bigger schools in town. Travel outside the county became popular, and highways were being built to form a network over the state. Jobs became more plentiful and industry located in the county provided even women a place to earn a salary. By the late 1940s, most of the rural areas had electricity, thus improving the quality of life.

Through all the changes, Clarke County has kept its identity. The people have kept a sense of integrity and worth that seems absent from society as a whole today. Looking forward to the 21st century, Clarke County will march at a steady pace, hopefully, holding on to the values learned from our ancestors, whose contributions we must never forget.

One

Open for Business
The County Seat

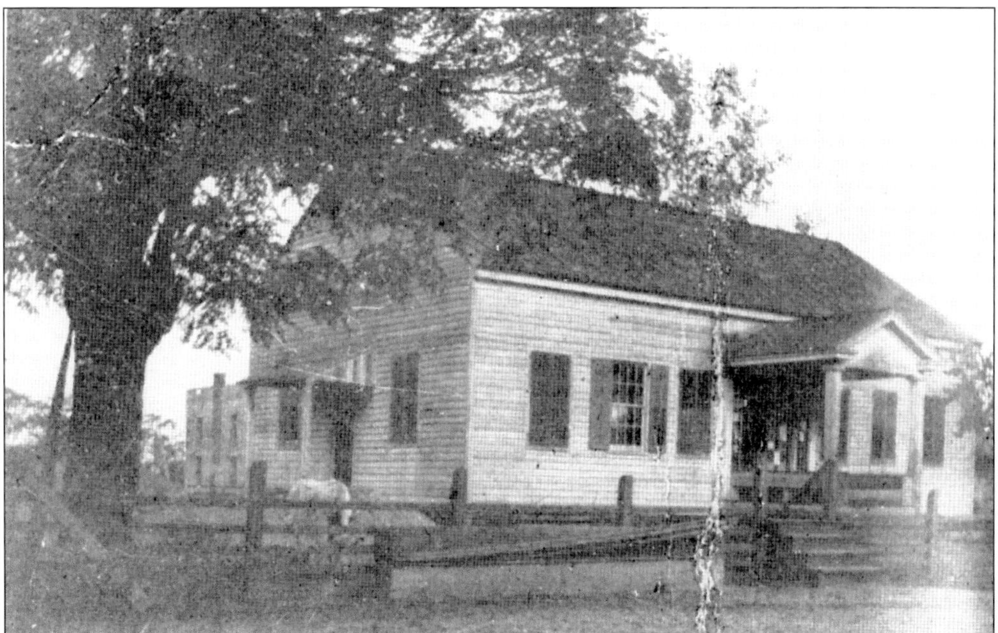

The first Clarke County courthouse was built in Grove Hill when the county seat was moved in 1832 from Clarkesville to Smithville, which was also known as Macon. The immediate area around the courthouse was referred to by both names until about 1850, when the post office moved closer to the courthouse. However, the name Grove Hill was given to the post office in 1828, when it was located 2 miles north of the present town. It had been established in 1820 and was then called Post Oak Level. This photograph supposedly was made by a Universalist preacher, Rev. Q.H. Shinn, in 1898, a year before the courthouse was torn down.

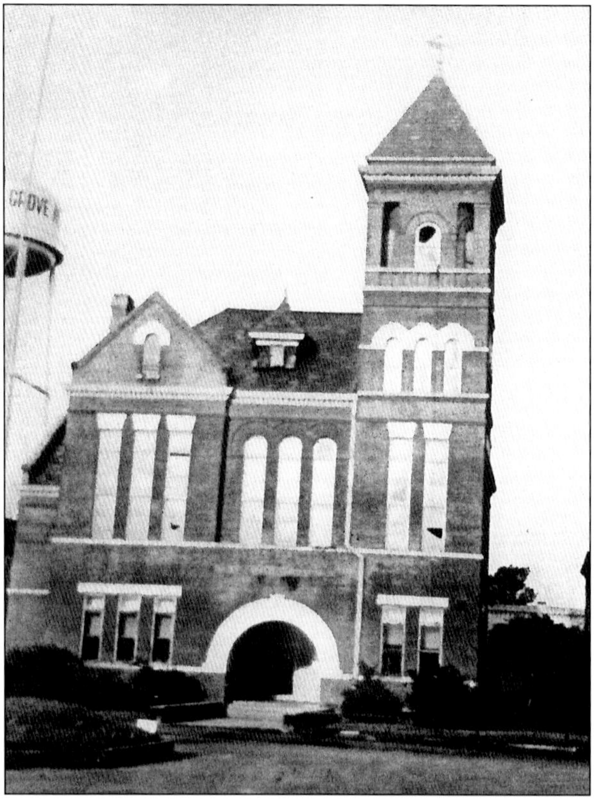

The second courthouse, built in 1899, stood where the present building is today. It replaced the wooden structure built in 1832, when Grove Hill became the county seat. The *Clarke County Democrat* noted the completion of the building in its November 23, 1899 edition, stating that "all rooms could be kept comfortable with fireplaces and stoves." This structure was torn down in 1955, when the present courthouse was built.

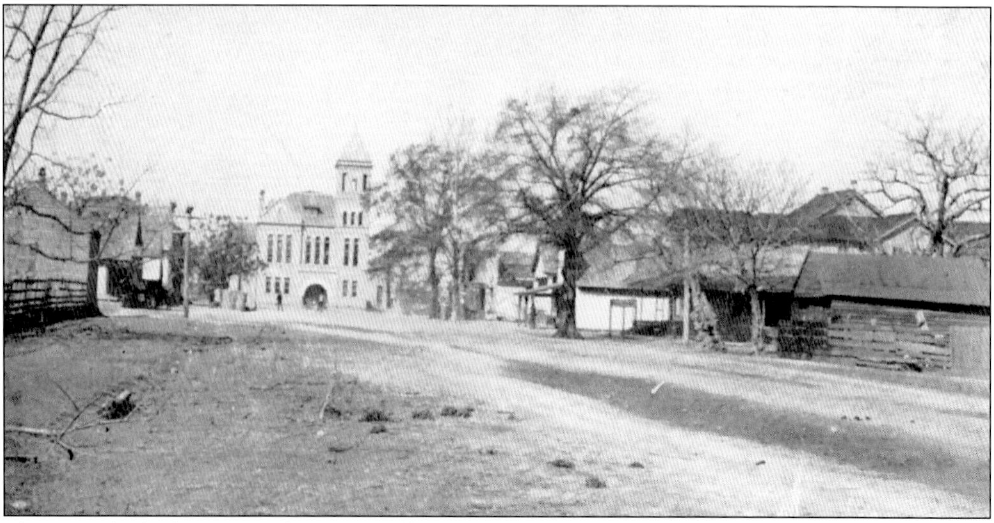

Photographed after 1899, this view still bears some resemblance to Main Street today. On the right is a blacksmith shop, the Wells-Morrow-Leggitte Hotel, Cobb Drug Store, Pugh Brothers Store, originally known as the W.L. Mitchell Store, and the W.W. Daffin Store. Farther down on the right is J.W. Cunningham's Store, known later as S.C. Gordon and Company, and a vacant lot which completes this side. On the left is Plez Rivers's Barber Shop, across the street on the corner, followed by the post office, a millinery, John S. Chapman's store, and the Cunningham Hotel.

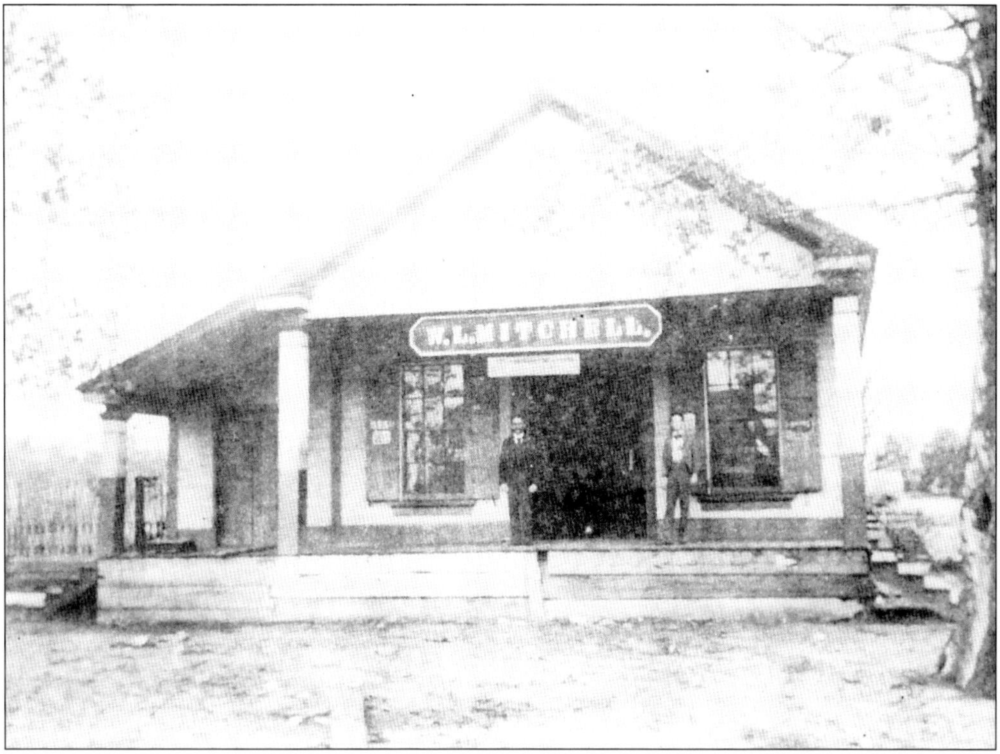

W.L. Mitchell's store became the Pugh Brothers Store, located next to the Cobb Drugstore (later the Newton Grocery). W.L. Mitchell is shown on the left and his nephew, Frank Bonner, is on the right.

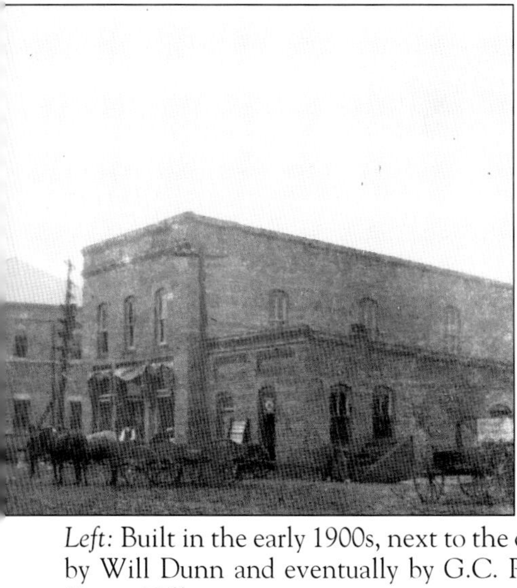

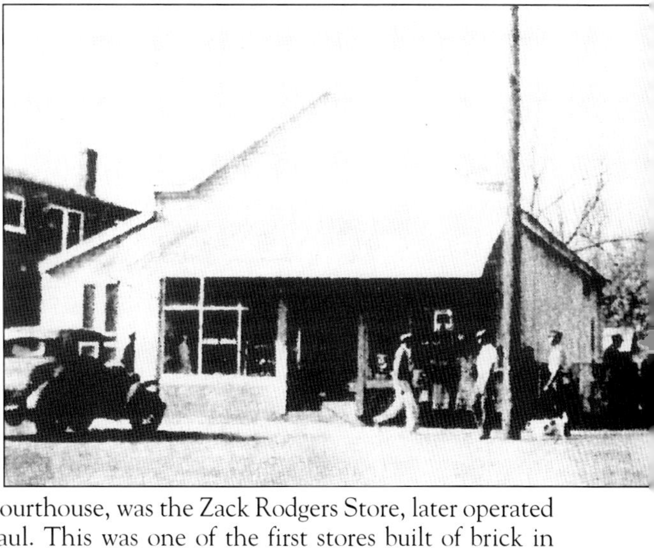

Left: Built in the early 1900s, next to the courthouse, was the Zack Rodgers Store, later operated by Will Dunn and eventually by G.C. Paul. This was one of the first stores built of brick in Grove Hill.
Right: The Pugh Brothers Store, owned by Jesse P. and Isaac Pugh, is seen here as it looked in the 1920s.

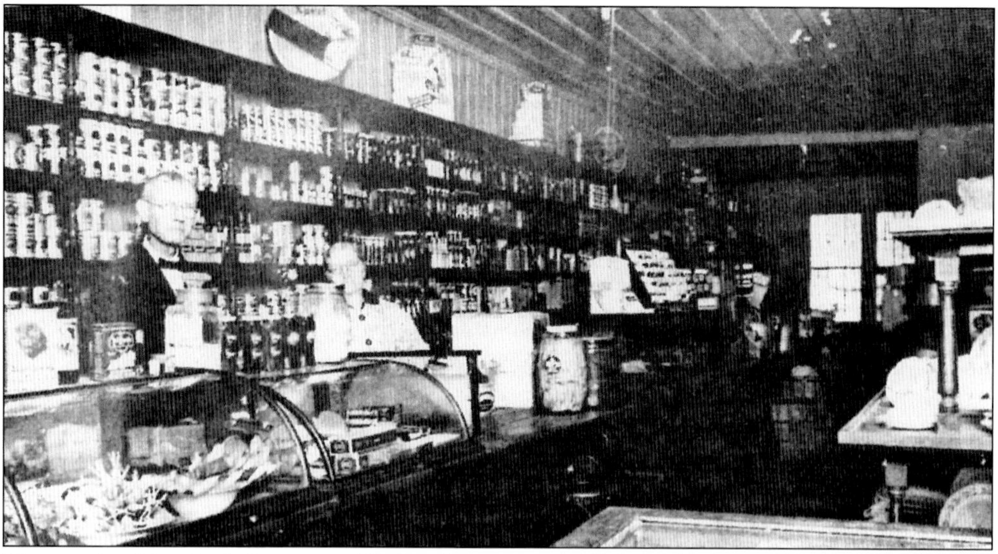

The inside of the Pugh Store was filled with groceries, candy, and even china. A spool of string hung from the ceiling for securing packages wrapped in paper, before paper bags came into use. Mr. and Mrs. Jesse Pugh served Grove Hill for over 45 years at this location.

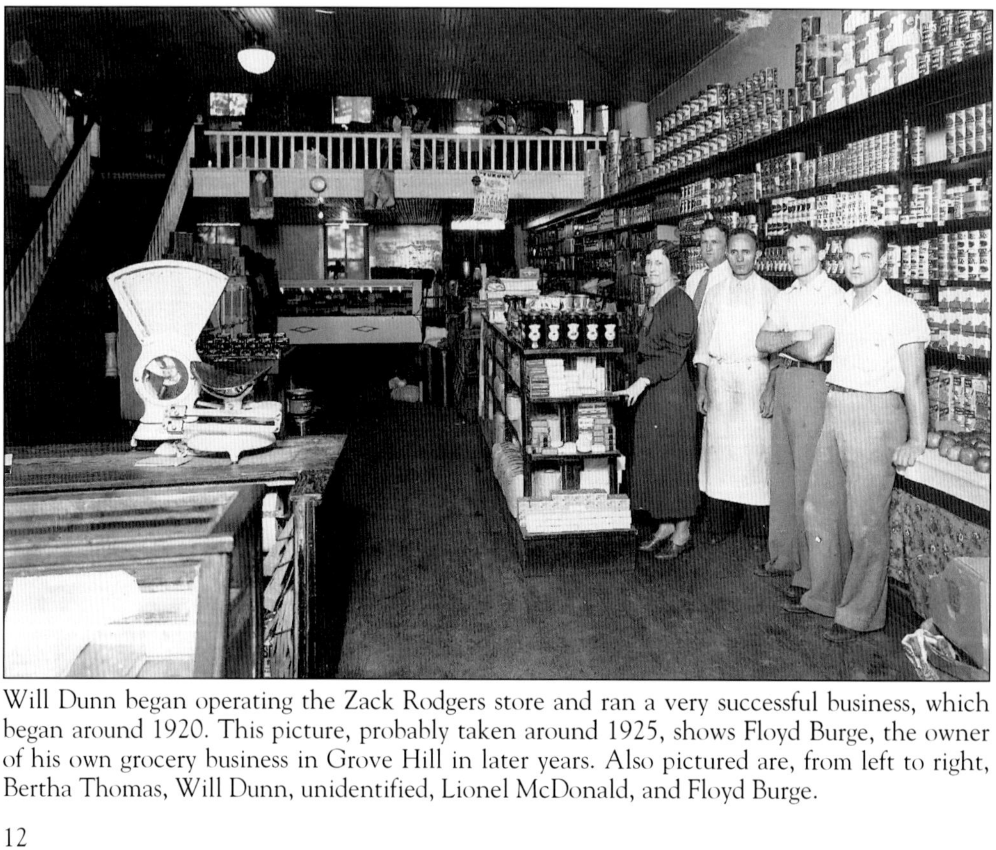

Will Dunn began operating the Zack Rodgers store and ran a very successful business, which began around 1920. This picture, probably taken around 1925, shows Floyd Burge, the owner of his own grocery business in Grove Hill in later years. Also pictured are, from left to right, Bertha Thomas, Will Dunn, unidentified, Lionel McDonald, and Floyd Burge.

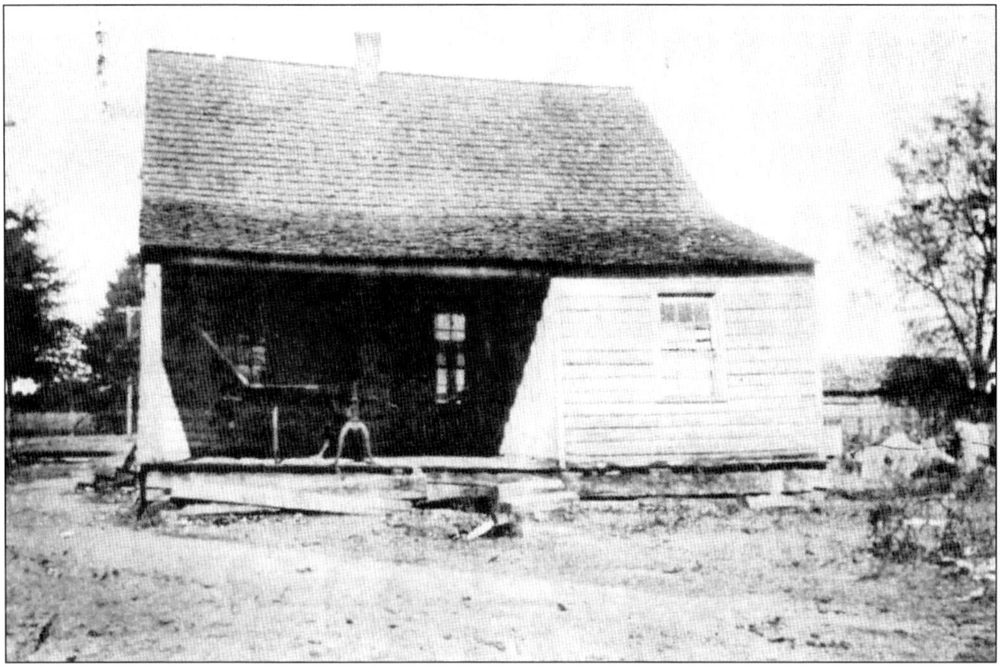

The *Clarke County Democrat*, the oldest business in Clarke County, has been in operation since 1856, when it occupied the building of a former saloon located across from the courthouse.

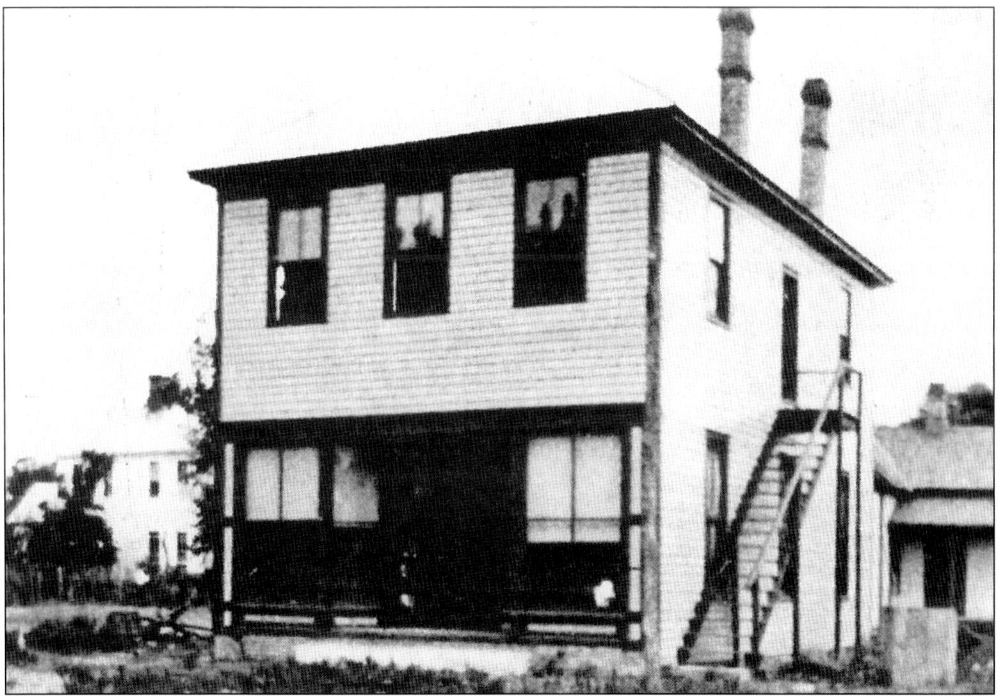

A two-story building was constructed in 1912 for the newspaper. Finally, a brick building was erected in 1941. In 1992, the editor and owner of the newspaper, Jim Cox, moved the business to Highway 43 to its fourth building, but only the second location of the weekly newspaper.

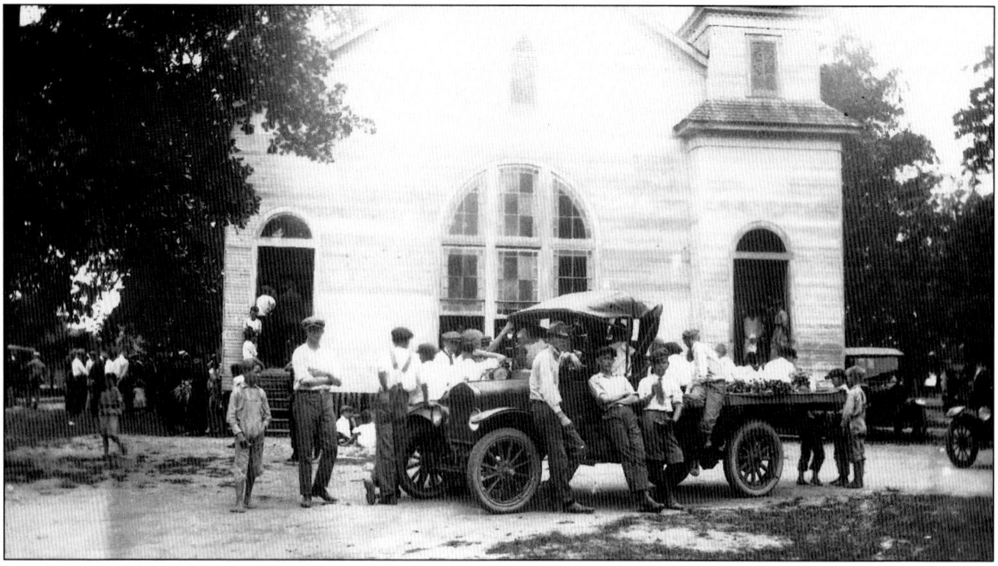

In this rare photograph, possibly the only one of the first Grove Hill Baptist Church, funeral flowers are visible on the truck in front of the building, which was nestled in a grove of oak trees—from which Grove Hill received its name. This church, begun in 1861, sat just out from the Graham Waite home and faced north. The funeral in progress is for John D. Lavender, a soldier killed in World War I. The photograph is dated around 1918.

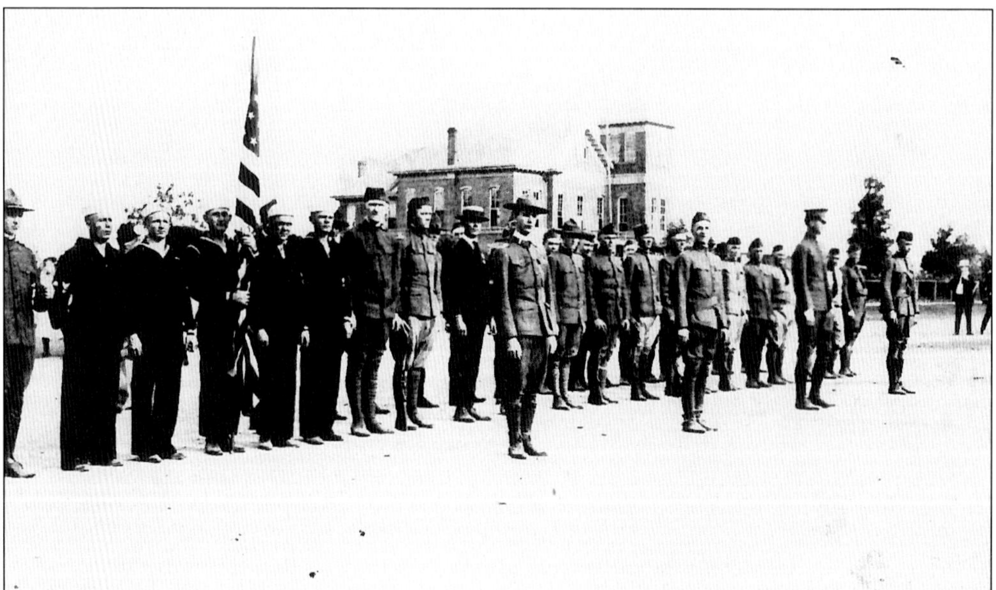

Clarke County High School can be seen towering over the military funeral for John D. Lavender about 1918. This photograph is part of the Mary Tucker Collection.

In the early 1900s, Dr. Tollie Pugh took his Holsman, the second car owned in Clarke County, for a spin down Main Street in Grove Hill. When purchased in 1907, the car was reported to be the only one in Grove Hill. The Holsman was manufactured in Chicago. The car was most likely made between 1903 and 1909 since it appears to have been pulled by a rope or cable, a mechanism similar to the one which propels a bicycle. Some early cars were pulled by a chain. The buggy wheels, made of solid rubber, were large and gave the appearance of a wagon. It had no radiator and was air cooled. The first car was owned by Carlie Stewart, then of Zimco.

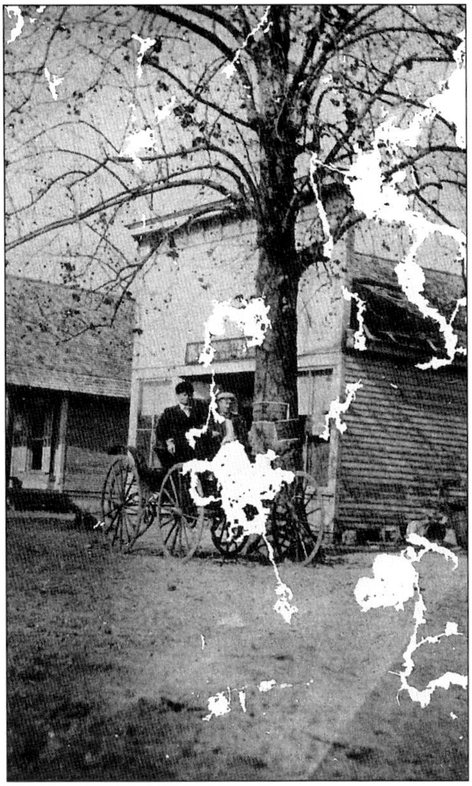

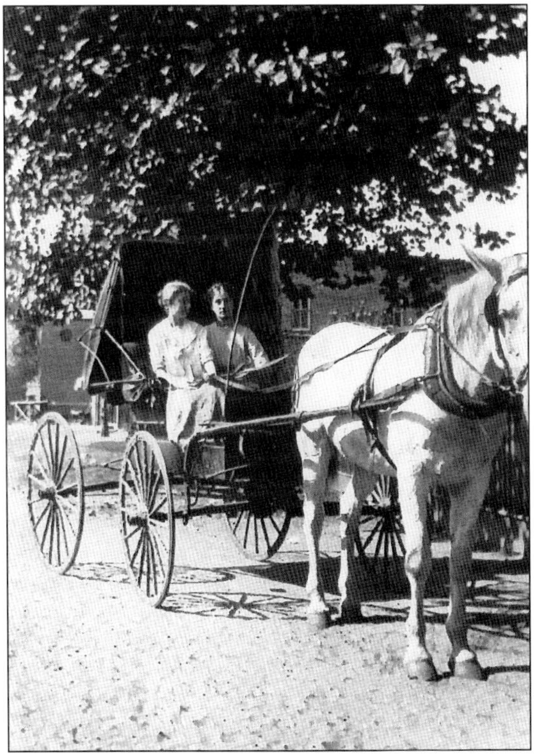

It was not uncommon to see young ladies in a buggy out for a ride on the dirt streets in 1910. The young women seen here are Kathleen Rodgers (left) and her sister, Bardee, in front of the Rodgers home, with their father's business, the Zack Rodgers store, in the background.

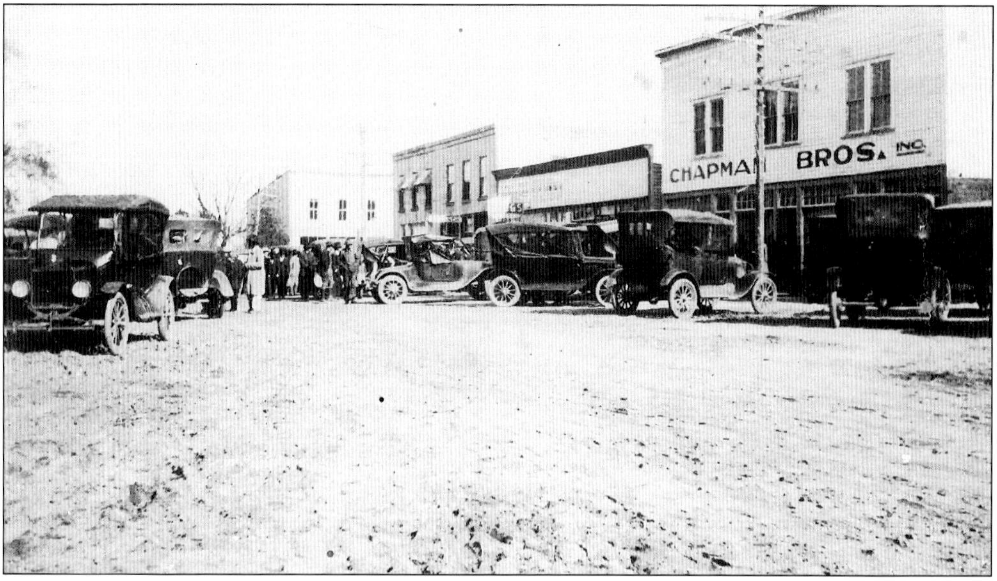

This gathering in Grove Hill was on March 31, 1923, when W.D. Dunn Drug Company gave away a new Model T Ford car. After a long, well-publicized promotion, the winner was selected. Billie Morton of Jackson was the new owner of the free car. Dunn Drugs was located next to Chapman Bros. (later Cowdens).

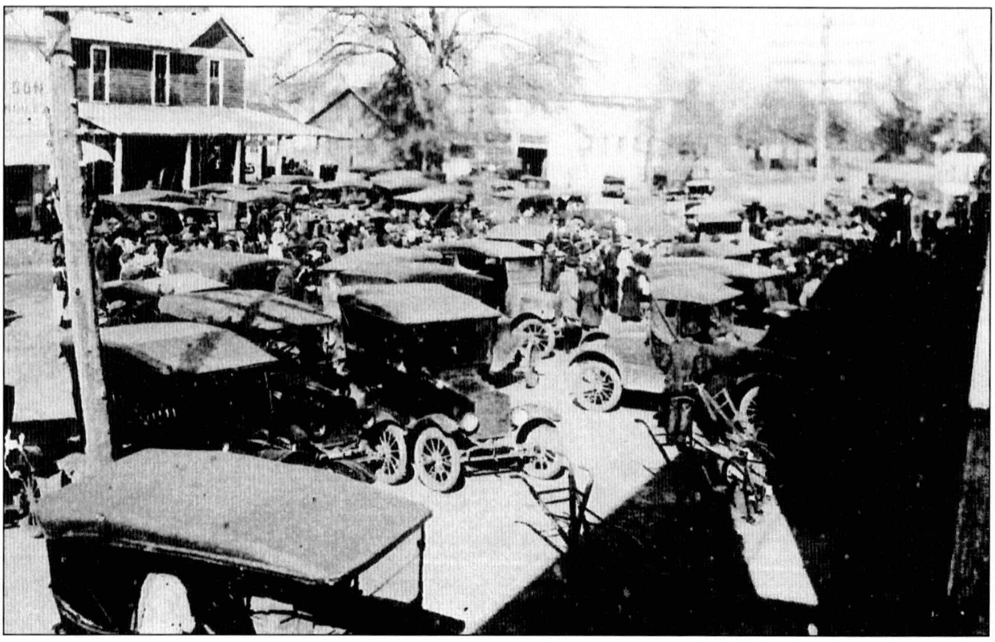

Giving away a new car in 1923 caused a traffic jam that makes modern traffic snarls seem mild. Note in the photograph the Wells-Morrow Leggitte Hotel on the corner in the background. The plow stocks on the sidewalk are in front of Chapman Bros. Hardware.

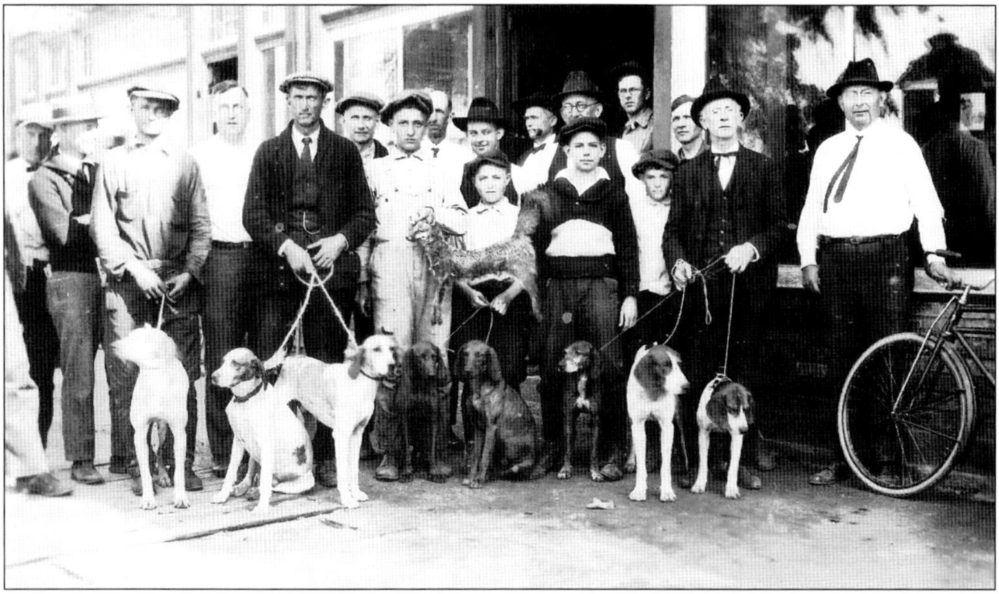

After a successful fox hunt in 1908, these Grove Hill men proudly display the fox as they gather in front of Chapman's store. Some of the persons identified are Clarence Thompkins, George Carlton, Will Dunn, Dr. Clim Pugh, Zack Rodgers, and Harold Carter (boy).

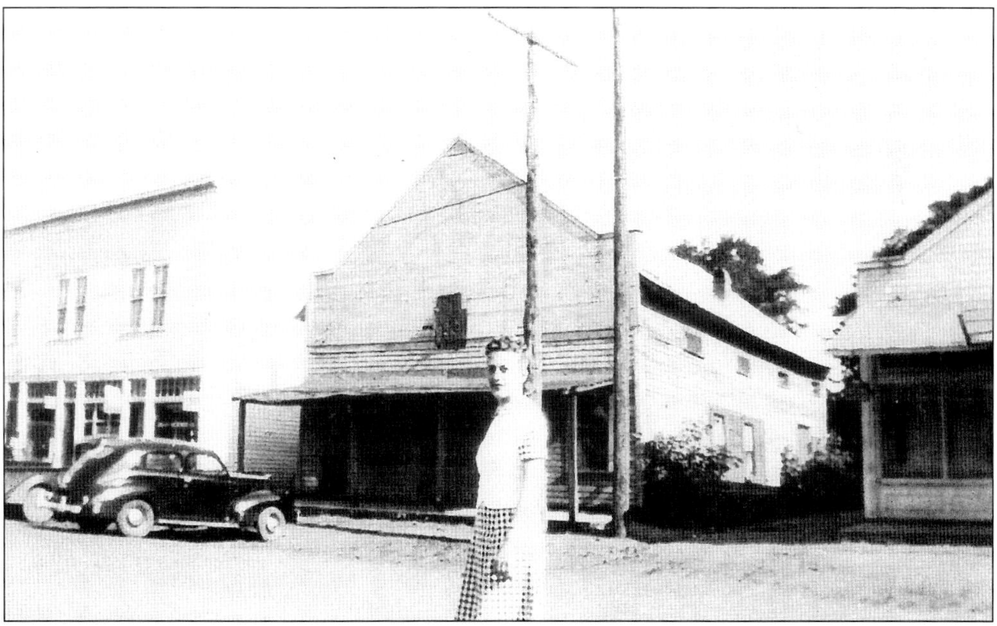

On the left is John Chapman's hardware store, in the middle is the theater run at one time by Vaughn Chapman, and on the right is Ed Burge's store, where the IGA is today. The theater had benches for seating, a player-piano, which everyone wanted to play during the movie (pumping with their feet), and a silent projector which was cranked by hand. Silent films were shown here in about 1919.

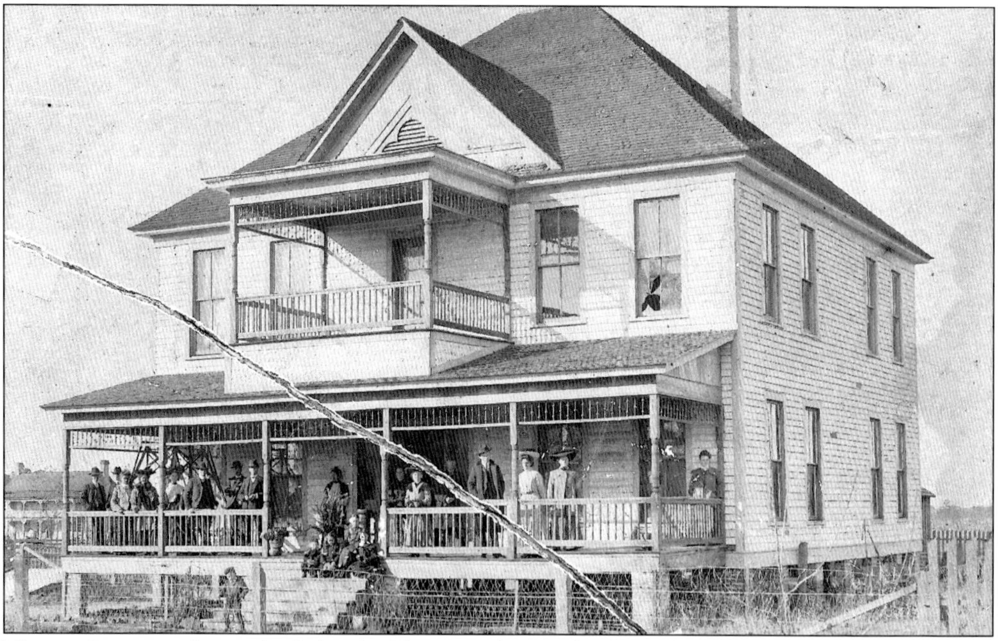

This early scene shows the John S. Chapman house, built in the early 1900s, in Grove Hill, between where the post office and the Cecil Chapman house are located today, facing south. In the distant area to the left of the house, the Alston-Cobb house (the present Clarke County Historical Museum) can be seen. In later years, "Miss Sallie," the wife of John S. Chapman, took in boarders. Folklore has it that she was in friendly competition with Mrs. Coate, her very best friend, who also took in boarders and lived where the Exxon station is today. Schoolteachers and others boarded in many houses in town.

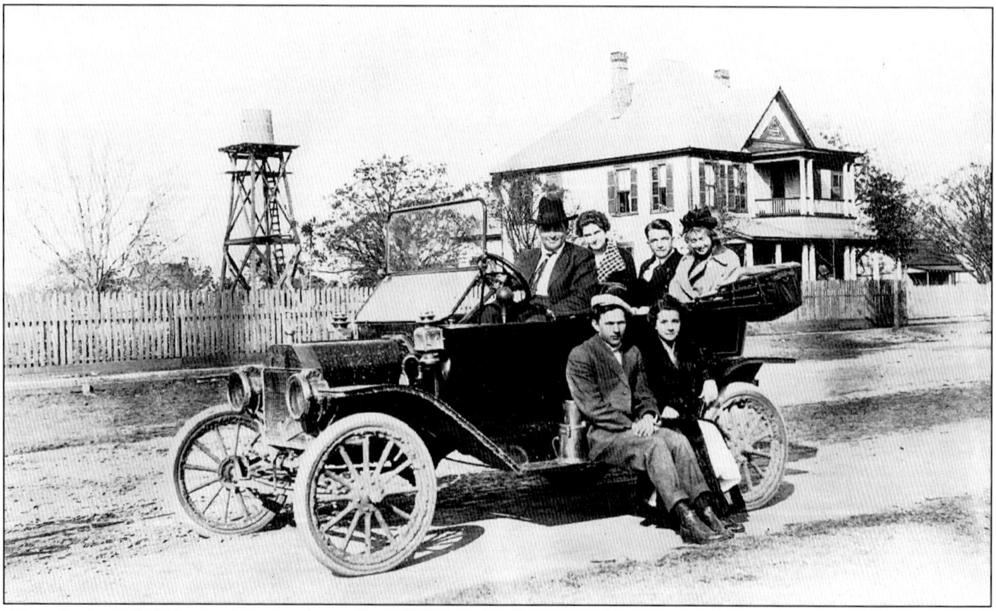

The driver of the car, Howard Hollingsworth, has stopped in front of the Chapman house with Hattie Belle Bush Chapman (wearing the hat) in the back seat with friends. J.C. Godbold, a doctor from Whatley, is seated on the running board with Ella Williamson Coleman.

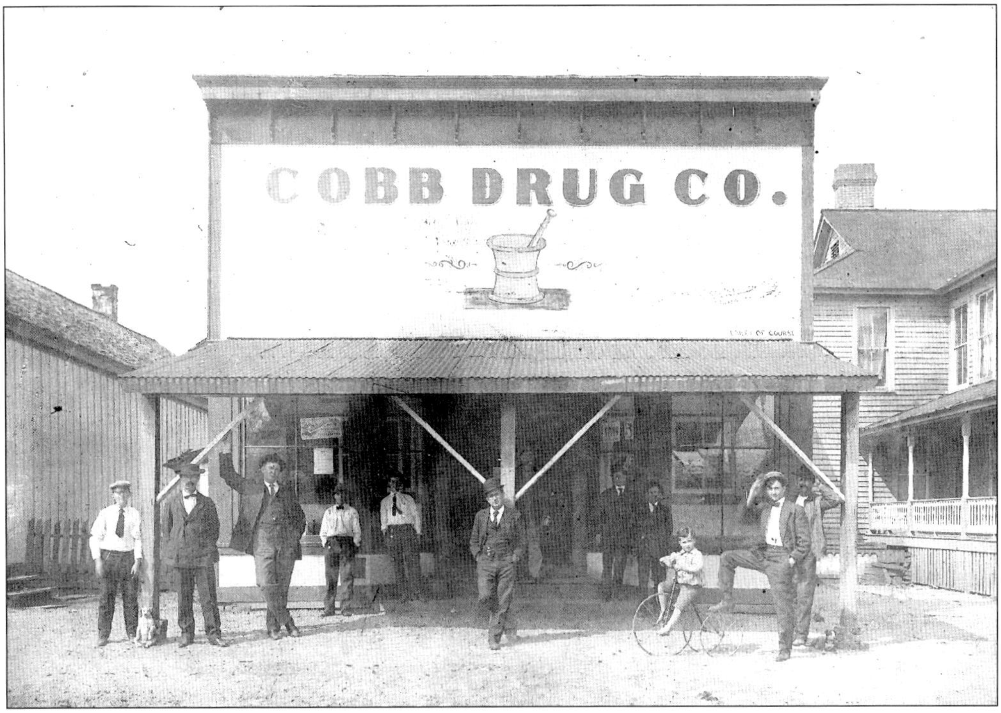

Cobb Drug Company, owned by Dr. Jesse M. Cobb, is possibly the first drugstore in Grove Hill. The building is still standing today and has housed many businesses over its long history. It probably is best known as the Ocie Newton Grocery.

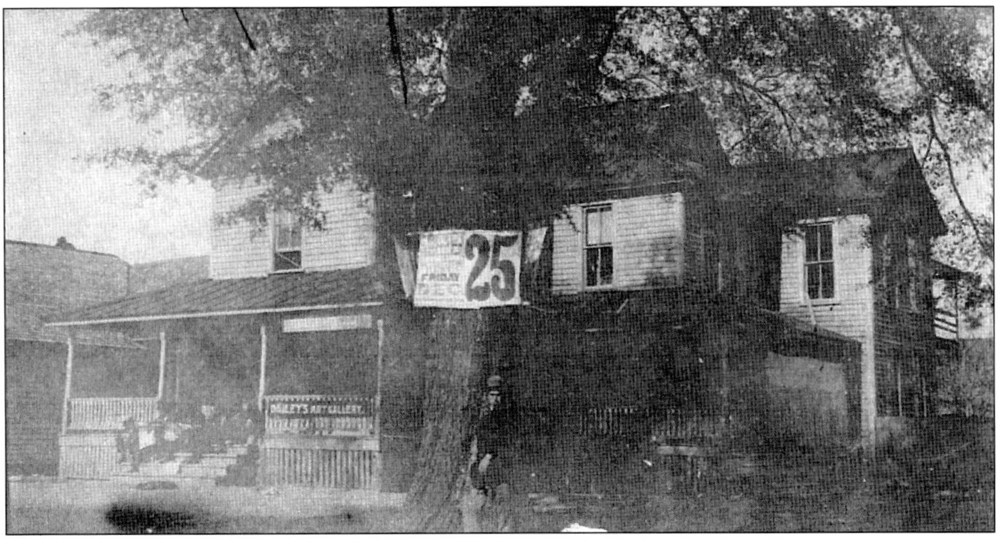

This picture of the Wells (later the Morrow and the Leggitte) Hotel was taken in December of 1908. It stood on the corner of Main and Jackson Streets and was built by Mr. T.W. Wells. John Morrow was an early photographer and had a studio there in the late 1890s. The advertisement on the oak tree is for the same circus being advertised in the next picture. On the front porch, facing Main Street (next to Cobb Drug Co.), is a sign advertising Dailey's Art Gallery, which was also located in the hotel.

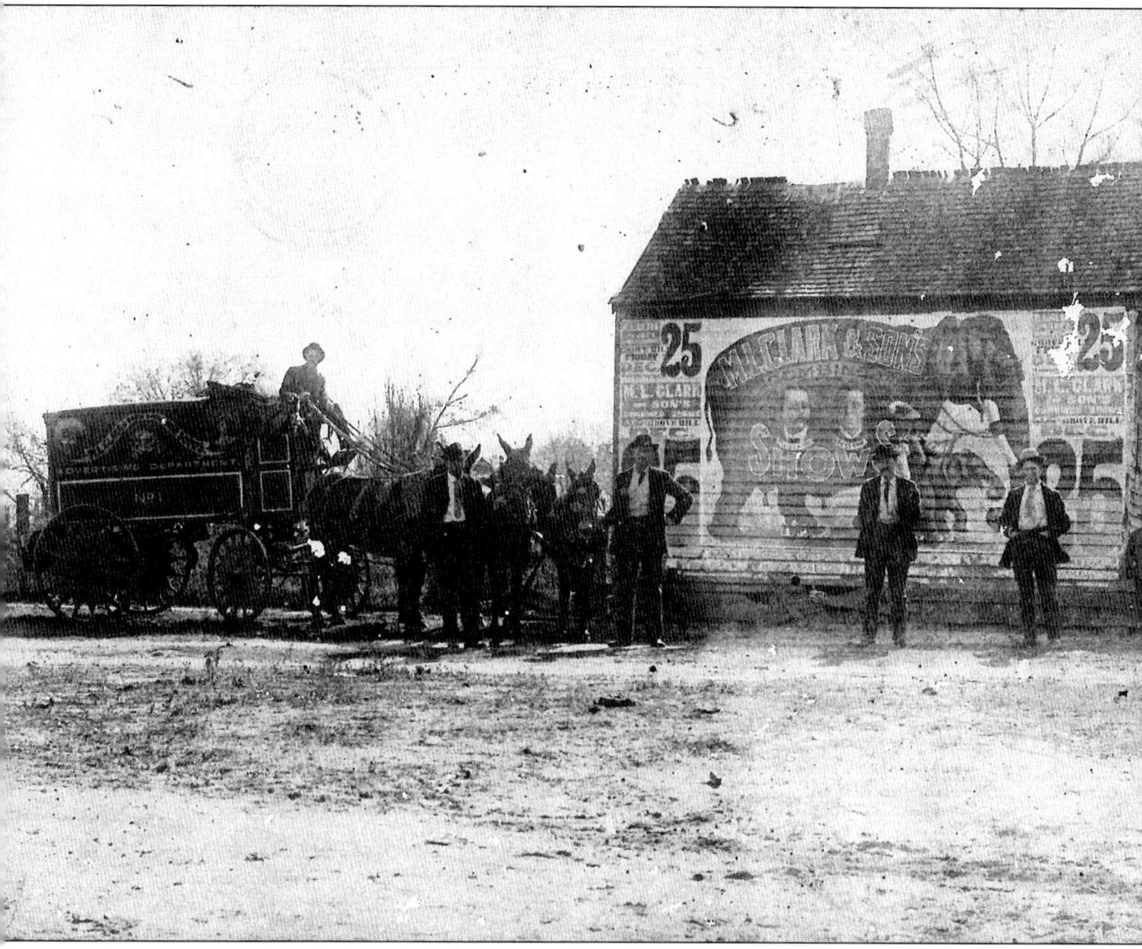

As entertaining for adults as for kids, the circus coming to town warranted an advertising wagon arriving a week or so ahead of the play-date to spread the word. Friday, December 25, was the date—some Christmas present for a small town!

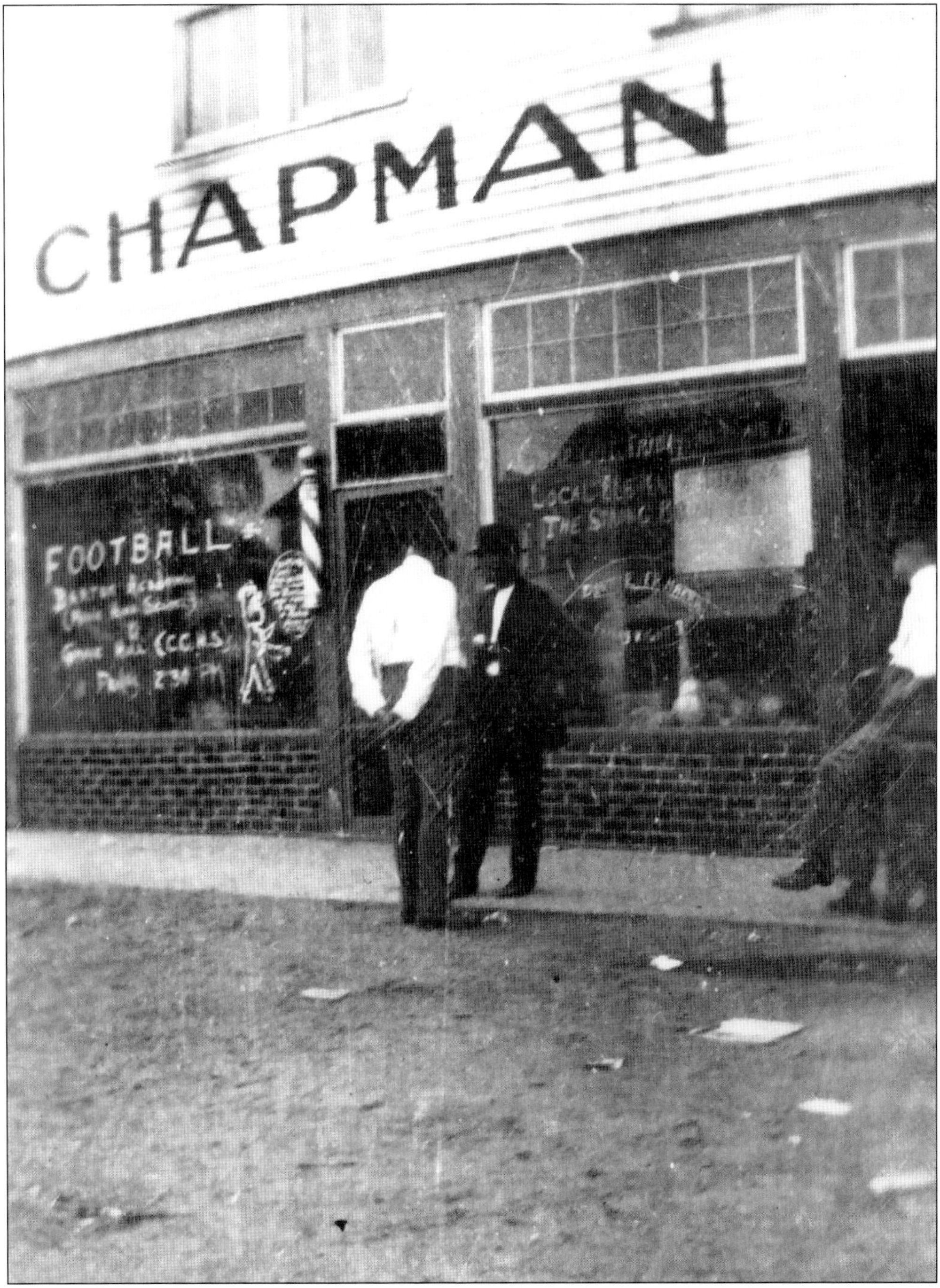

On Main Street, Chapman Bros. Hardware used their glass-window to advertise the up-and-coming sport of the 1920s—football. This building became Cowden Hardware in more recent times. The left window reads, "Football, Bartow Academy, (Grove Hill School), vs. Grove Hill (CCHS), Friday, 2:30 p.m." Afternoon games were a necessity since there was no electricity and the game was played for the students and the town. Lack of transportation kept the game of local interest only for a few years.

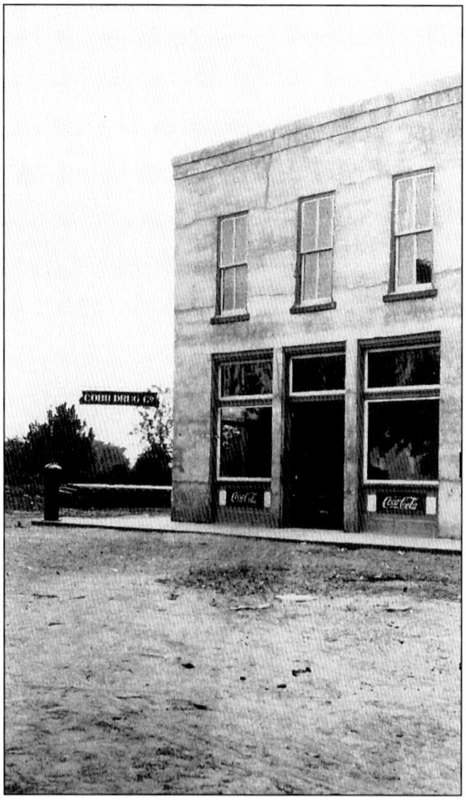

On the corner, the Cobb Drug Co., featuring the new soda, Coca-Cola, moved from across the street to this building, where two brothers, A.B. and Foscue Tucker, druggists, later maintained a drugstore from the early 1900s until the 1960s called Peerless Drugs.

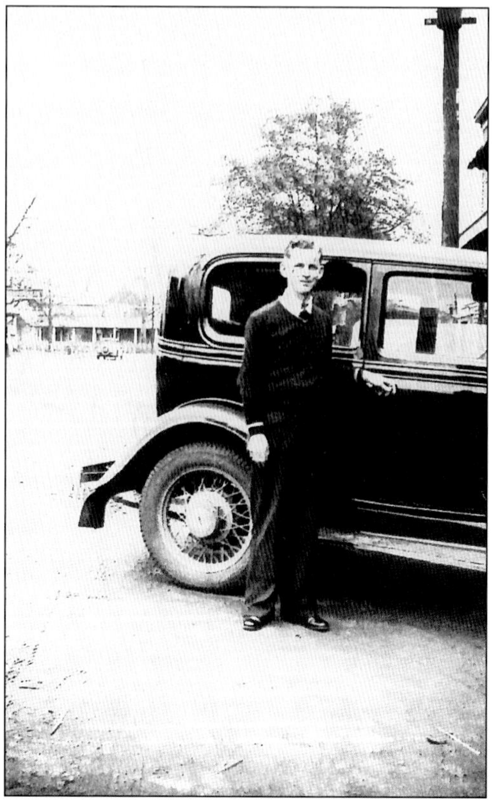

In 1931 and 1932, the soda jerks for the Peerless drugstore were Sheldon "Tuttie" Megginson (shown here), Quincey Waite Jr., and Charles McDonald. Looking south toward Jackson, the Charlie Coates home can be seen in the spot where the Exxon station is today.

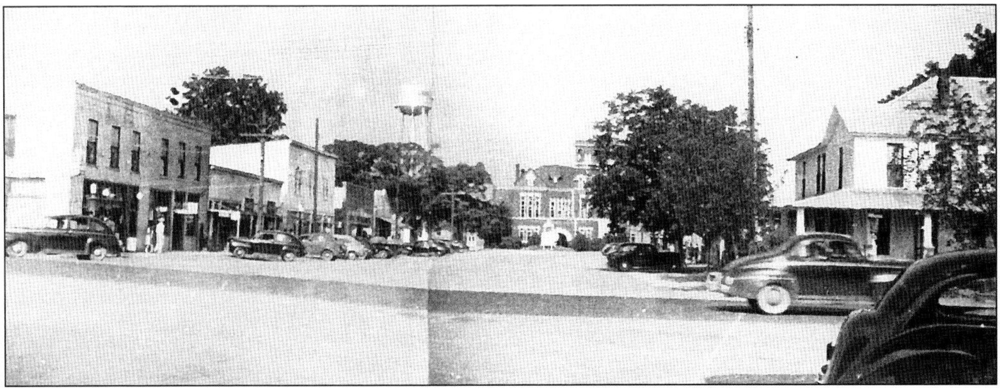

The wide dirt street leads to the courthouse, with the war monument shown in front. The dark strip, the only pavement in town, is Highway 43, running north and south from Mobile to Selma. The Wells Hotel, on the right, faces Peerless Drugs across the street on the corner.

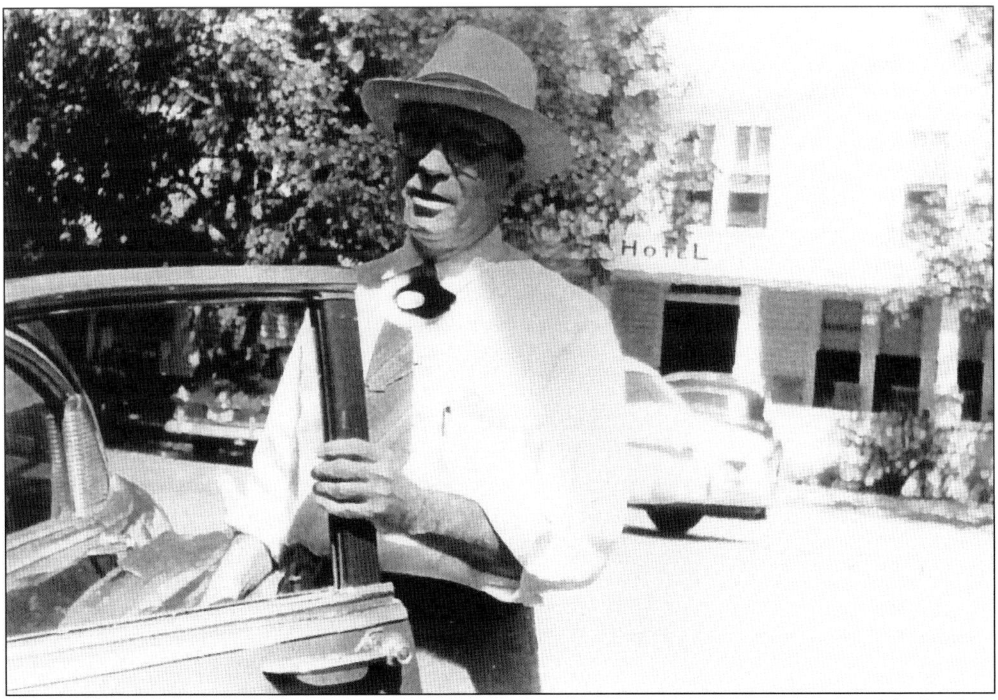

Dr. R.D. Neal Sr. is parked in front of Peerless Drugs in the late 1940s. Dr. Neal helped to transfer the first hospital in the county from Jackson to the newly constructed Grove Hill Hospital facility in 1948. He gave many years of dedicated service to the Grove Hill area.

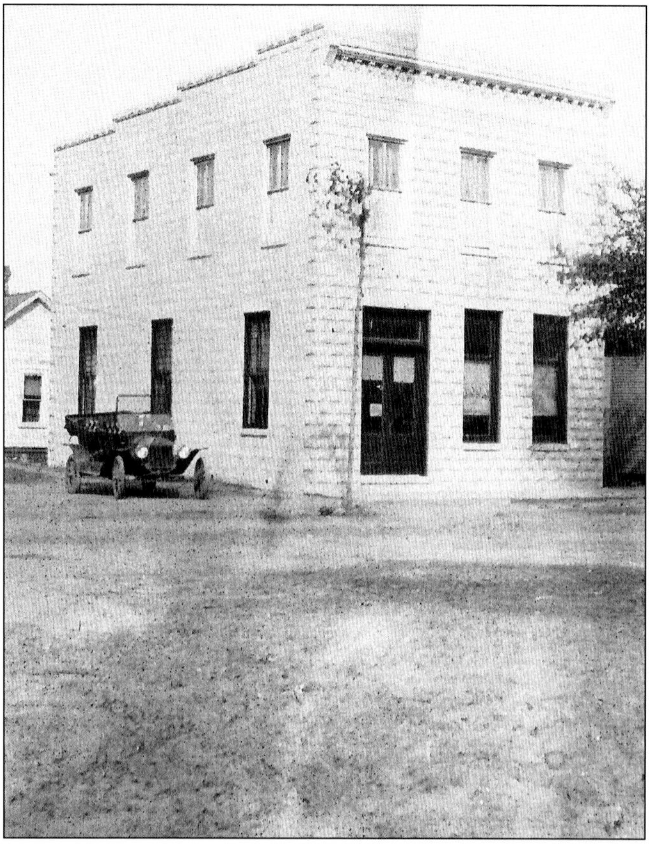

The First Bank of Grove Hill opened for business on August 1, 1936, in this building on the lot next to J.W. Cunningham's store, which later became S.C. Gordon and Company. The bank began with a $30,000 capital investment, and, by 1982, when Grove Hill was 150 years old, its assets were valued at $30 million.

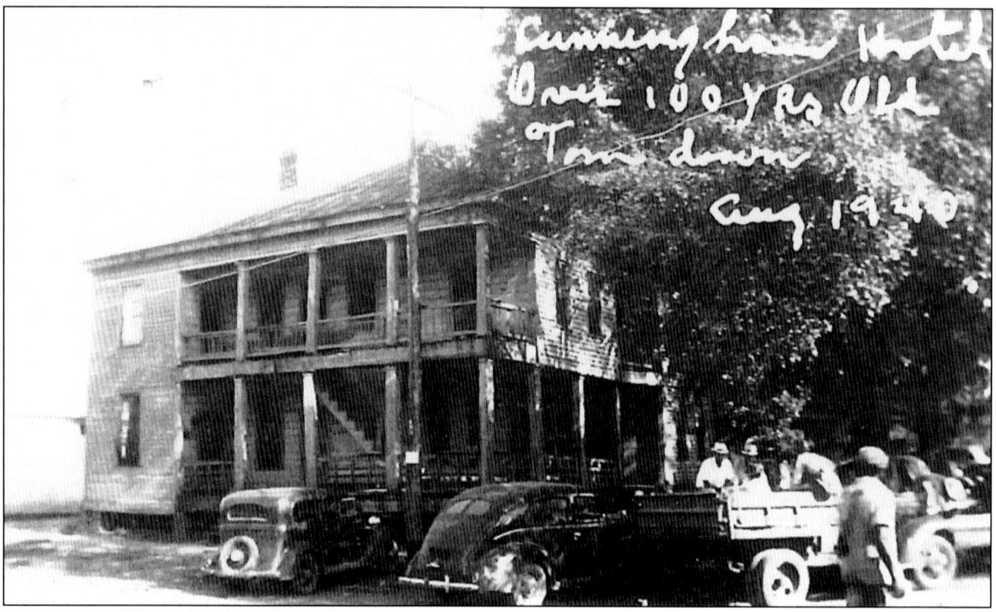

One of many establishments that offered rooms to visitors, the Cunningham Hotel sat where Watrous Garrett's law office was later located, to the right of the Ed Burge store on Main Street. The hotel, owned by Mr. and Mrs. Joseph W. Cunningham, was built in the early 1890s.

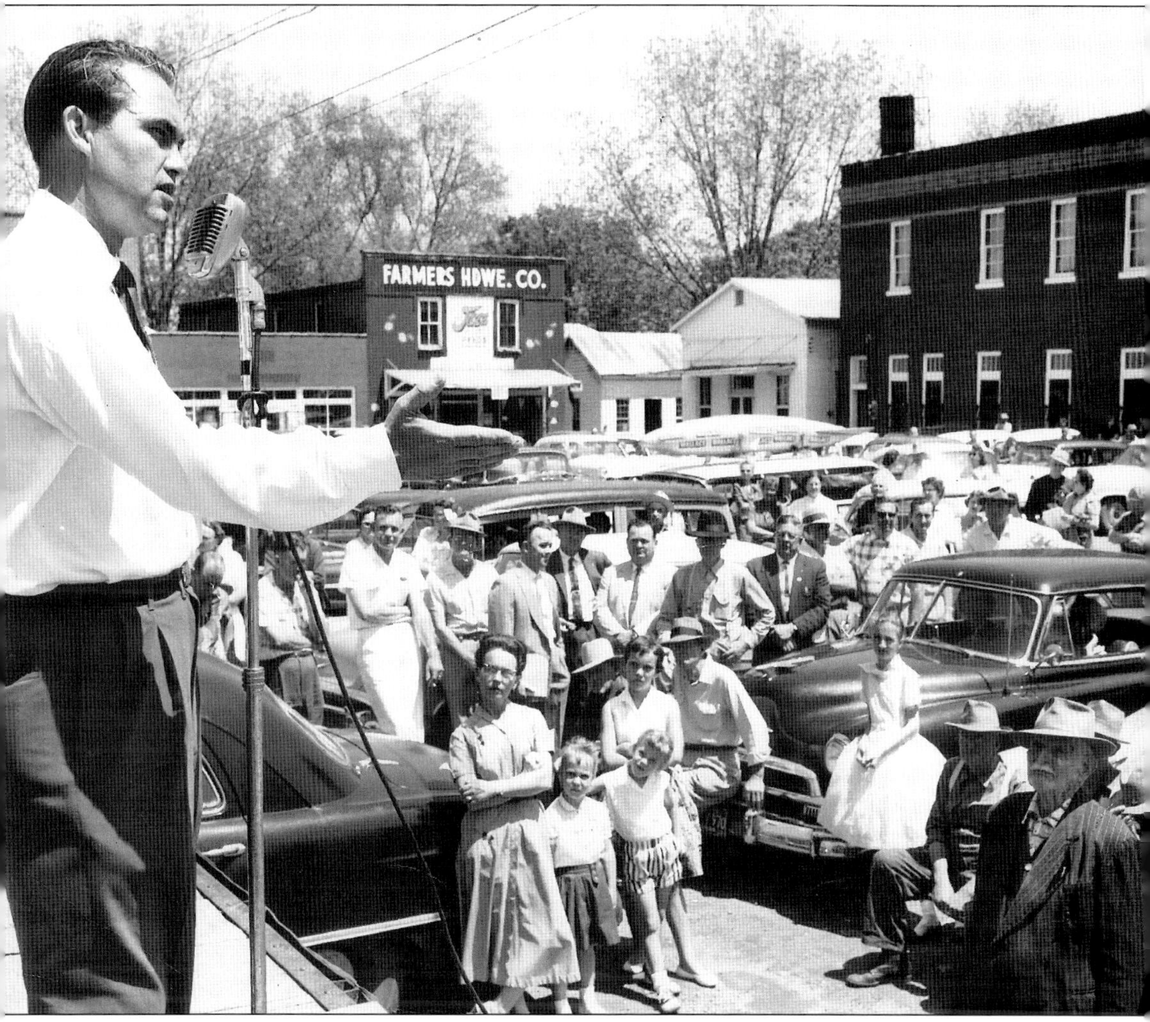

The young George Wallace, former governor of Alabama, makes a speech in Grove Hill around 1950, during the years when Jimmy Hurd was mayor and when Wallace was a young politician. The white building between Farmer's Hardware and Paul Jones's law office was the first public library in the county seat. The library was started by Lucille Burson, who collected books at first and put them in her office until she could find a building. Kitty Hicks was probably the first librarian.

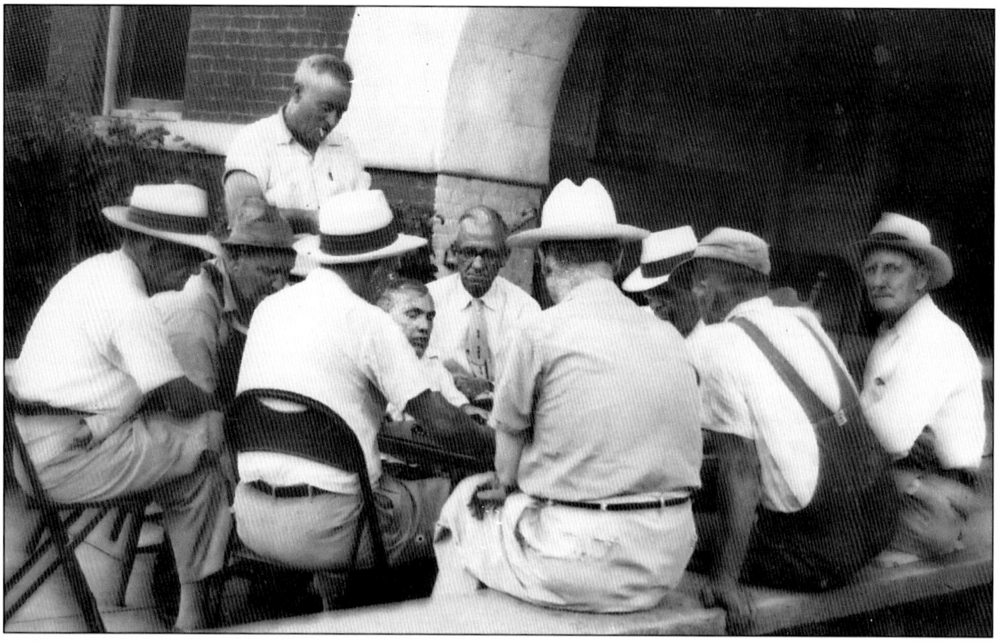

A domino game, the traditional pastime of Grove Hill, is in progress in this picture. This scene, photographed around 1949, portrays Will Edge sitting idly by watching the game that is in front of the old courthouse. Identified, from left to right, are Charlie Calhoun, Thad Sigler (overalls and hat), Gary Coleman (standing), Howard Calhoun (white hat and facing away from camera), Ernest Thompkins, R.A. Bumpers (wearing a tie), Vaughn Chapman (wearing a hat and facing away from camera), Robbie Coleman, Carter Williamson (overalls and cap), and Will Edge.

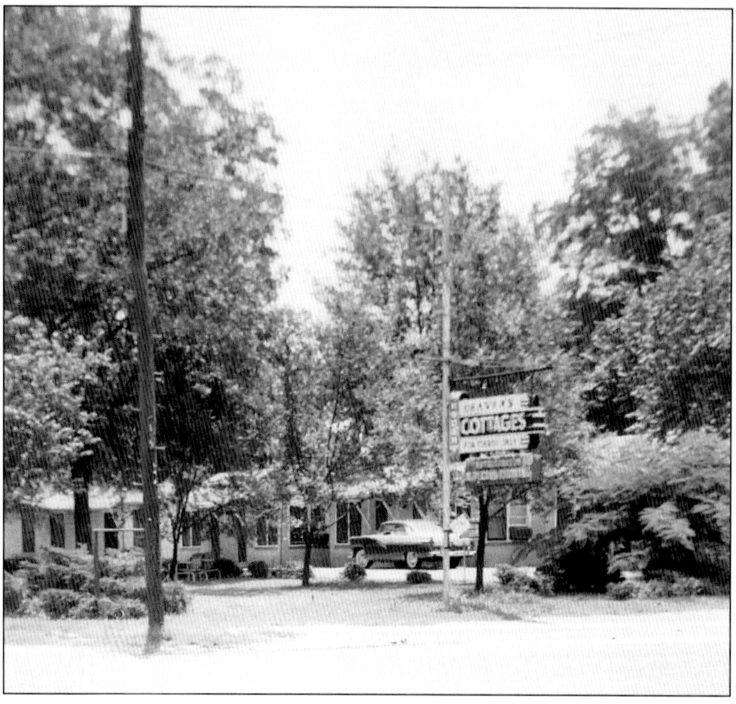

A whole new concept in travel lodging was the Deavers Cottages, located north of the Grove Hill Methodist Church on Highway 43, where motorists drove up to their room, which they then secured for the night.

Two

Open for Business

Jackson

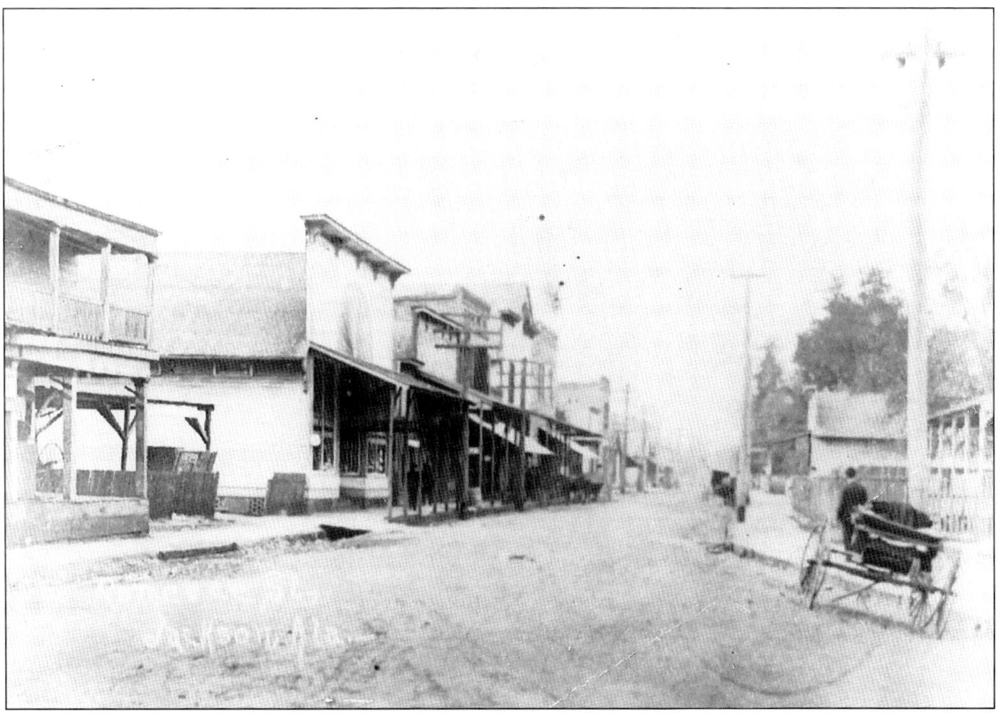

Taken in the first year of the new century, this 1900 photograph shows a wonderful view of downtown Jackson. From the Curve on College Avenue, we look toward the Tombigbee River down Commerce Street. Most of what we see from Prim and Kimbell General Merchandise to halfway down the block was destroyed by fire in 1924. Telephone poles are visible since Jackson had a locally owned telephone system, which was bought by Southern Bell in 1906.

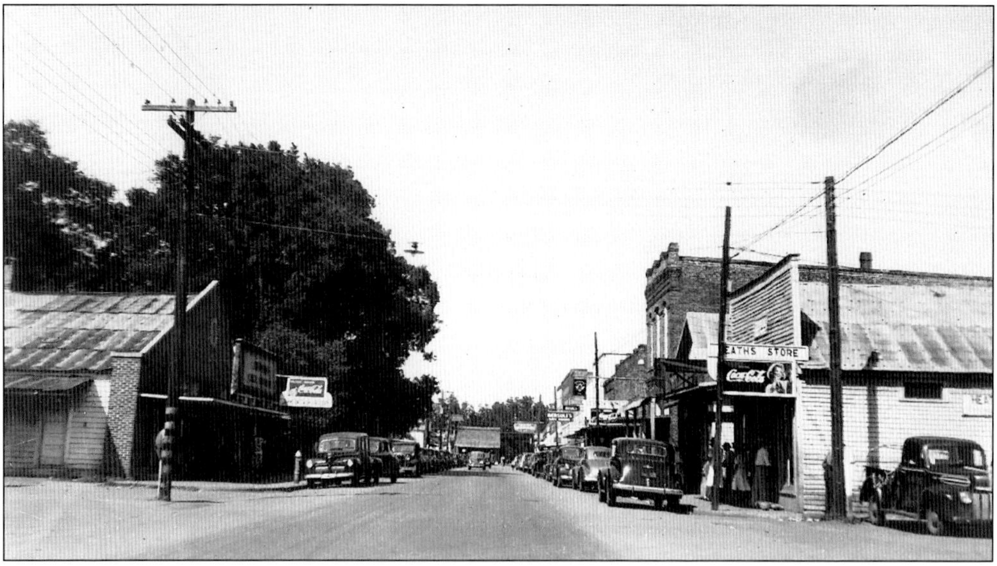

In this 1943 Jackson photograph which looks north on Commerce Street, the J.A. Savage & Son General Store (the tallest building on right), built at the turn of the century, has become the Woodson Furniture Company, which began business in 1925. At the end of the street, facing south, is the old Jackson Bank & Trust building, which, before 1910, had housed the Planters Bank & Trust.

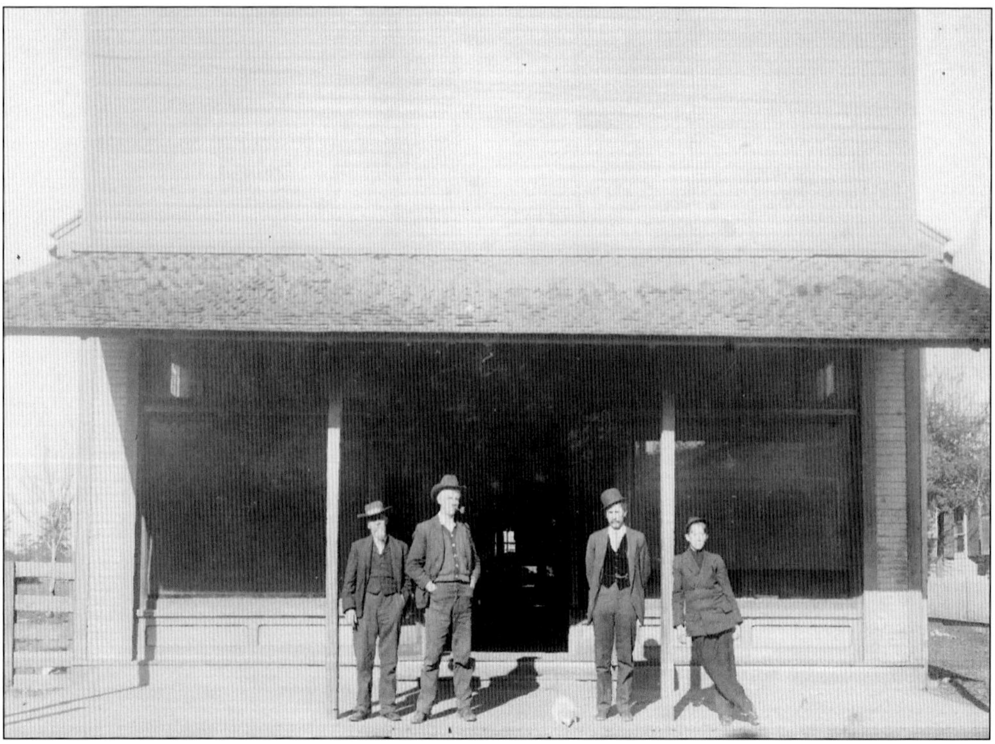

Thomas Marion Bradford, wearing the derby, ran this store from 1910 to 1913. His family lived in Jackson for three years before moving to Scyrene. The white, pet coon posed for this picture also. Bradford later built his own store in Scyrene.

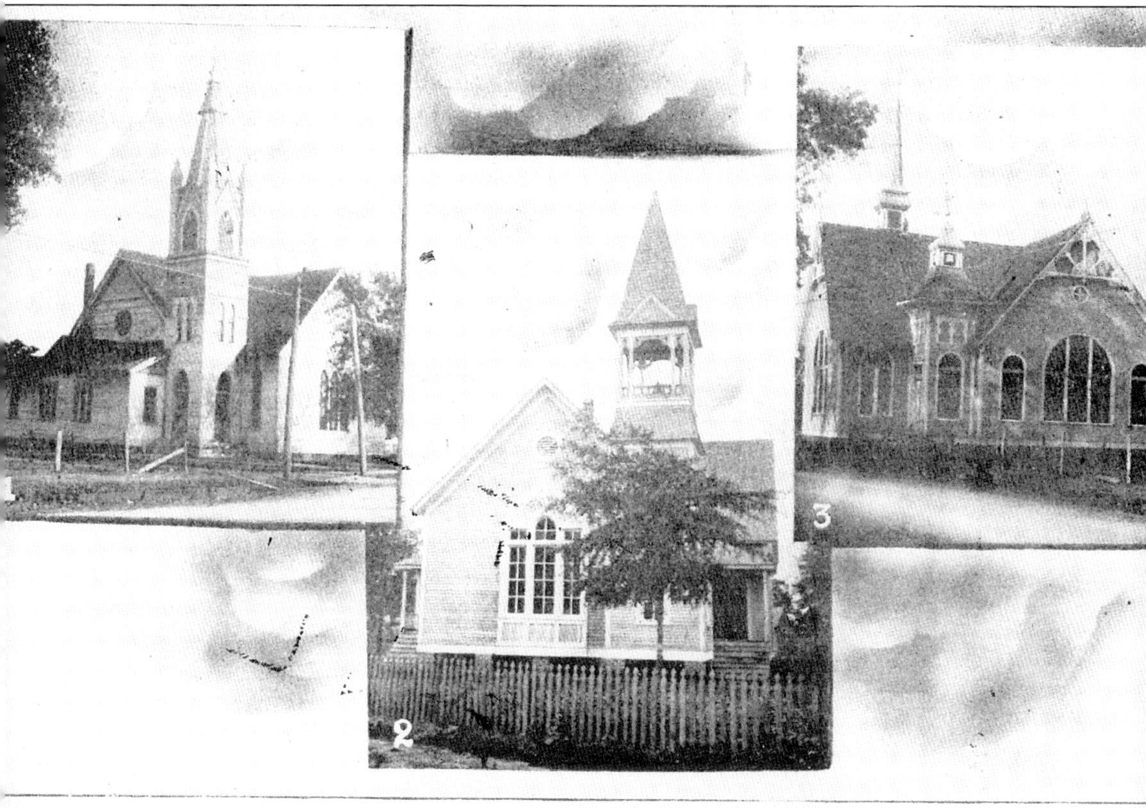

JACKSON CHURCHES
1. Methodist. 2. Presbyterian. 3. Baptist.

According to John Graham, a Jackson author, there were two churches, no schools, one or two stores, a blacksmith shop, and a post office in Jackson in 1875. The Methodists began meeting in a small church near the present cemetery sometime between 1840 and 1845. In the early 1890s, a church was erected on the north side of Commerce Street. The Presbyterians organized a church here in 1873, and, in about 1920, they built the church pictured here. The Baptists organized and built a church in 1858, which they gave to the Presbyterians in 1873. In the 1890s, the Baptists built a church on the lot where the Nichols residence was located (in 1923).

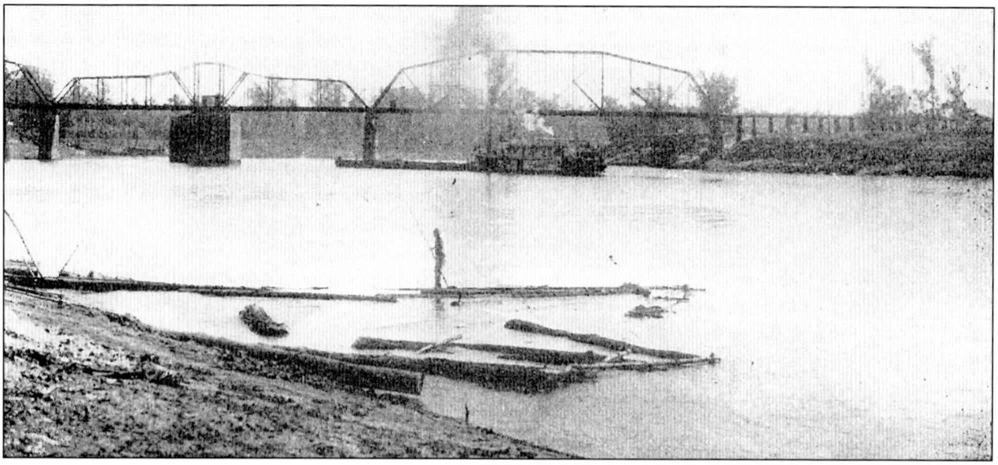

The Jackson Ferry was in sight of the Southern Railroad Bridge. J.C. Rivers leased and operated the ferry.

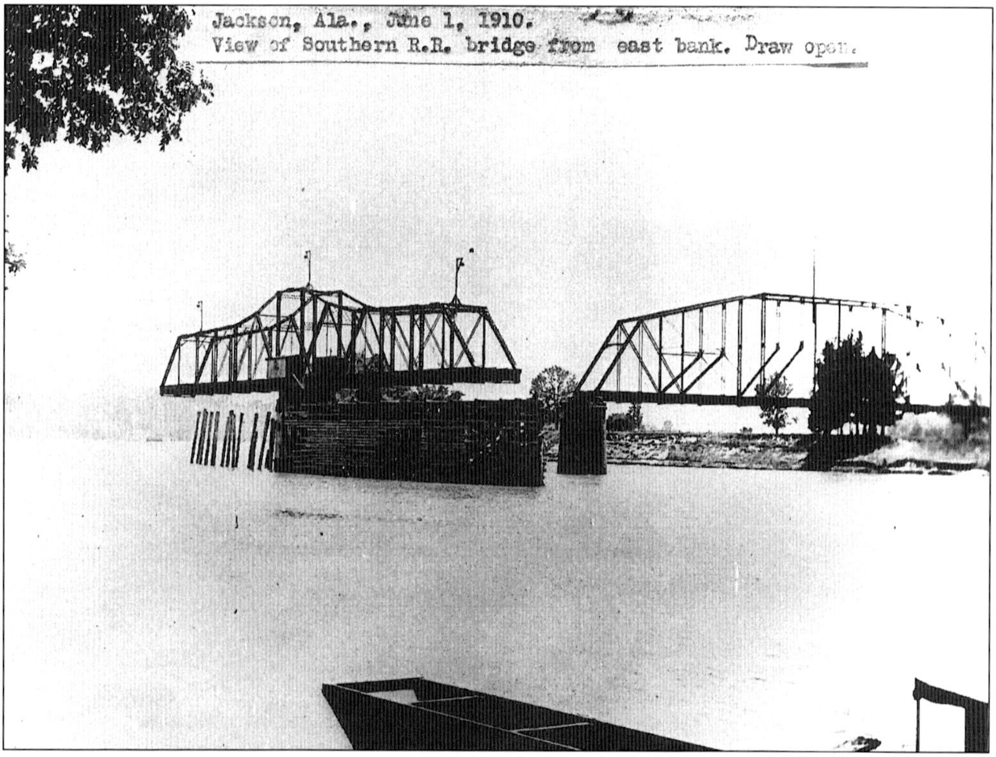

The original railroad bridge across the Tombigbee River was completed in 1888 and joined Jackson on the east side of the river to Carson and Prestwick on the west side. Built by Mobile and West Alabama and Georgia Railroad Company, the first boat to go through the draw span was the *R.E. Lee* on December 31, 1887. A mishap occurred on Sunday, January 16, 1892, at about 4 a.m., when the engine tender and a coal car rolled off the bridge into the river. From Jackson to Choctaw (now Thomasville), daily mail service was provided by way of the railroad, starting in October 1888. The railroad and the bridge also opened up the pine timber industry in the same year. In these earlier times, trees were a nuisance because agriculture ruled this part of the world.

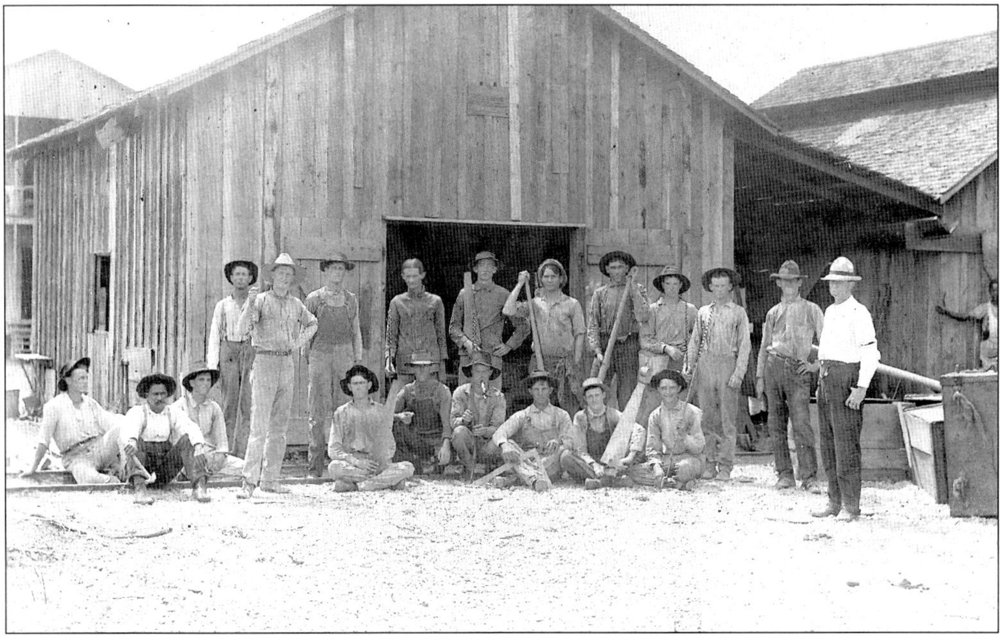

Old Lock No. 1 was constructed in the 1890s or early 1900s near Salitpa on the Tombigbee River. It opened for traffic in 1909 and was in operation for 50 years. Coffeeville Lock and Dam replaced it in 1960. Congress approved funds which allowed for more locks and dams to be built. By 1915, the last of 17 structures was completed. Each had been assigned a number, with the first one above Mobile called Lock No. 1. This lock was located at McGrew's Shoals, a popular crossing for Native Americans and early settlers.

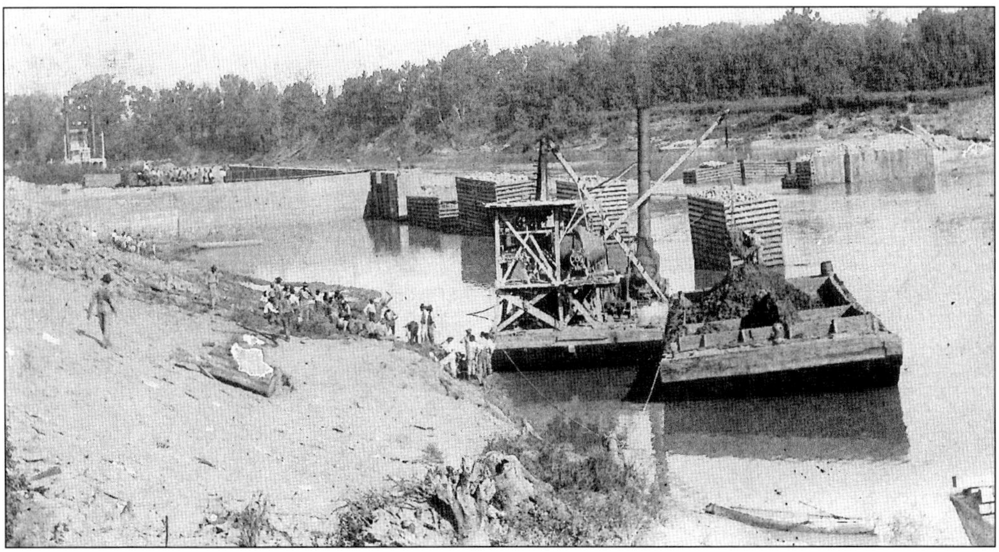

During 1895–1896, buildings for laborers and mechanics were constructed. A blacksmith shop, material storehouses, dwellings for engineers and superintendents, and other structures cost $3,419.35. Work was underway in 1896. It cost $152 for 4 and 8/10 acres on the Clarke County side and 2 41/100 acres on the Washington County side. In this picture, excavation of the upper approach looking downstream from the Clarke County side is in progress. Note the steamboat behind the wall (upper far left).

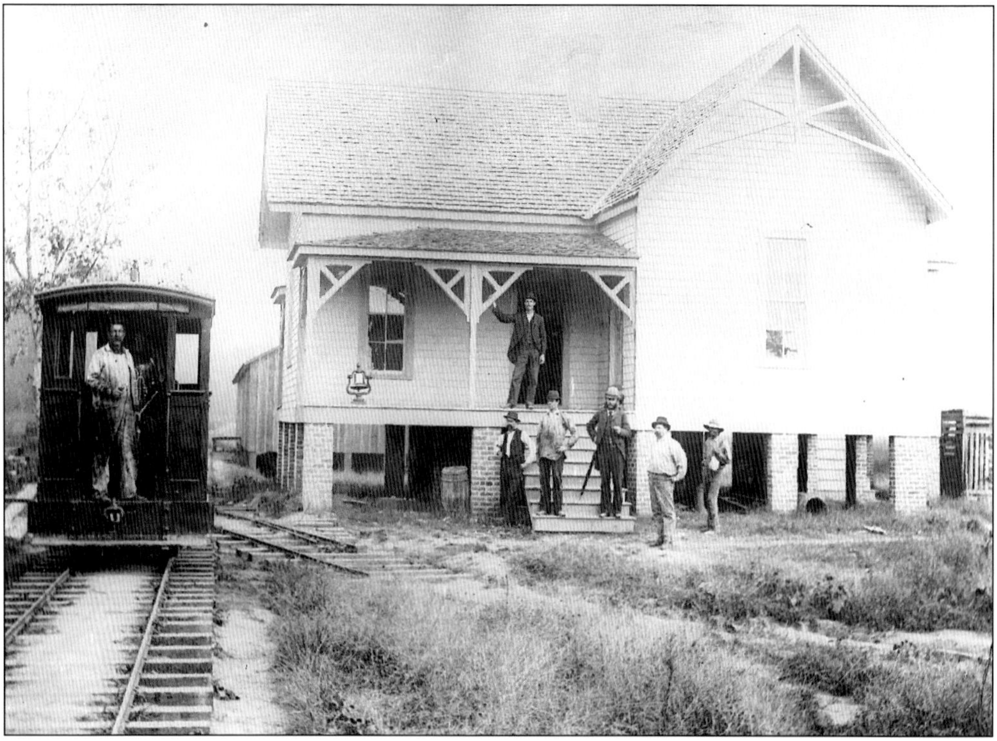

The lockhouse pictured in this 1898 photograph was destroyed by a 1953 tornado. The locomotive *Harding* is seen here.

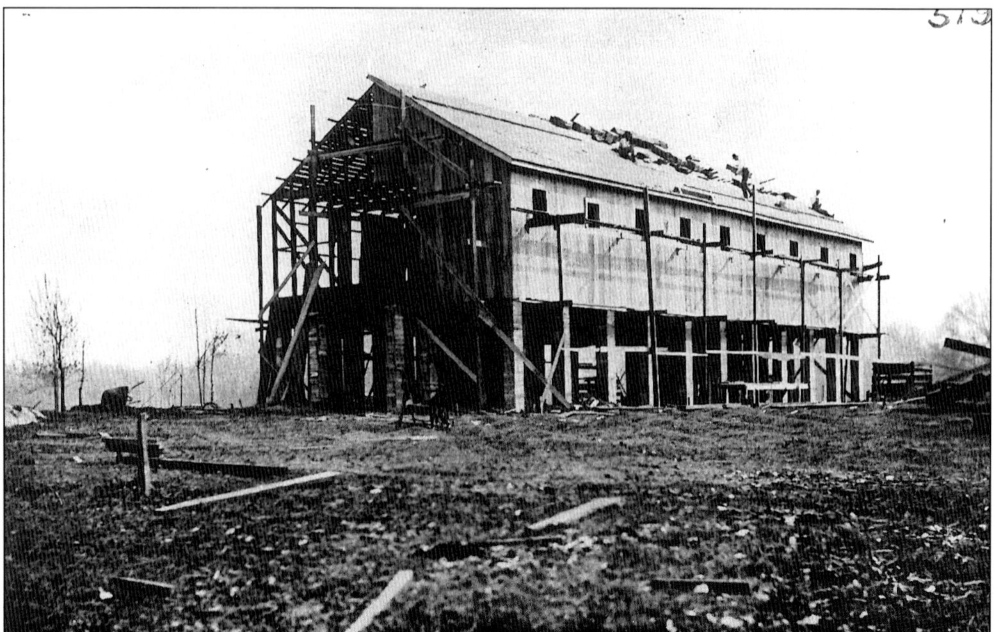

During the improvement of the Tombigbee River, at Lock No. 1, on March 7, 1911, when this picture was taken, the warehouse was under construction. The tornado of 1953 destroyed it also.

Three

Open for Business

Thomasville

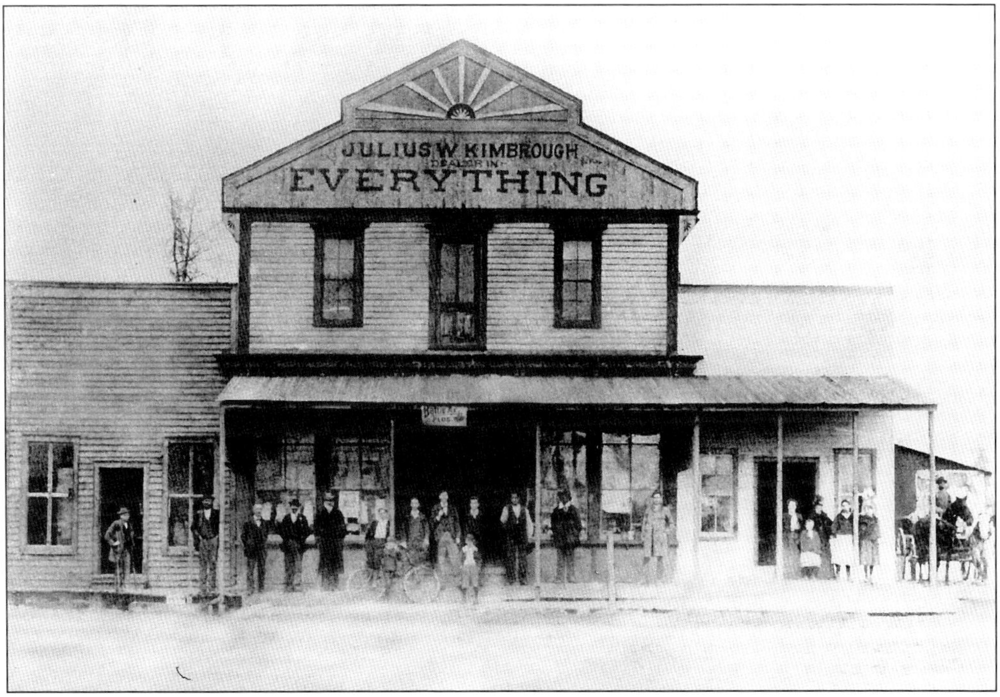

J.W. Kimbrough, "Dealer in Everything," built his store before 1899. After the fire of 1899, Kimbrough rebuilt and his slogan read, "The Great General Store." Julius W. Kimbrough was one of Thomasville's first merchants. His second store was rebuilt on the same spot on Wilson Avenue, but, this time, was constructed of brick. Due to the coming of the railroad, many stores had been hastily built with a wood-frame construction, and to these structures the fire showed no mercy as it swept away about 24 business establishments.

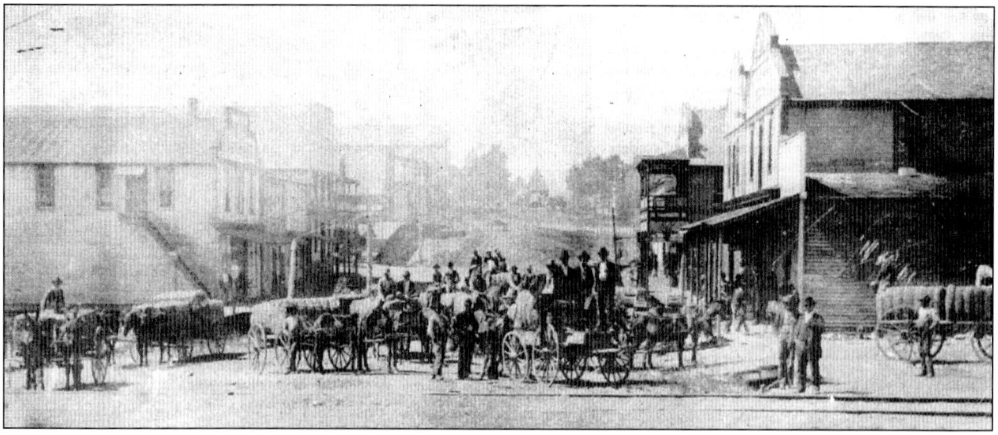

This is a clear view of Thomasville before the fire when the buildings were of wood-frame construction. Notice Kimbrough's store on the right and the town well in the top center of the picture.

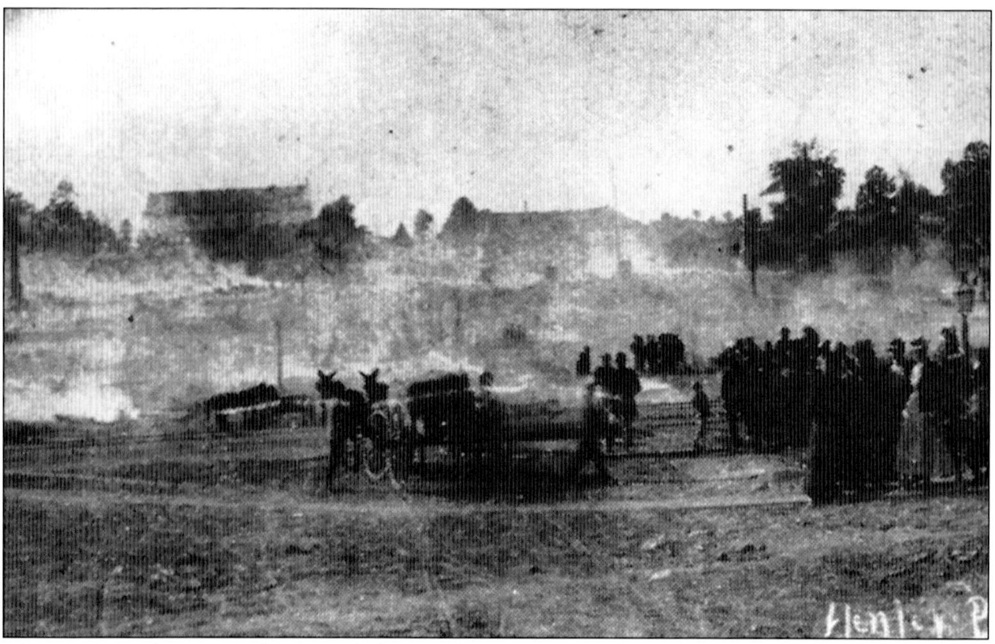

The scene in this 1899 photograph by Henley's Photography shows the devastation of the fire that claimed the businesses on both sides of the street.

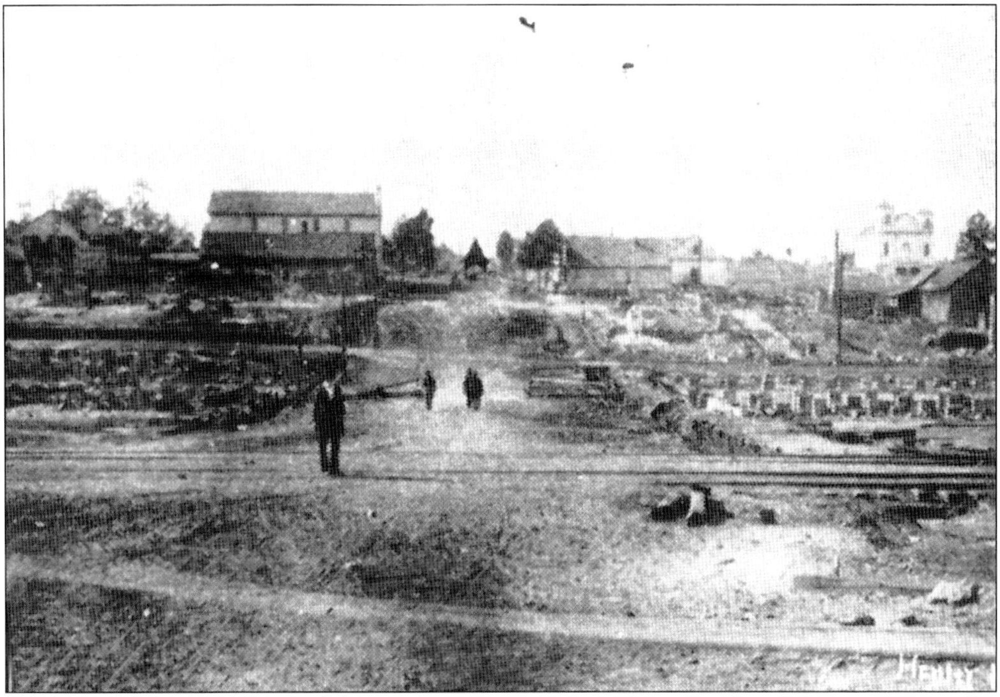

Henley's photograph gives a picture of the devastation after the smoke cleared. The view of Wilson Avenue, looking west up the hill, lets us see the Thomasville Baptist Church (upper right corner) standing where the parking lot of the Baptist church is today. Notice the town well is still visible in the middle of the street. It is easily recognized by its cupola roof.

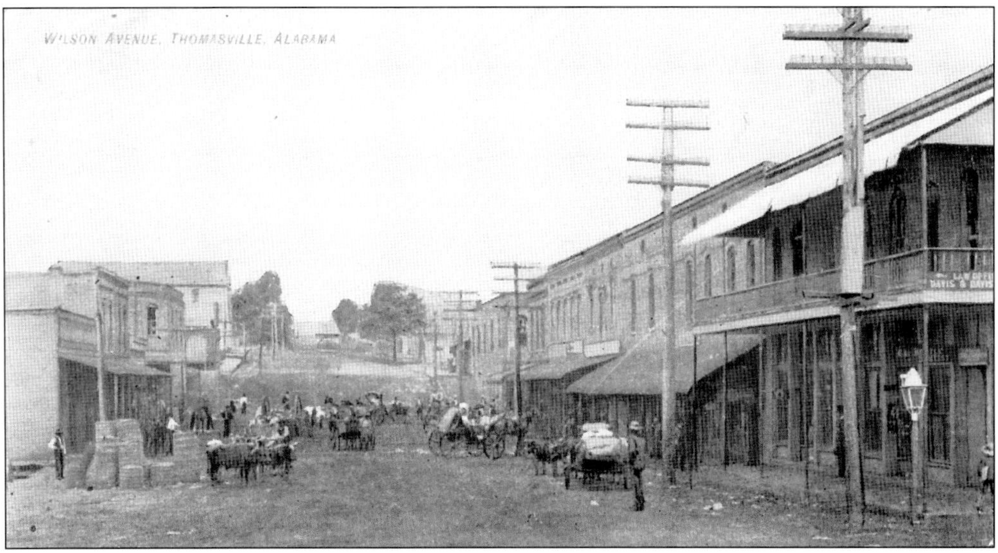

This downtown scene, in the early 1890s, was taken from the railroad tracks, looking west. After the fire, stores were rebuilt with brick. The public well served both man and beast. Every morning after opening up, the clerks from the stores rushed to the well for a bucket of water for use in the stores, since there was no running water in town. A water trough was provided for horses when their owners came to town to trade from outlying areas. The well was housed under a red, pointed roof.

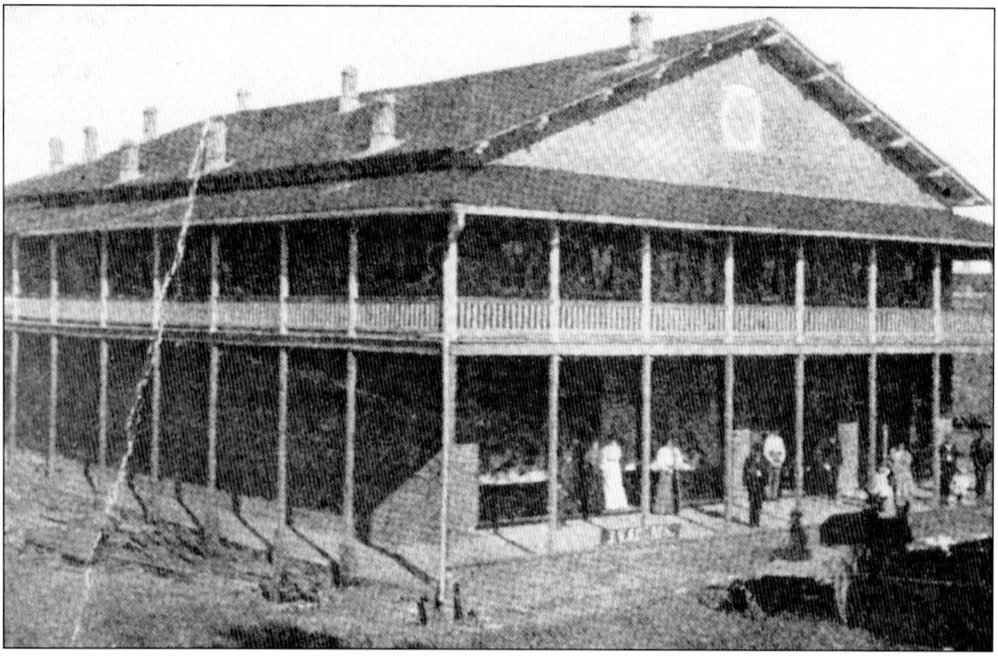

The J.V. Adams store and hotel seen here is still standing today on West Front Street in Thomasville, though without the porches. Many businesses have been housed here, including the Yellow Front, a grocery store. J.V. Adams was the son of one of Thomasville's pioneer residents, Mr. Monroe Adams.

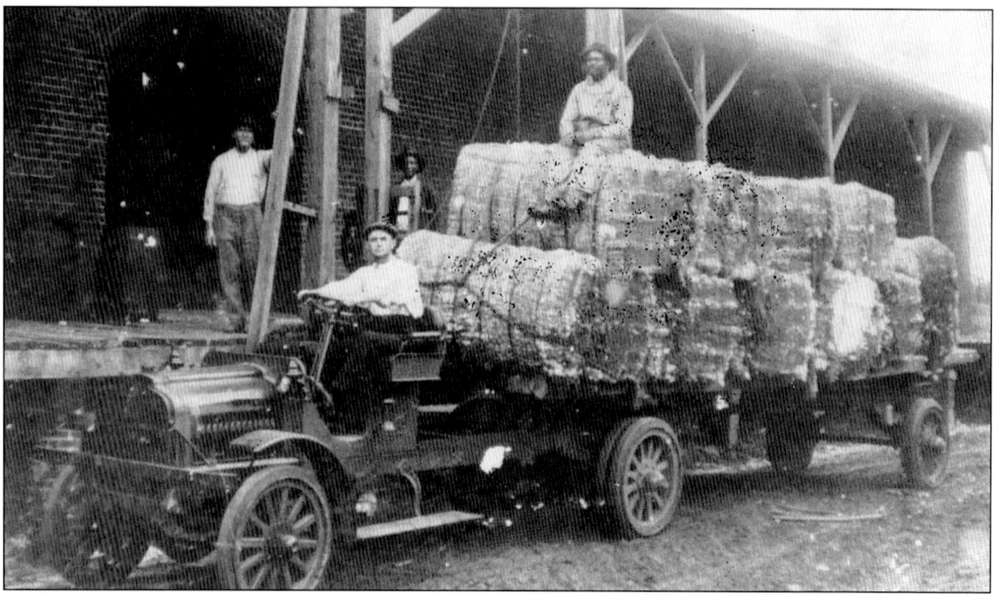

When cotton was king, bales piled high in the station's freight warehouse was a usual scene. The average shipment per season was 10,000 bales. This picture shows cotton being unloaded for shipment on the railroad out of Thomasville. The Southern Railway completed the railroad from Birmingham to Mobile in 1888. The first train pulled out of the station in February of that year. Passengers left on the first train for the Mardi Gras celebration. Thomasville became an important shipping point for a large agricultural area.

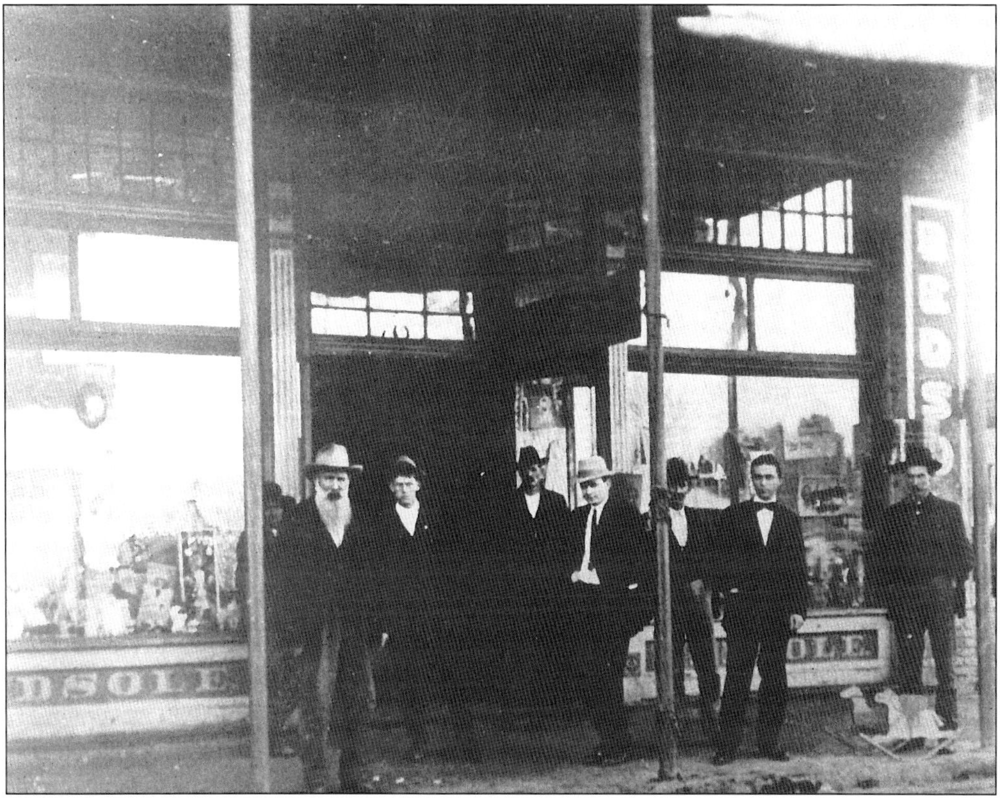

This 1902 photograph is of the early Bedsole's Store. O.A. Bedsole is next to the post, to the right of the door. The gentleman with the long beard to the left is identified as Joe Ballard.

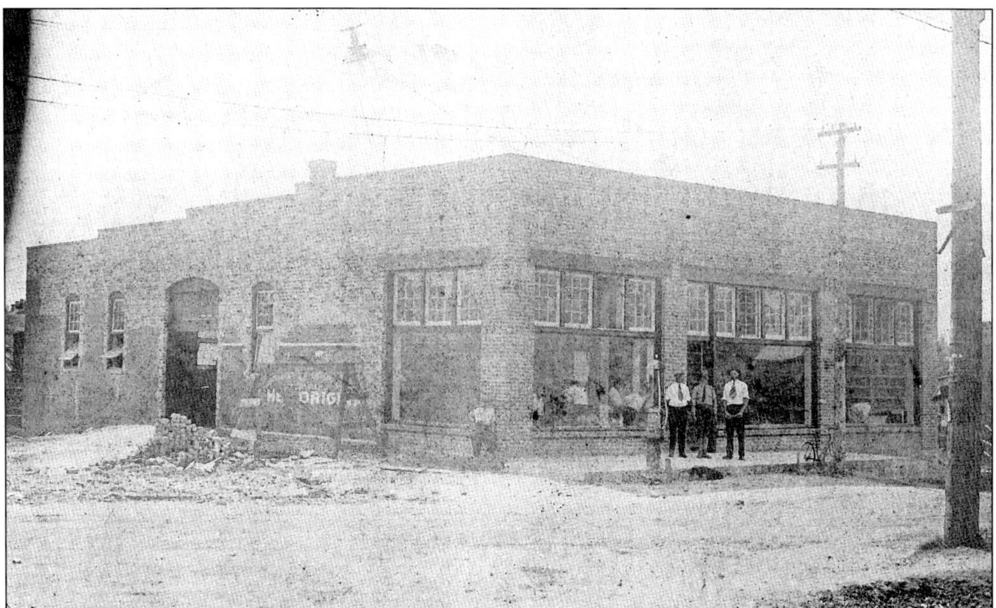

The Ford dealership owned by J.K Ashley was built in the early 1900s. This building later housed the Hall Motor Company. It sits vacant today, across from the post office.

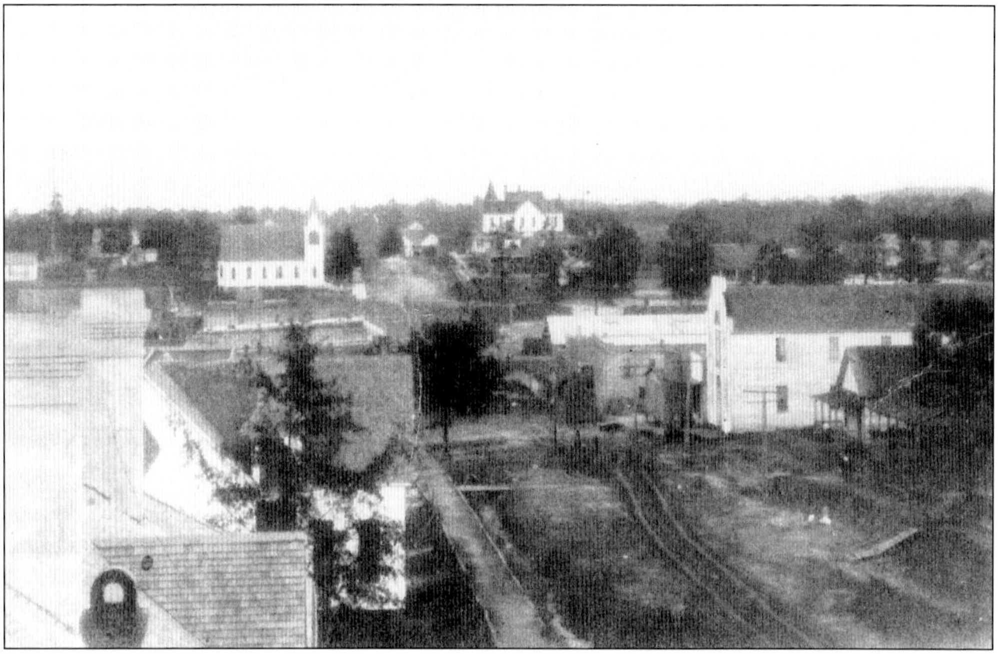

Mr. N.B. Boyles traded a milk cow for all the land north of Highway 43, on both sides of the road, in North Thomasville. His house, seen in all the pictures before the fire, is in the upper part, to the right, in the picture and was located at the site of the late Dr. R.A. Irons's residence.

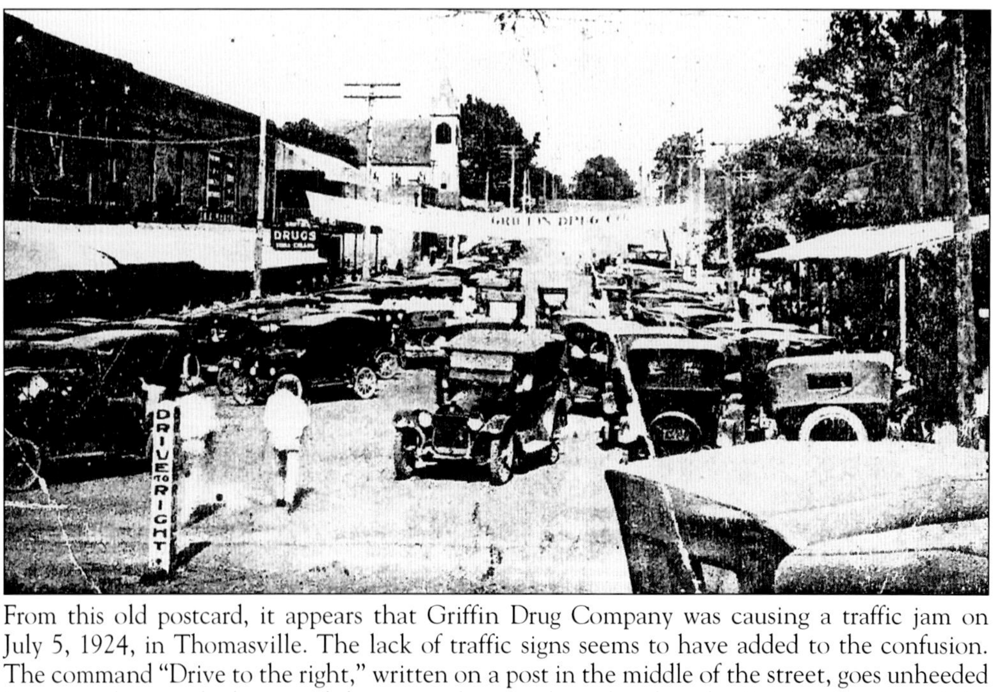

From this old postcard, it appears that Griffin Drug Company was causing a traffic jam on July 5, 1924, in Thomasville. The lack of traffic signs seems to have added to the confusion. The command "Drive to the right," written on a post in the middle of the street, goes unheeded it seems. The view looks toward the east and across the railroad tracks. W.W. Bettis owned the first car back when parking was not a problem in Thomasville.

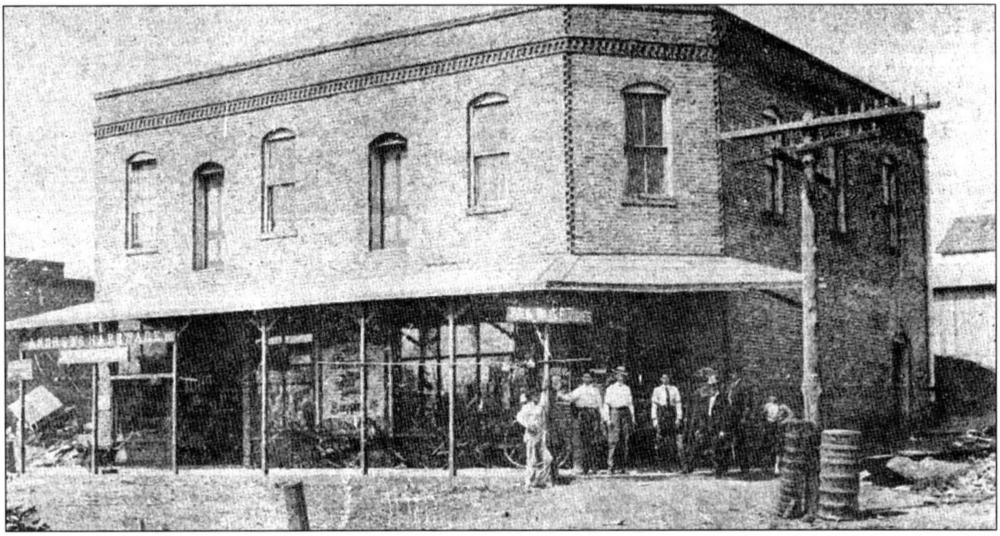

Andrews Hardware, on the corner of West Front Street and Wilson Avenue, where People's Drug Company was located, was a successful and enduring business. The store was started by W.H. "Hamp" Andrews in 1903. Later, the business merged with Dozier Hardware and moved across the street.

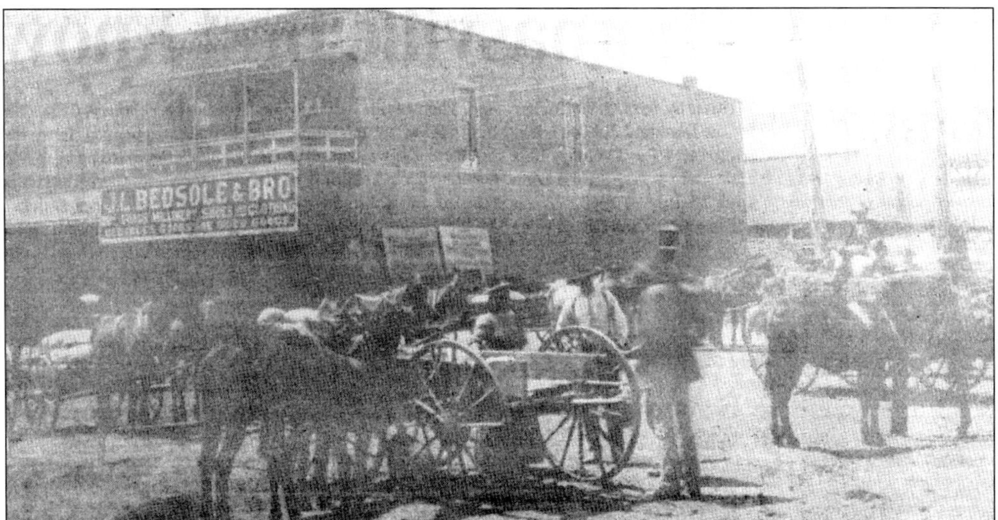

In 1913, the Bedsole store in Thomasville held a sale to dissolve its general mercantile business with plans to devote its efforts to the dry goods business, as well as going from credit business to cash business. This is the crowd on hand for the sale.

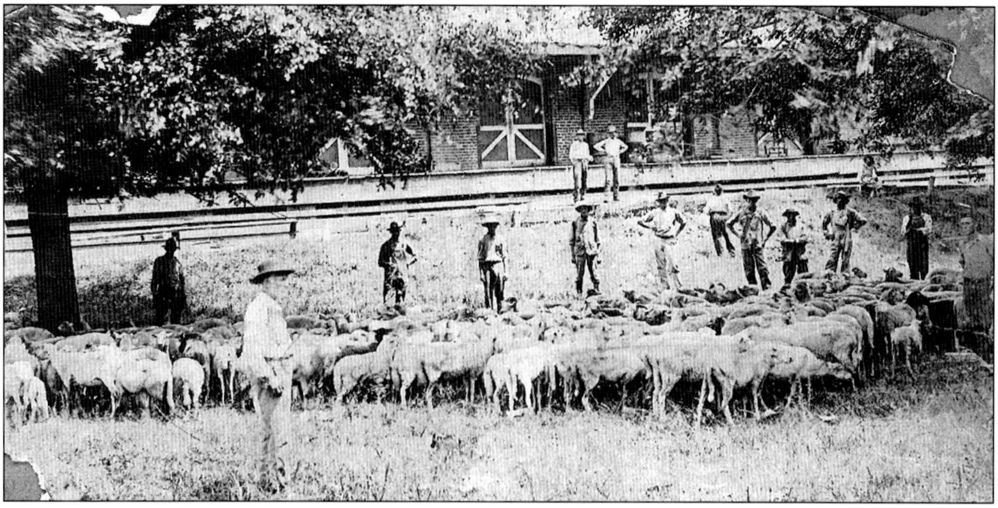

Levi Harrison's sheep are at the Thomasville railroad station waiting to be loaded on the train to go to market. His drovers include Wallace McIntyre, Joe Williams, Diston Harrison, and Ira Harrison. Levi stands in the left foreground of the picture. He and Bill White, as well as Warren Pugh, raised sheep in the early 1900s in the Chilton community and drove them to Thomasville when the time came to sell them.

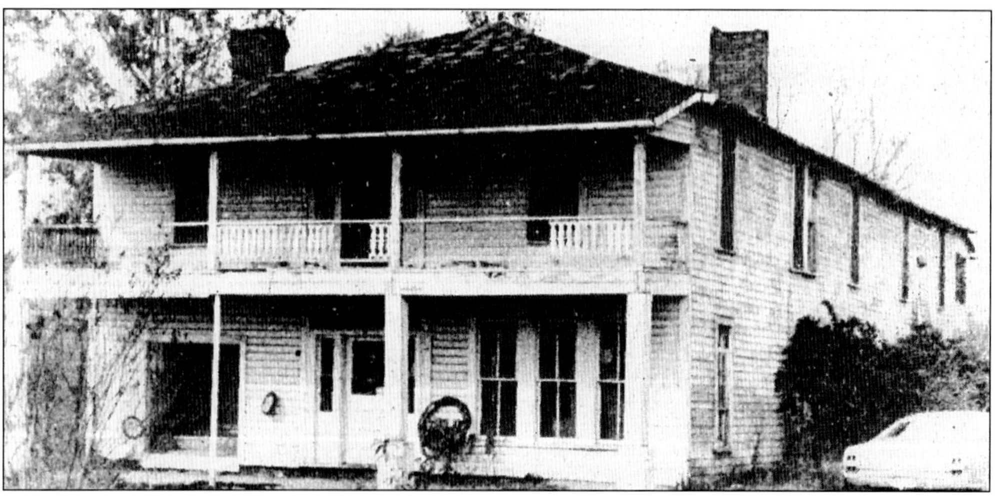

The White Hotel in Thomasville was built around 1910 after Dave White bought an old warehouse down by the railroad. The hotel was really a boardinghouse for drummers, teachers, and others. Many of the young, single men in town who worked as clerks in the stores also stayed there. This picture was taken just before it was torn down.

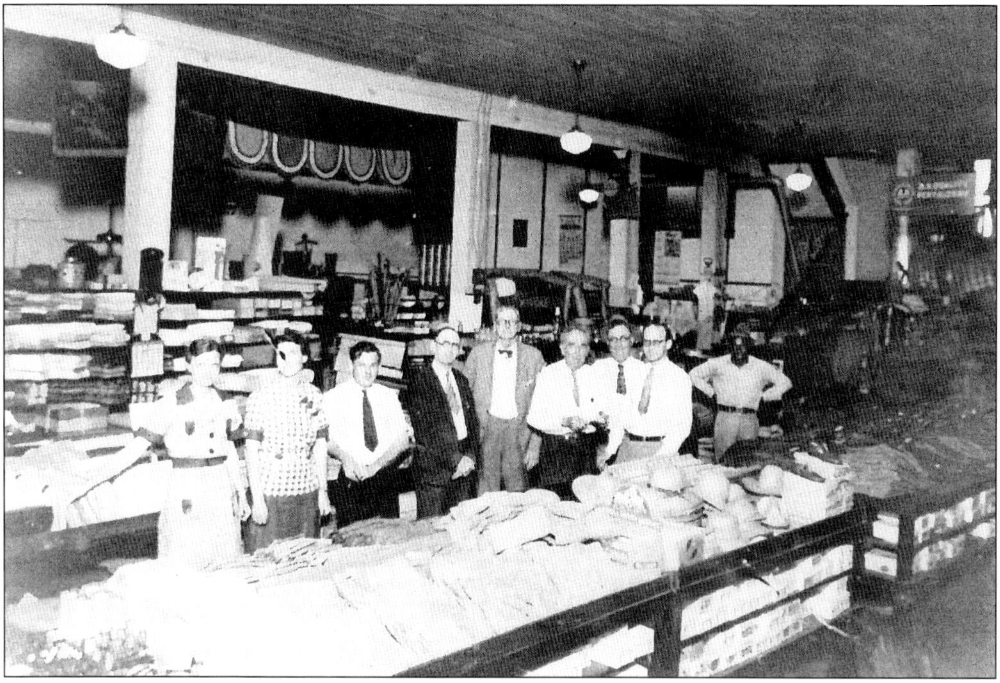

This view of the interior of J.W. Kimbrough's store was taken in the late 1930s or early 1940s. From left to right are Millie McCurdy, Flora W. Kimbrough, A.K. Smith, ? Pickens, J.W. Kimbrough, Bud Adams, W.J. Miller, W.A. Kimbrough, and L.J. Johnson.

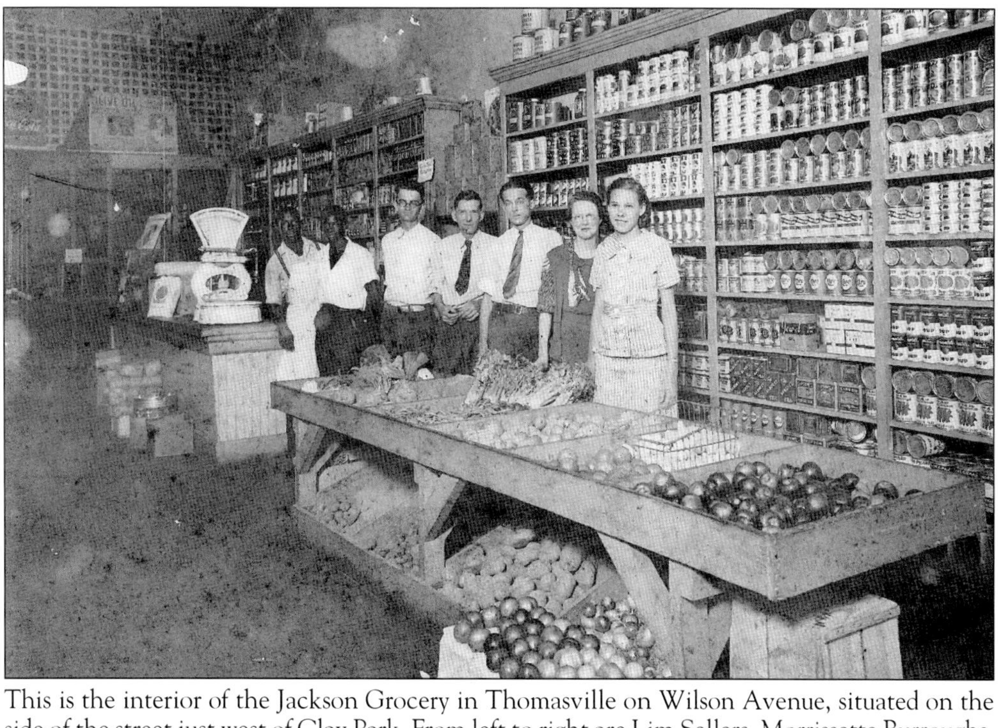

This is the interior of the Jackson Grocery in Thomasville on Wilson Avenue, situated on the side of the street just west of Clay Park. From left to right are Lim Sellers, Morrissette Burroughs, Bracy Gates, Elio Jackson, Eddie Tucker, Dolly Jackson, and Peggy Jackson.

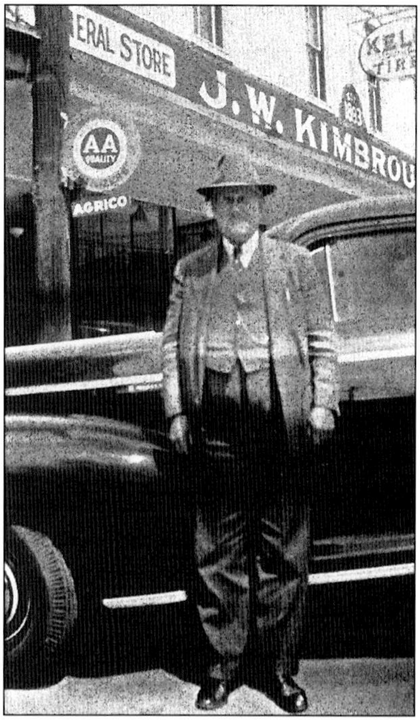

In 1941, Dr. A.L. White, 75 years old, stood in front of J.W. Kimbrough's store in Thomasville. He began his practice in 1907 after graduating from Vanderbilt University around the turn of the century. He was the son of Ennis Loftin White of Chilton. He had one daughter, Myrdie, who married Vance Nored, also of Thomasville.

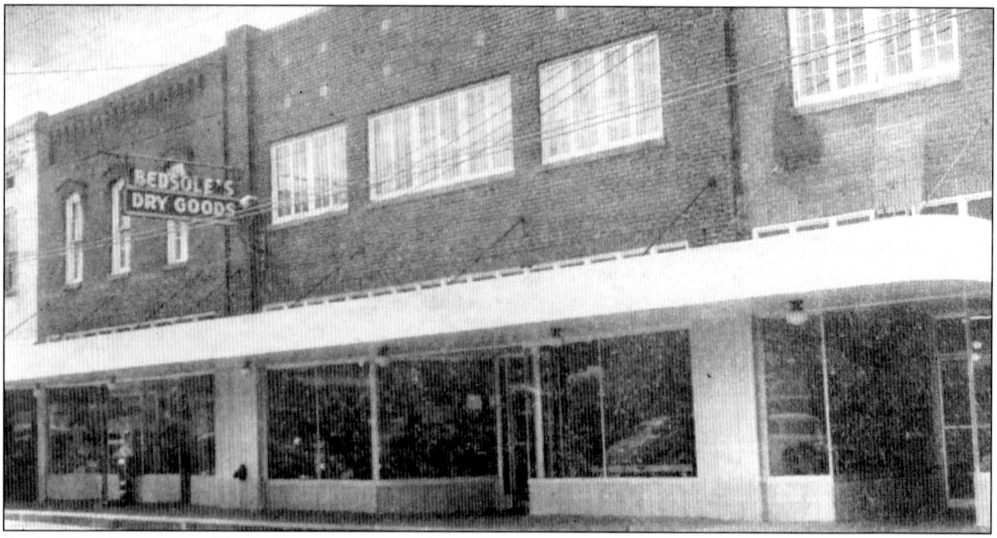

Bedsole's Store, established in 1902, in Thomasville, had its 50th birthday around the time this picture was taken in 1952. In 1898, Travis L. Bedsole moved his store from Tallahatta and, in 1902, took in his son, J.L., as a partner. In 1907, Travis Bedsole retired, and J.L. took in Ocie A. Bedsole, his brother. In 1908, the store began selling for cash, a drastic move for the times, since most stores at that time provided credit and furnished goods until the cotton crop was baled and sold, at which time, the farmer paid his bill and hopefully paid off the mortgage on his property that he had taken out in the spring. Cash was limited since there was no industry with a cash payroll, except a few sawmills. Yet J.L. Bedsole took a risk and began selling on a cash basis, and, in 1913, a department store, instead of a general store, was established. J.L. Bedsole's grandfather's nephew, Rafe Bedsole of Mitcham Beat, had the first Bedsole's Store in Clarke County.

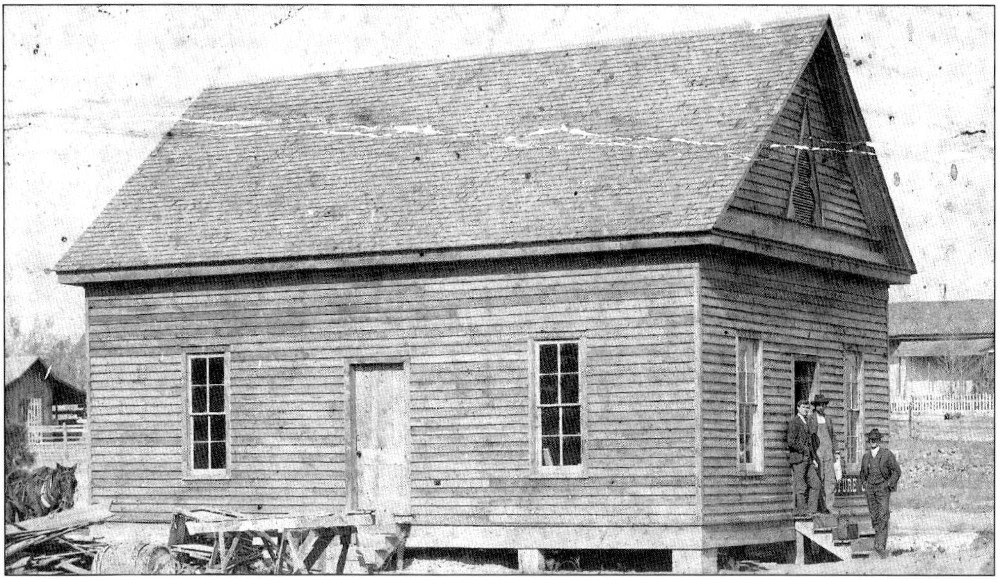

This picture, taken before 1888, is of the David Augusta Megginson Store in Choctaw Corner. Even though the railroad was coming through Thomasville, Choctaw Corner continued to plan and build in the early 1900s. A few companies, like Carlton and Slade, moved their business from Choctaw Corner to Thomasville.

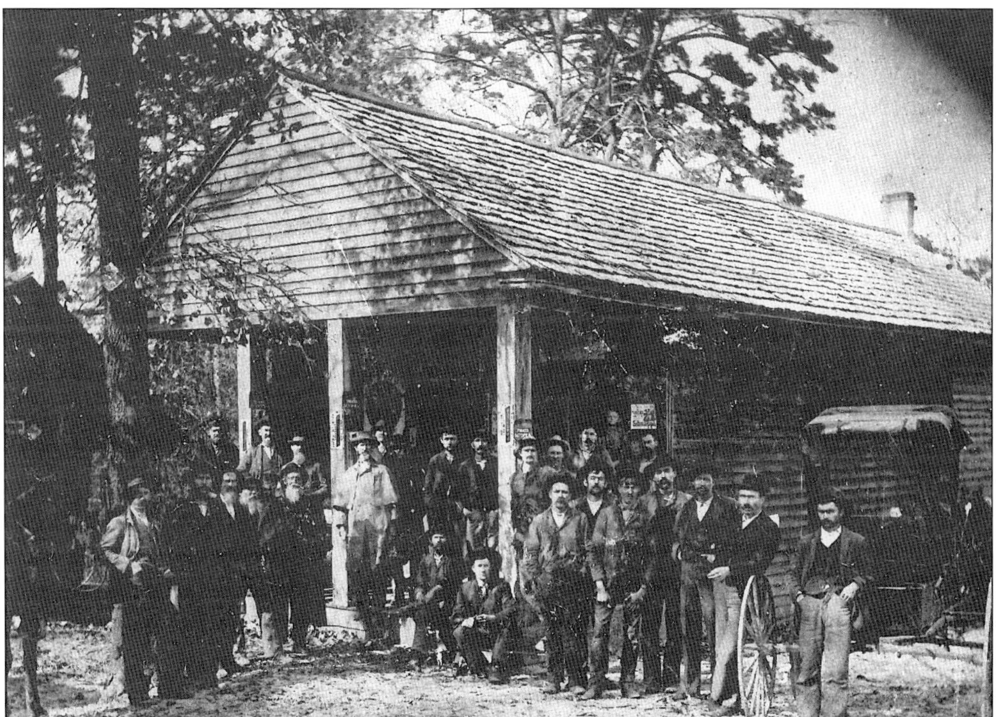

Leaving the Thomasville area and heading for Coffeeville, one could find Sandy Norris's store, seen in this picture around 1893. On the porch and steps are men reported to be members of a posse riding through Mitcham Beat.

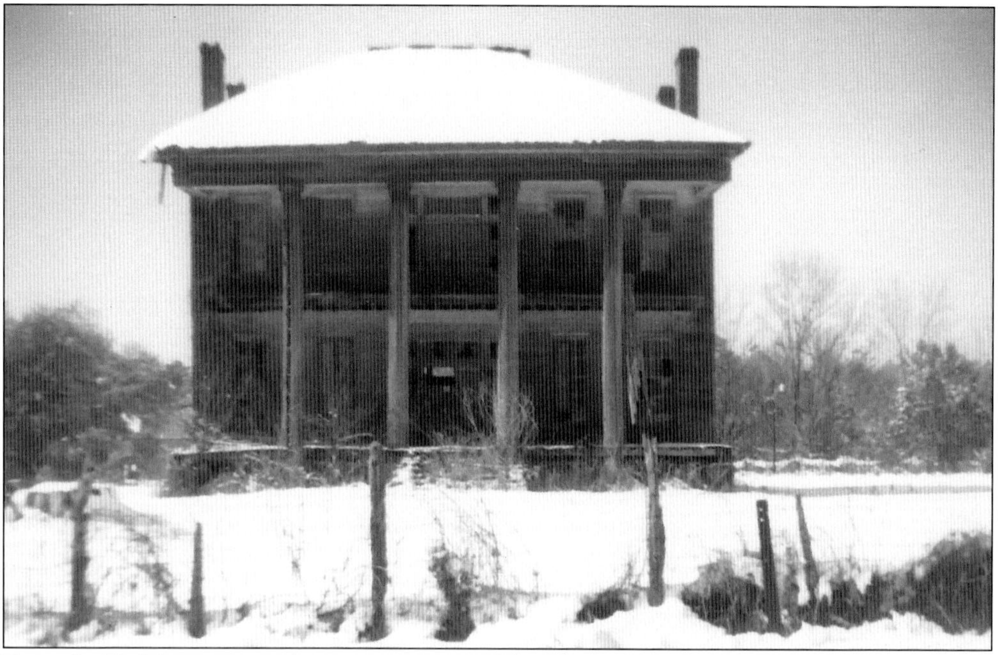

From the York home, steamboats were seen and heard as they came to Coffeeville Landing on the Tombigbee River. This home was built in 1856 by John Figures. He operated a gin and a store and was postmaster before the Civil War. Having lost everything in the Civil War, John Figures put the house up for sale. At public auction, John Cunningham bought it for his son-in-law, Oscar York, as a wedding present for his daughter. Figures died in 1868 a poor man, all his cash was worthless Confederate money. The house stood from 1856 to 1983. This shot was taken after snow had fallen in Coffeeville.

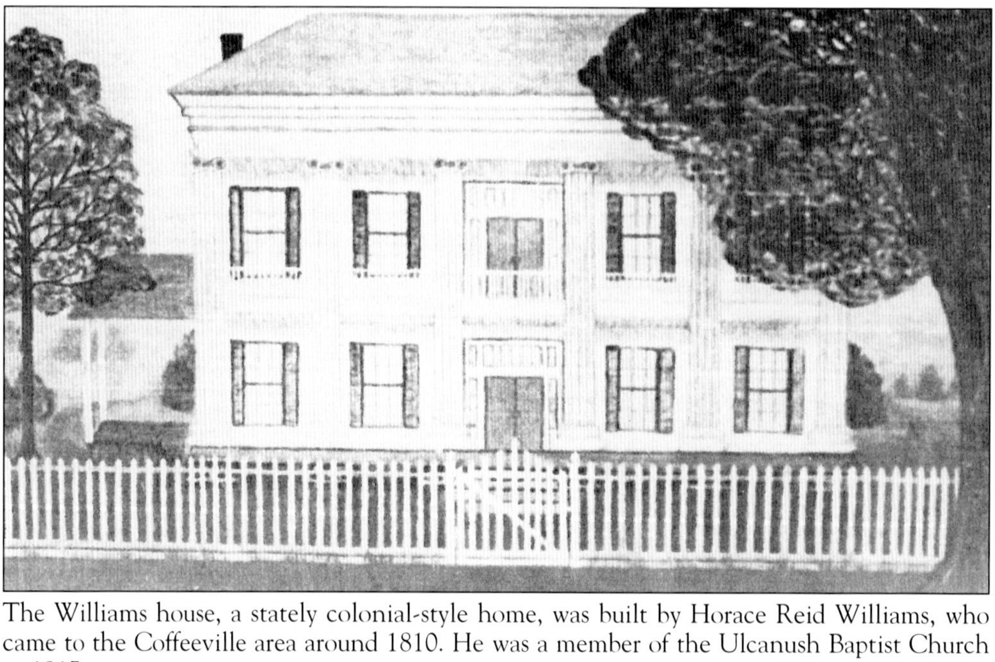

The Williams house, a stately colonial-style home, was built by Horace Reid Williams, who came to the Coffeeville area around 1810. He was a member of the Ulcanush Baptist Church in 1817.

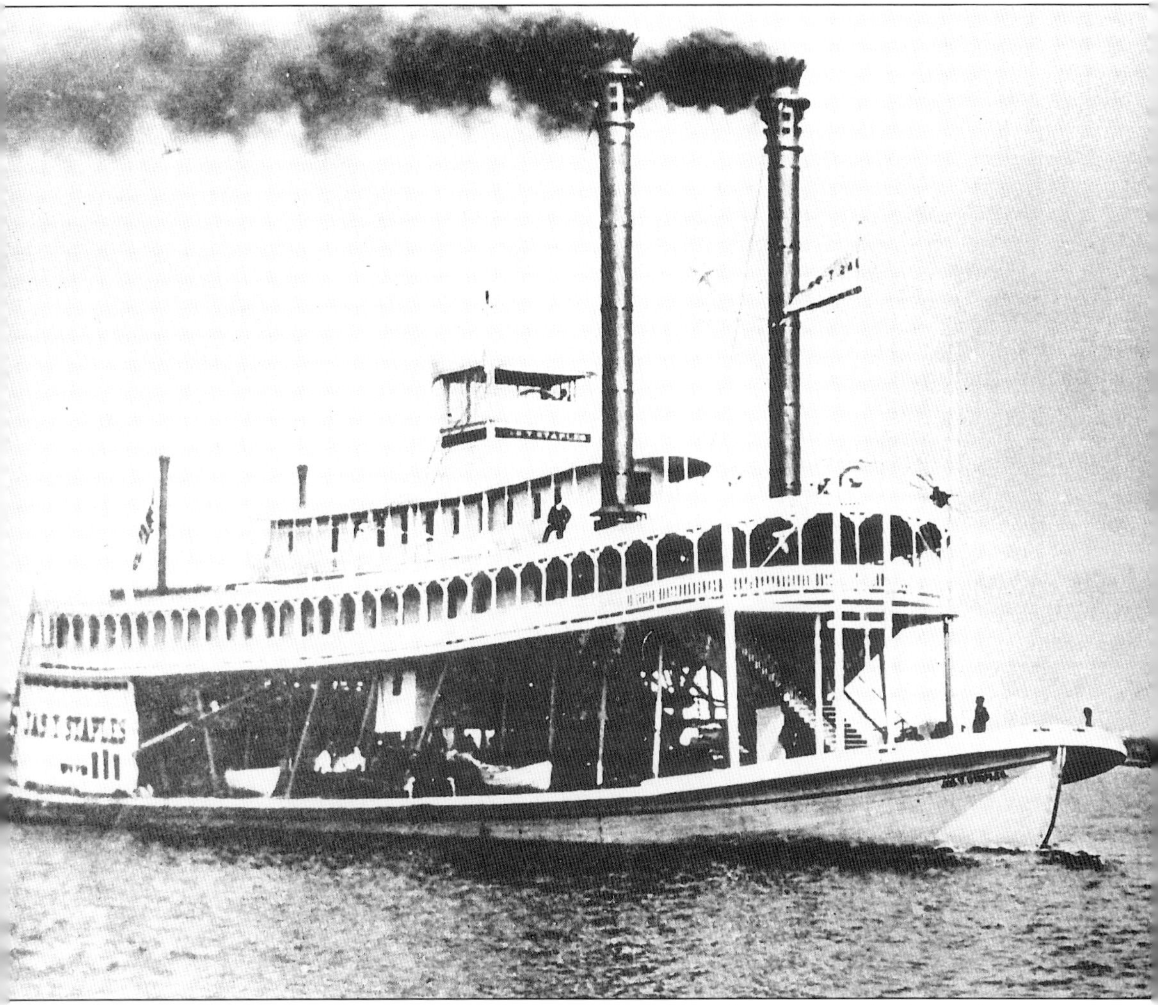

The *James T. Staples*, or the "*Big Jim*" *Staples*, one of many early steamers which traveled the Tombigbee River, is pictured in this photograph from the University of Alabama Library's Special Collection. The *James T. Staples* exploded in 1913, causing one of the worst disasters associated with steamers.

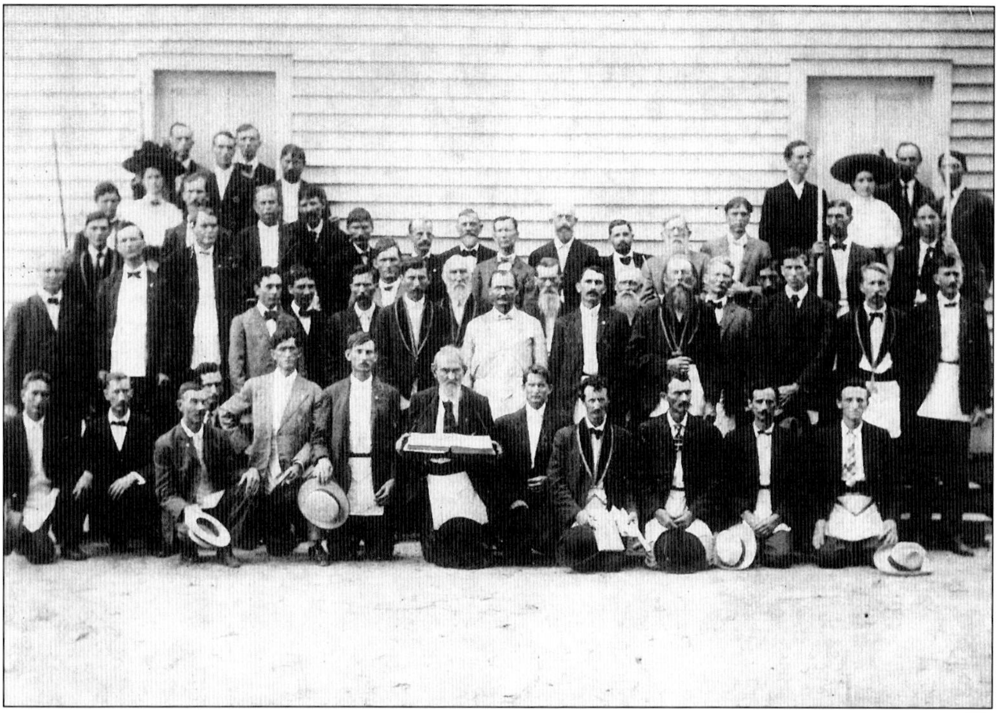

Masonic Lodge #122 of Coffeeville, seen here *c.* 1920, was chartered on January 25, 1850. The Masons have been very active throughout the history of Coffeeville.

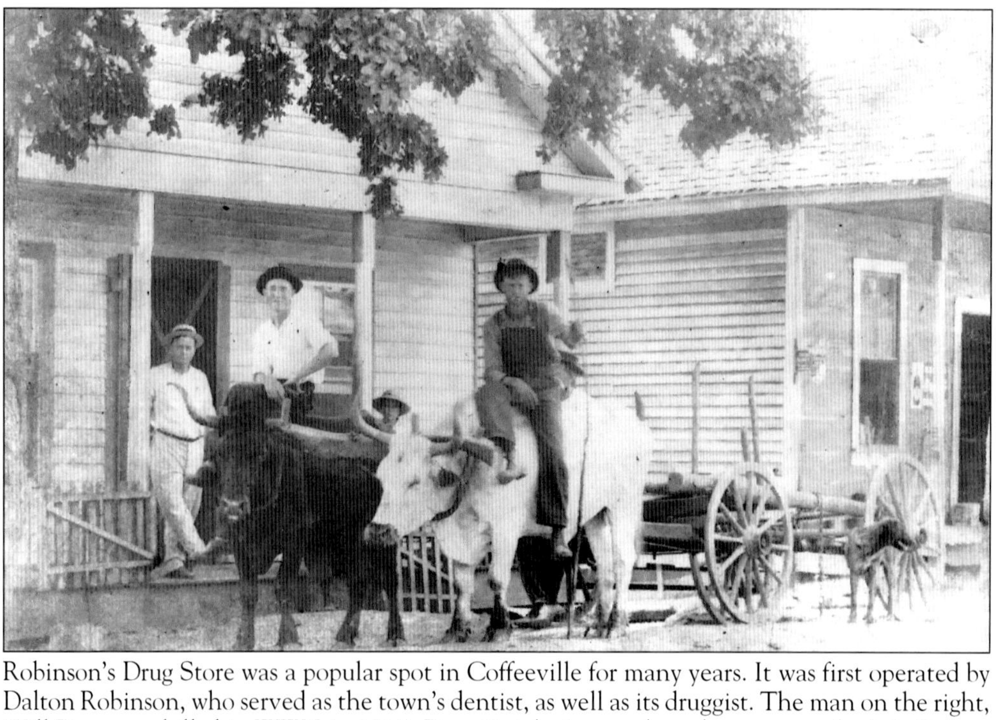

Robinson's Drug Store was a popular spot in Coffeeville for many years. It was first operated by Dalton Robinson, who served as the town's dentist, as well as its druggist. The man on the right, Will Deas, was killed in WW I in 1918. Dent Knight is seated on the oxen on the left. Dalton Robinson is in the doorway.

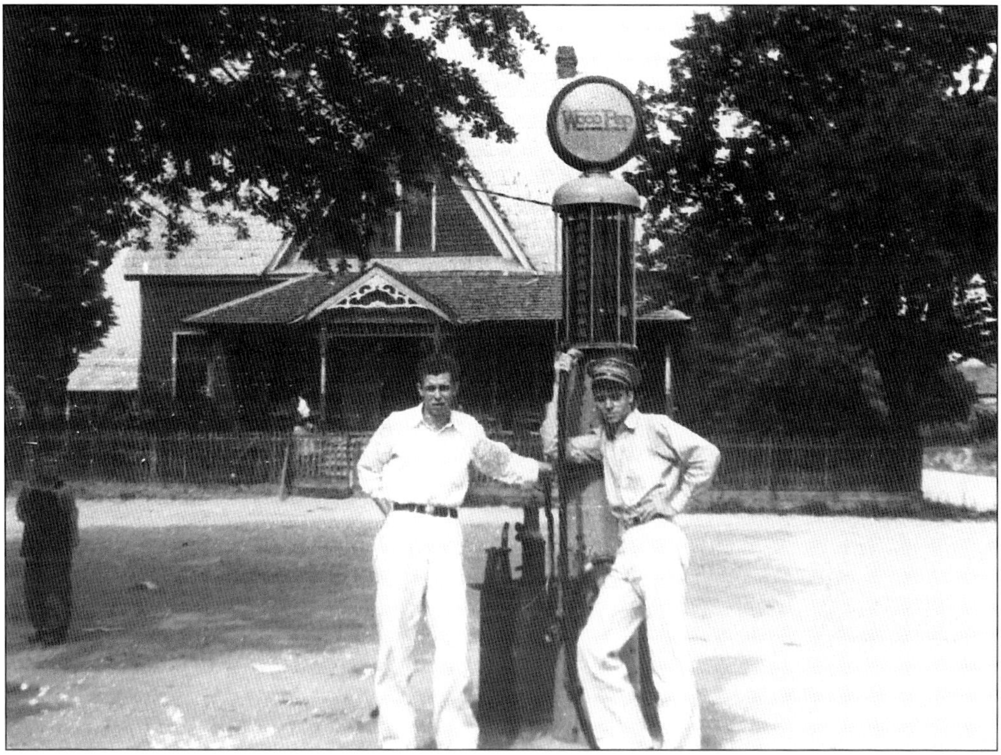

Looking toward the Myrick home in Coffeeville from Odie May Benson's Greasy Spoon, the first restaurant in Coffeeville, these young men are leaning on the Woco Pep gas pump, a sign of the progress in transportation.

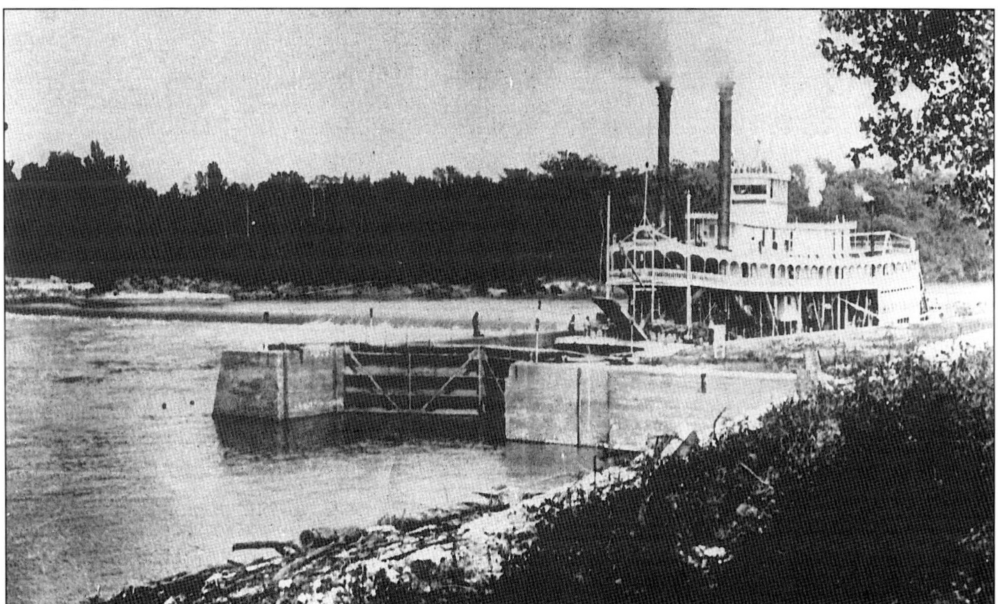

The steamer *Mary S. Blees* was "bound down" on the Tombigbee River on August 13, 1910, when this picture was taken at Lock No. 1.

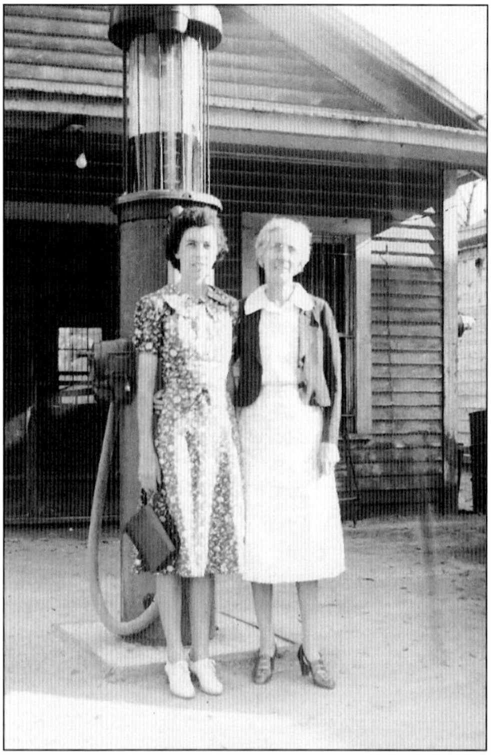

This T.M. Bradford Store in Dickinson was open until February 1950, when a new store was built. The original store was built early in Dickinson's history. Tommie Dee Bradford Kennedy and her mother, Martha Wilson Bradford, are seen here in front of the old store. Tommie Dee's father ran a store all his life; his first store was in Jackson.

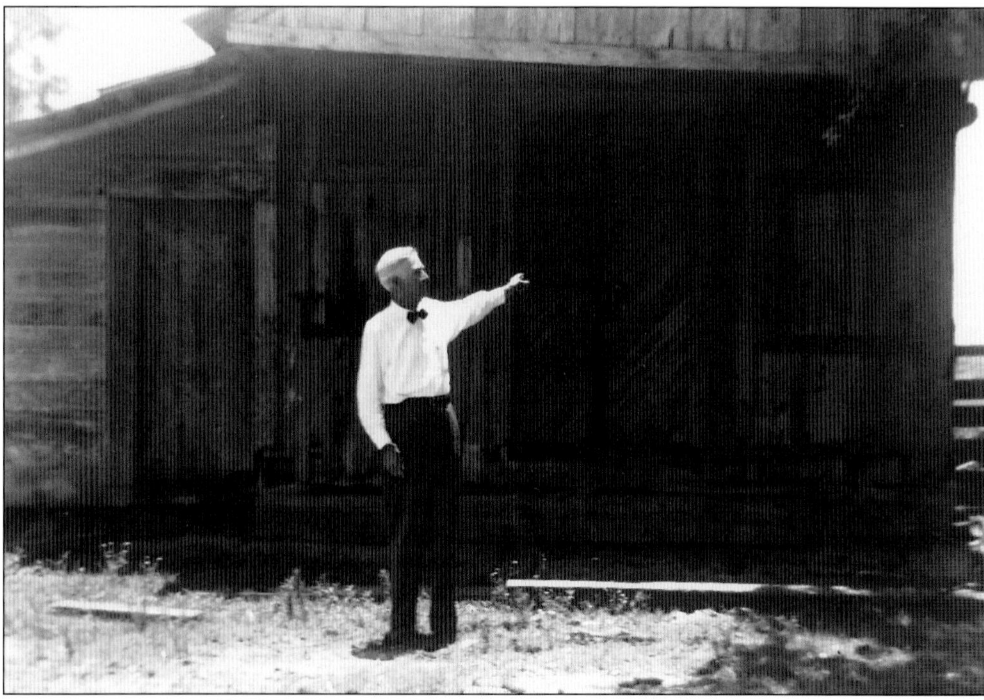

Thomas Marian Bradford, the father of Tommie Dee Kennedy, is seen here in front of his store in Scyrene in 1948. Bradford started this long line of Bradford stores when he moved from Jackson to Scyrene with his family in 1913.

Four

Open for Business

Other Places

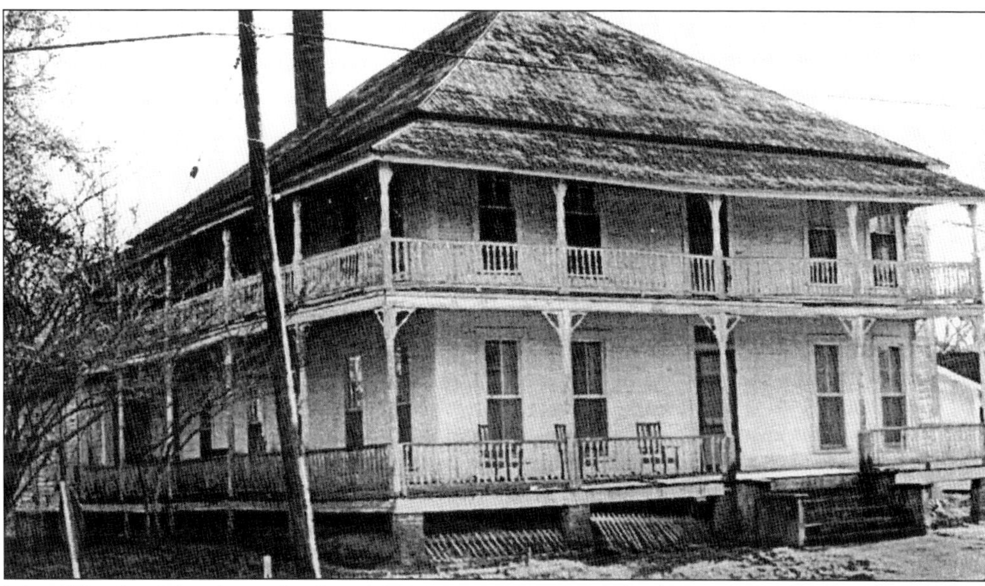

The Whatley Hotel was built in 1888 by Mr. A.D. Whatley and was owned by Nettles and Dacy. The hotel prospered and gained fame throughout southern Alabama up through the 1960s for its family-style meals. The hotel, now a prominent landmark of Whatley, was under construction in 1888, and the *Clarke County Democrat* kept up with its progress. In the February 24th issue, one could read that "Mr. Aleck Whatley lays the foundation this morning for the hotel near the Station." The issue from August 9, 1888, reports that "Messrs. Nettles and Dacy are putting up a handsome and commodious building at Whatley, to be used as a hotel." Then, on August 25, 1889, the paper reads, "Whatley, now one year old, has two stores, one doctor's office or drugstore, one blacksmith shop, one hotel, and one gin house under construction." The building standing today is presumed to be the same one spoken of in the above material.

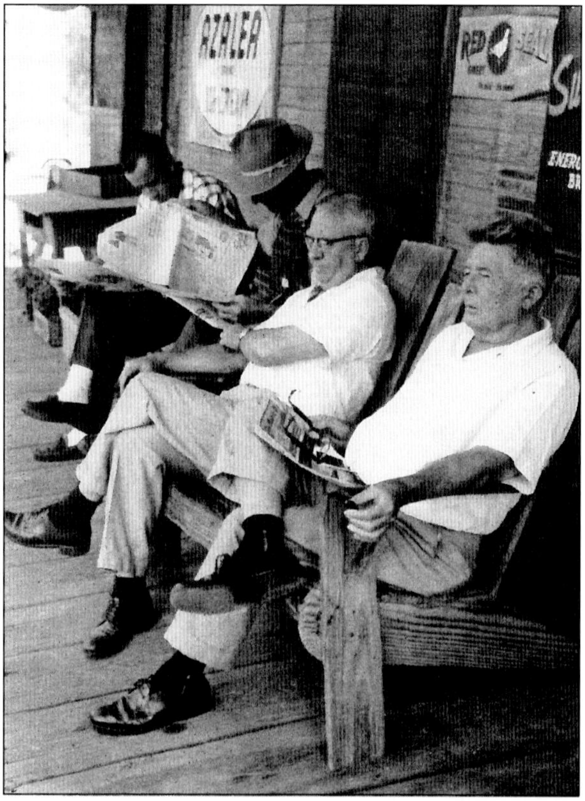

On the porch of Coleman's Store in Whatley are, from left to right, Percy Lee Haskew, Bert Coleman, and Danny and Lee Coleman. Coleman's Store was built sometime in the late 1880s by David Daniel Coleman, who ran it until his death in 1921. After their father's death, Coleman's sons, Lee and Bodie, operated the business as Coleman Brothers. In 1932, after Bodie's death, the business continued as L.L. Coleman's.

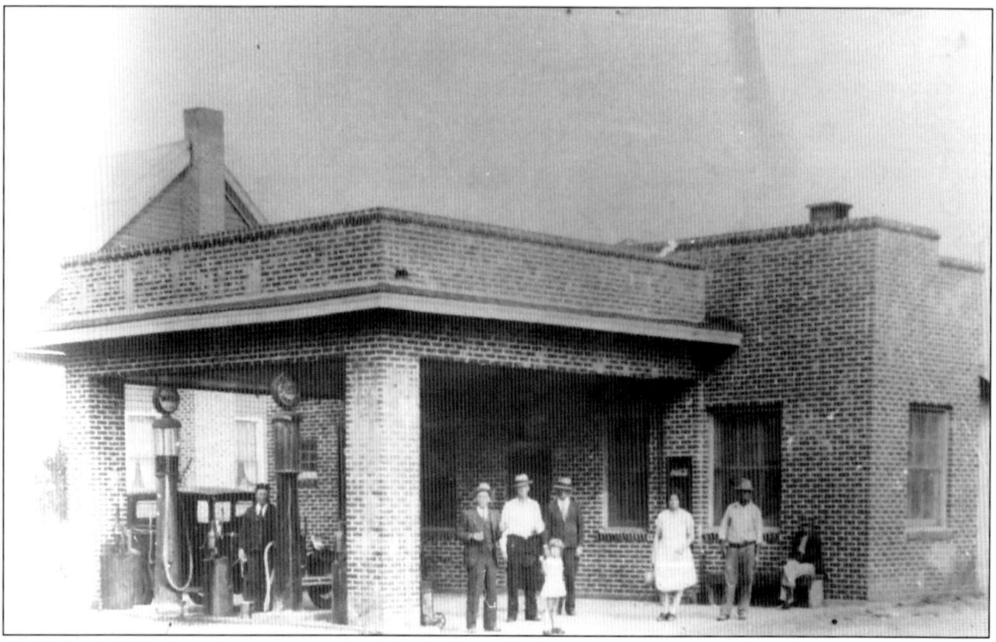

Whatley's "Piggly Wiggly" was built in 1930 to meet market needs. Oil and gasoline for automobiles and groceries were sold there. The new concept of selling for cash at a cash register at the front of the store was employed here. The store was strictly cash and carry.

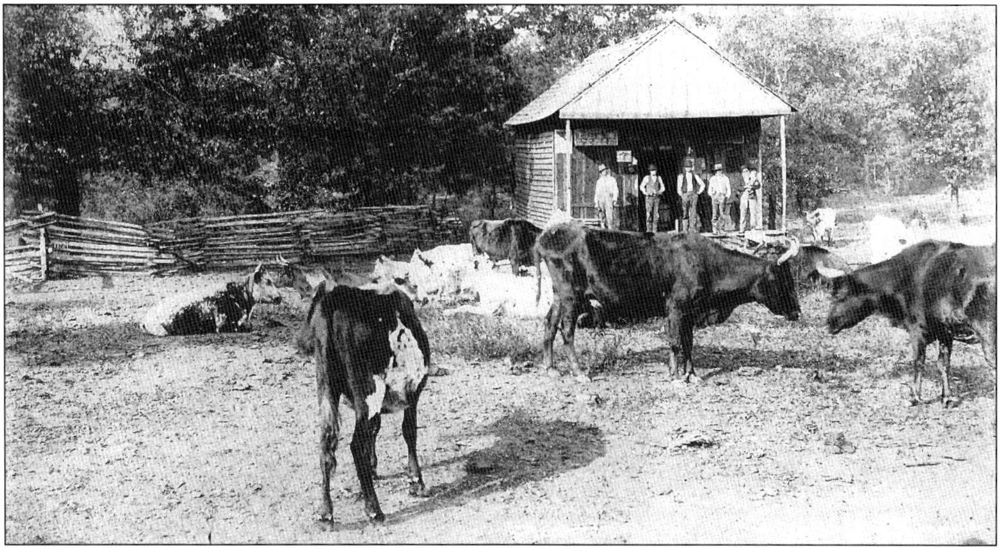

The store of George Thomas Reid of Tallahatta Springs was built in the 1880s in the community where many springs were located. Long before the settlers arrived in the area, it was called Tallahatta ("talla" meaning "town" and "hatta" meaning "many springs or brooks"). The area has also been called Louder Springs, named for the first white settler, and "Celebrated Watering Place" because, in 1847, the town became known for its health and resort vacation facilities.

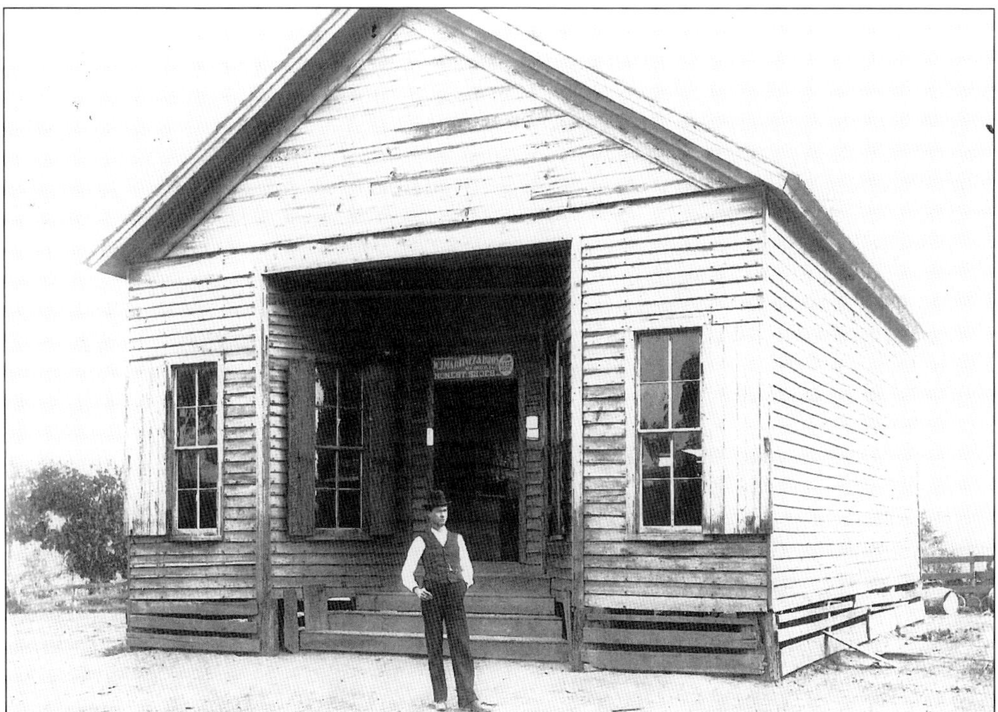

This photograph of the Jesse Pugh Store in Morvin before it moved to Grove Hill shows Jesse as a young man. He was the second postmaster in Morvin, and, later, he owned the Pugh Brothers store in Grove Hill with his brother, Isaac.

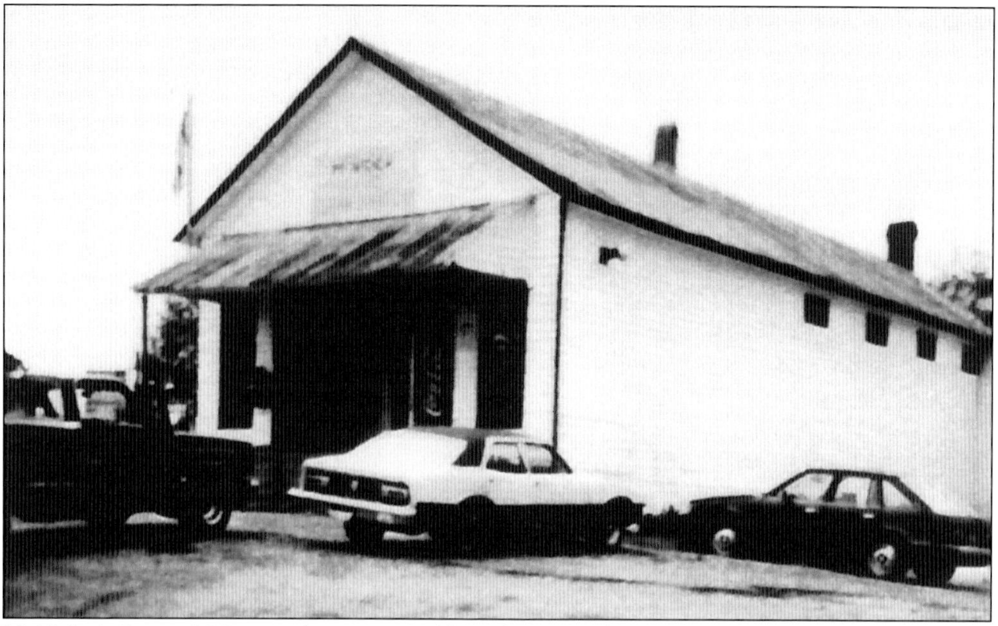

McNider's General Mercantile was owned by John McNider. The store was located in Morvin, where the McNider family has lived for many years. John McNider left the store to his sons. Then a cousin, Otis McNider, owned the store, leaving it to his son, Bruce.

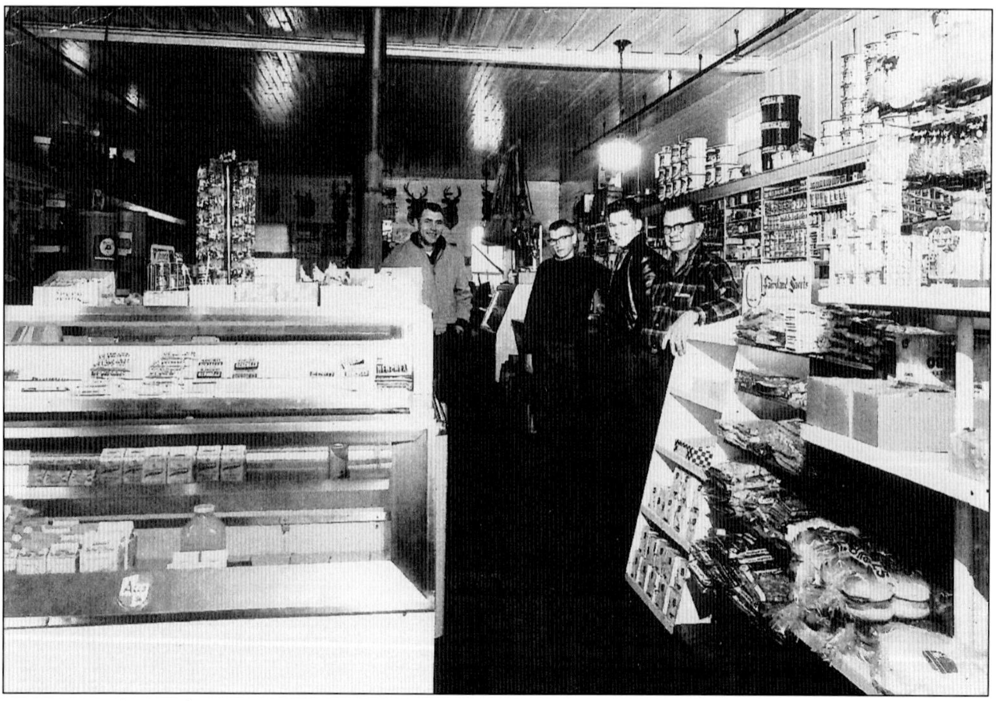

Otis McNider and sons are in the General Mercantile store with a customer in this photograph. Notice the high shelves filled with groceries which could only be reached by the sliding ladder attached to a rod near the ceiling. The pipe of the pot-bellied stove can be seen in the middle of the store.

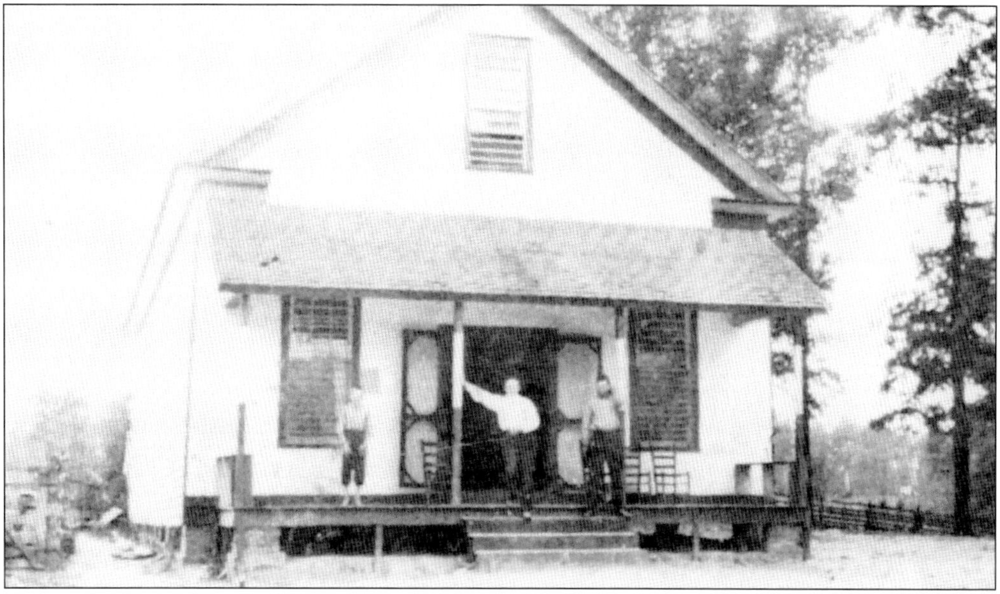

Pickens Store in Campbell was purchased in 1803 by Benjamin Franklin Pickens from Joseph Pickens, an early settler in the Campbell area. In 1815, John Pickens originally came from South Carolina. The Pickens family continued to operate the store in the building shown here until the 1930s.

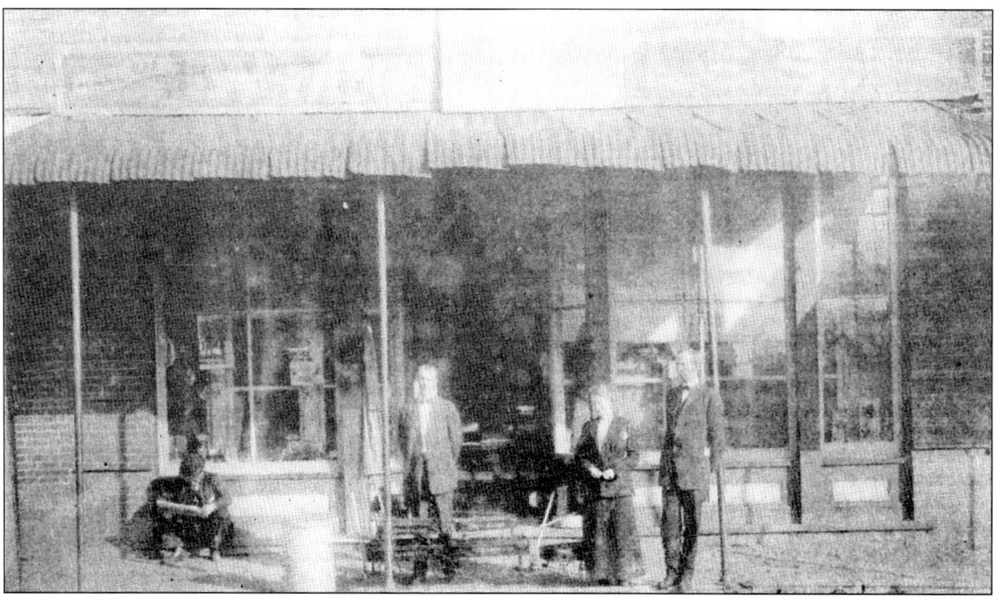

In the early 1800s, the Nored Store was located between Kimbrough's Great General Store and the Gunn store. In this picture, Ed Nored is leaning against the post and his wife, Hattie, is standing nearby. The seated man reading the newspaper is Dr. A.L. White, one of Thomasville's most beloved physicians.

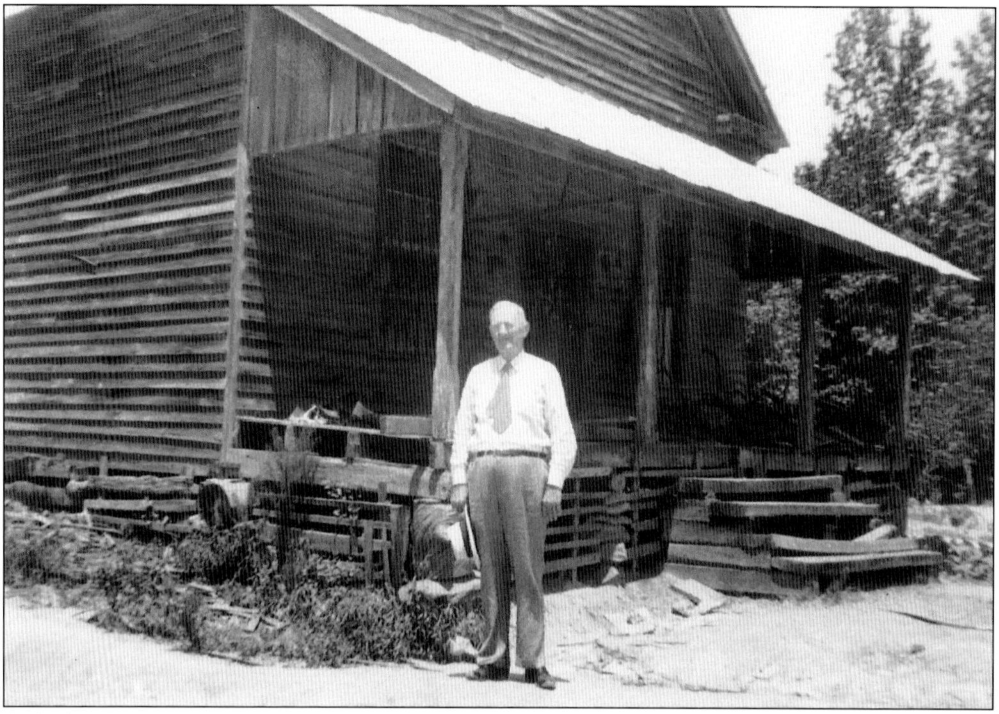

Bedsole's Store in McEntyre, a part of Mitcham Beat, was first owned by Rafe Bedsole in the mid-1870s. The first building was blown away in 1910. The building in this picture was rebuilt in 1910, and J.L. Bedsole is seen here some years later in front of the store.

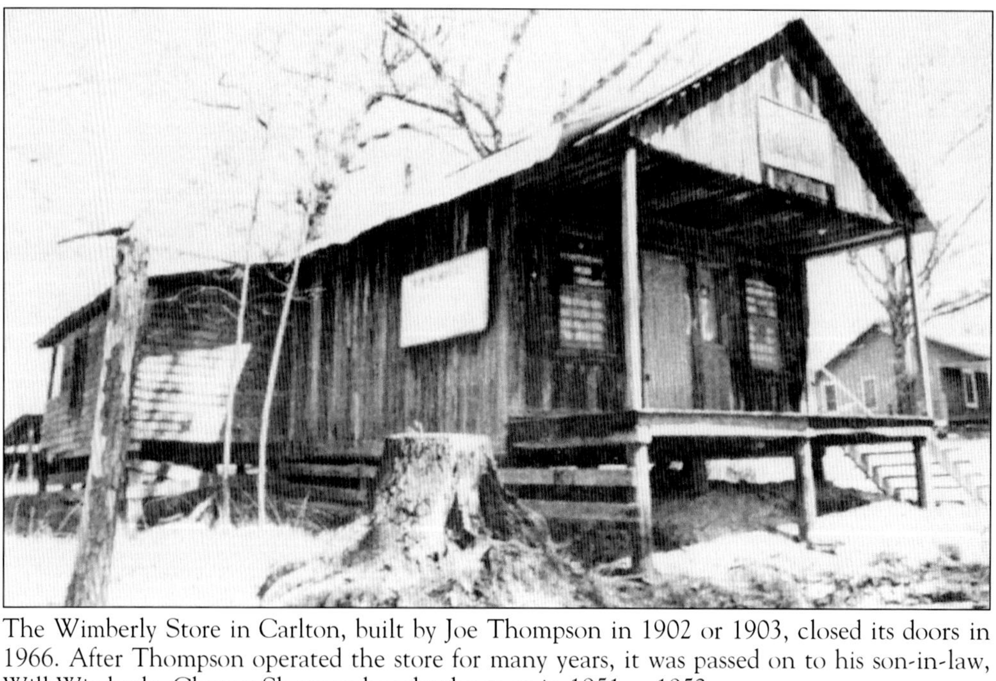

The Wimberly Store in Carlton, built by Joe Thompson in 1902 or 1903, closed its doors in 1966. After Thompson operated the store for many years, it was passed on to his son-in-law, Will Wimberly. Clayton Sherman bought the store in 1951 or 1952.

Five

Houses of Worship

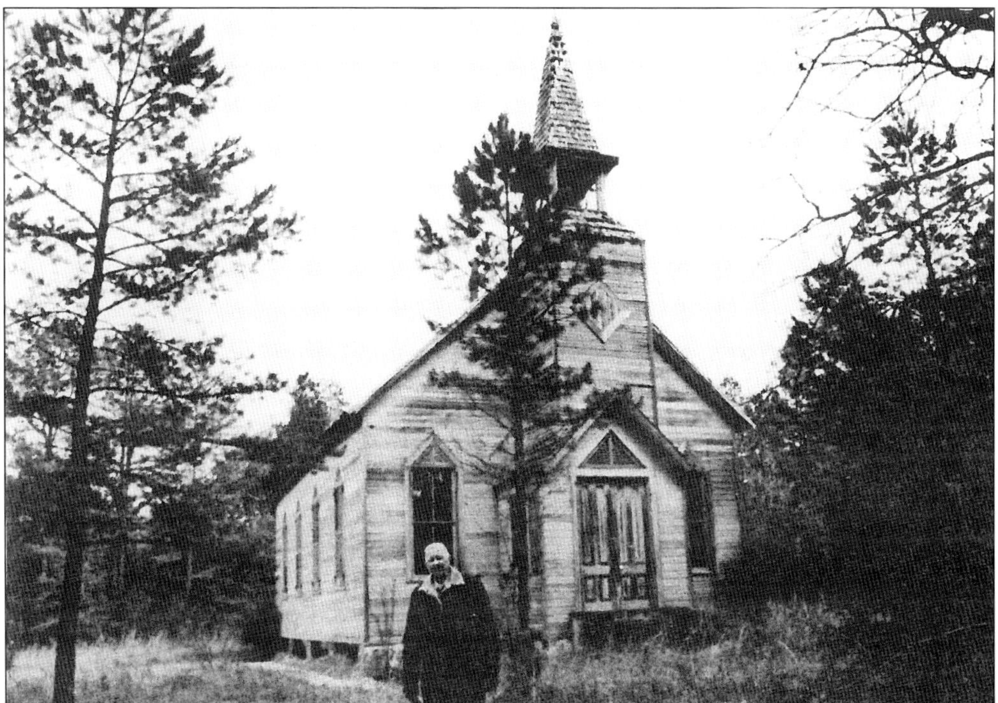

Although abandoned long ago and recently moved from these premises to a new location in Georgia, this Methodist church in Suggsville, Clarke County's most prominent town prior to the Civil War, shows, in its architecture, wealth, culture, and religious influences. The building was made of cypress at a cost of $750 in 1894. A.C. Levi of Columbus, Georgia, whose ancestors were from Suggsville, later moved the structure to his farm and restored it. The church began under a brush arbor during the town's early years. The town grew up around the residence and store of William Suggs, who moved to the area in 1814, when Clarke County was only two years old. The county's first newspaper, the *Clarke County Post*, began publication in Suggsville in 1836. The much-respected historian D.C. Mathews is pictured here in the foreground.

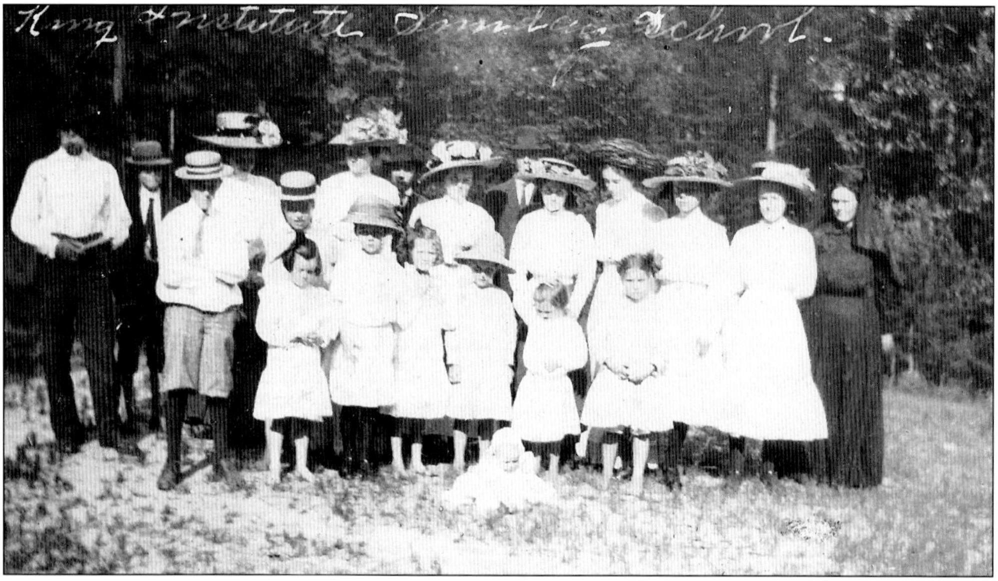

Sunday school was held at the old King Institute School, which was in existence from 1880 to 1910. This picture of a Sunday school class at King Institute was taken prior to 1913, when the school was consolidated with Zimco.

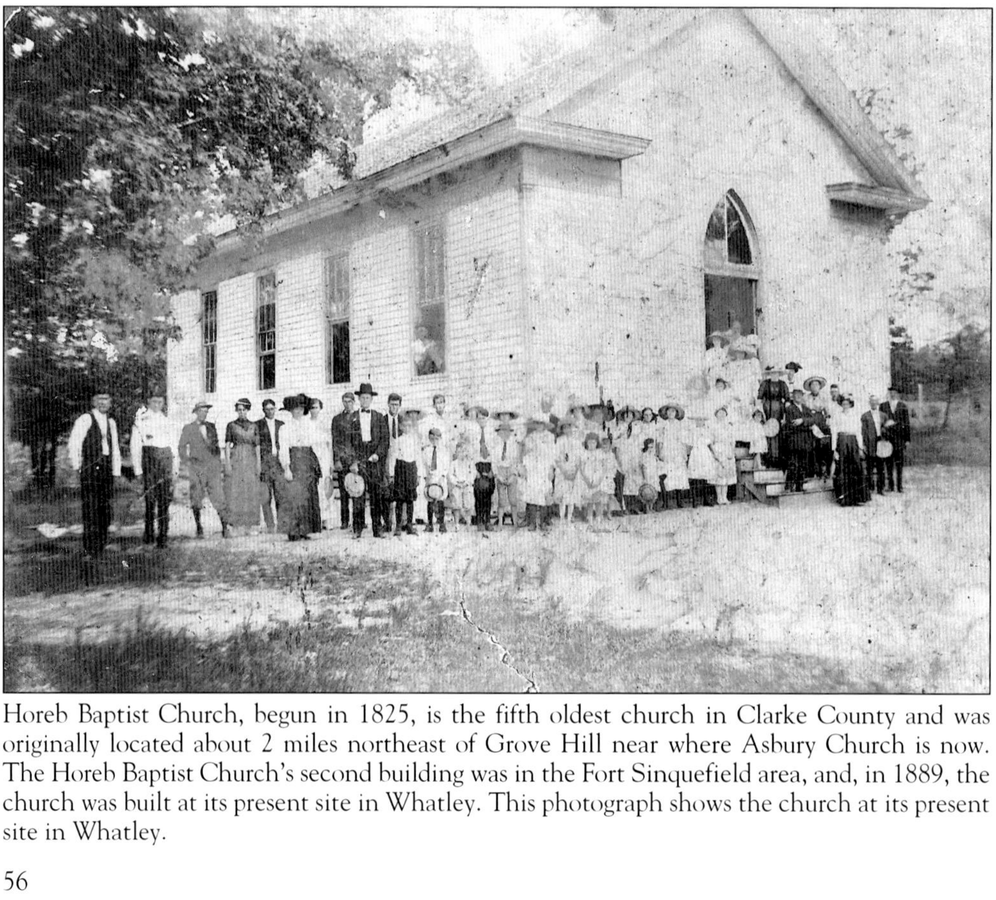

Horeb Baptist Church, begun in 1825, is the fifth oldest church in Clarke County and was originally located about 2 miles northeast of Grove Hill near where Asbury Church is now. The Horeb Baptist Church's second building was in the Fort Sinquefield area, and, in 1889, the church was built at its present site in Whatley. This photograph shows the church at its present site in Whatley.

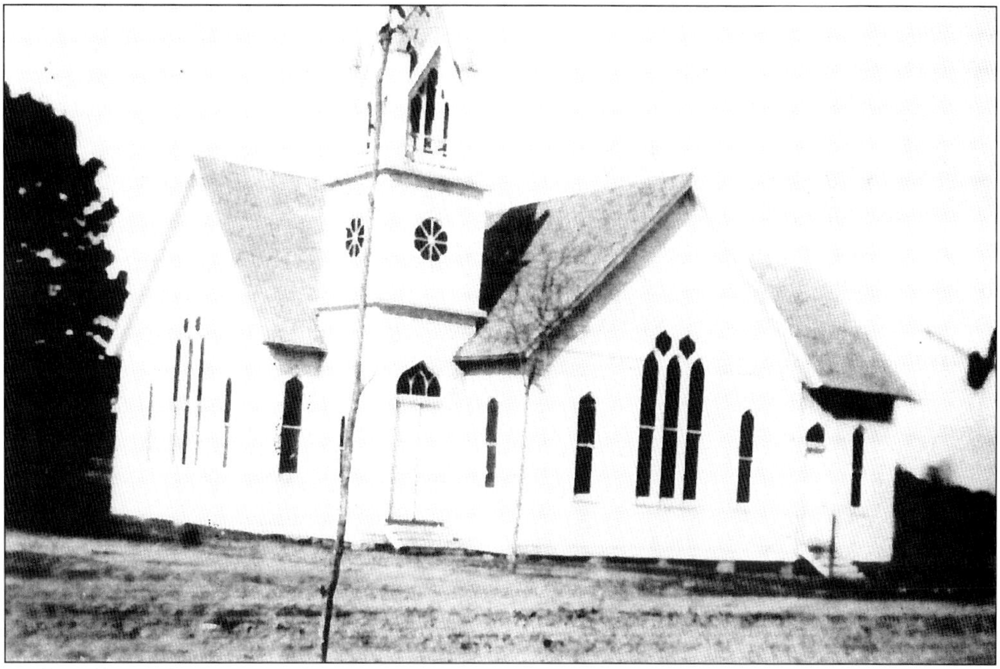

Coffeeville Methodist Church's first building was completed in 1904 while Rev. H.W. Chambers was the pastor. In 1940, that building was replaced by the present brick building, constructed while Rev. Ray M. Jones was the pastor of the church.

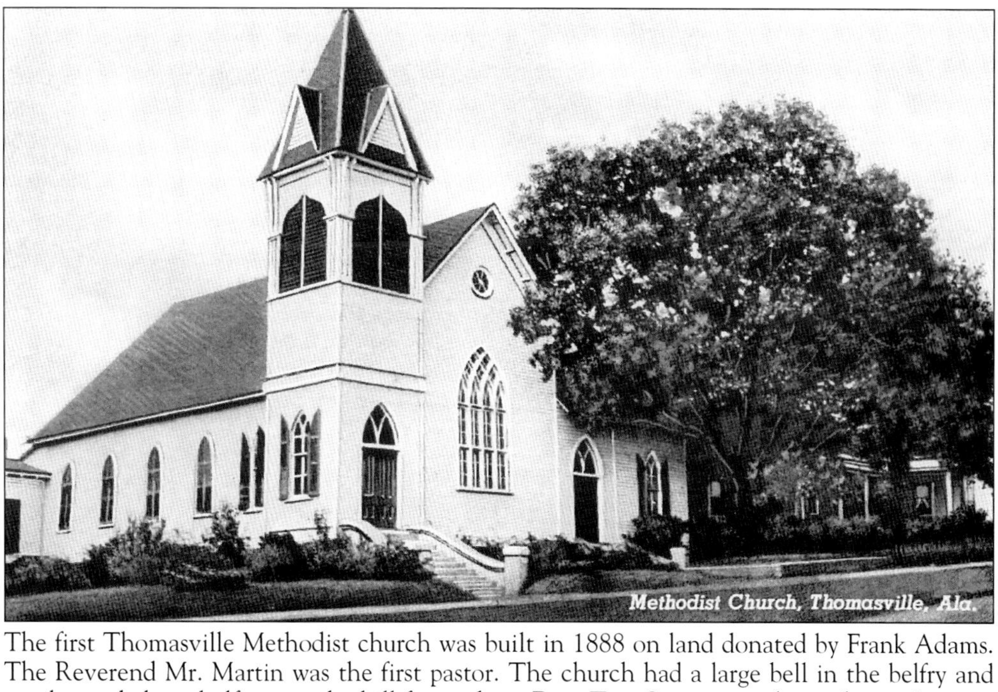

The first Thomasville Methodist church was built in 1888 on land donated by Frank Adams. The Reverend Mr. Martin was the first pastor. The church had a large bell in the belfry and was located about halfway up the hill from where Deas Tire Company is located now. Later, a second building, shown in this picture, was built and, then in 1953, was removed, when a new, larger church was built northeast of the old building.

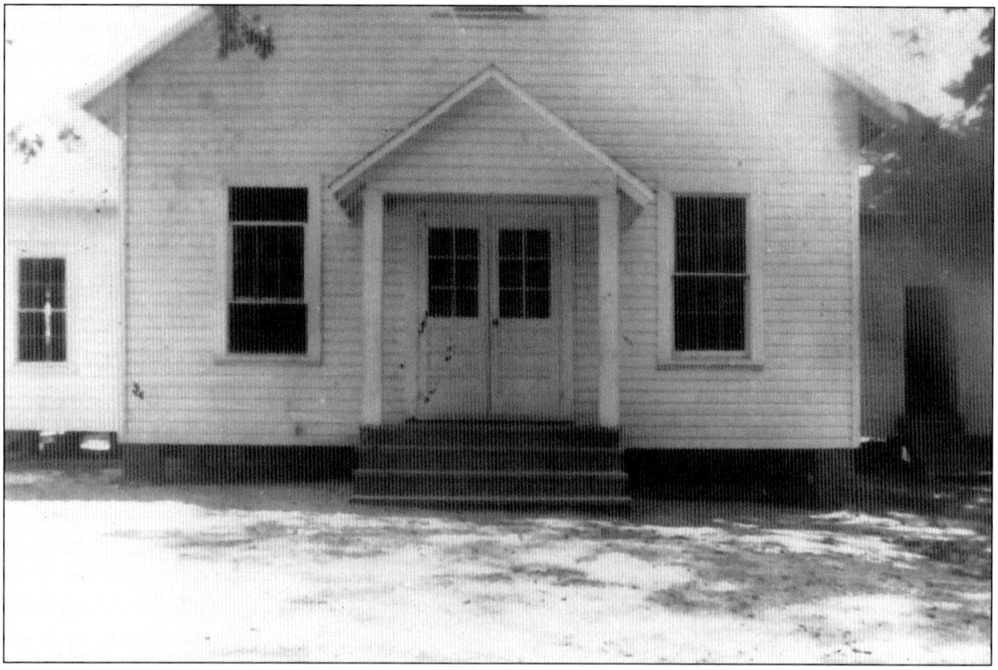

In 1859, three Baptist ministers drew up a constitution and rules of decorum for the Stave Creek Baptist Church and its 15 charter members. Church meetings were first held in a log cabin. The building pictured here was built around 1889 and was used until 1950, when the present building was erected.

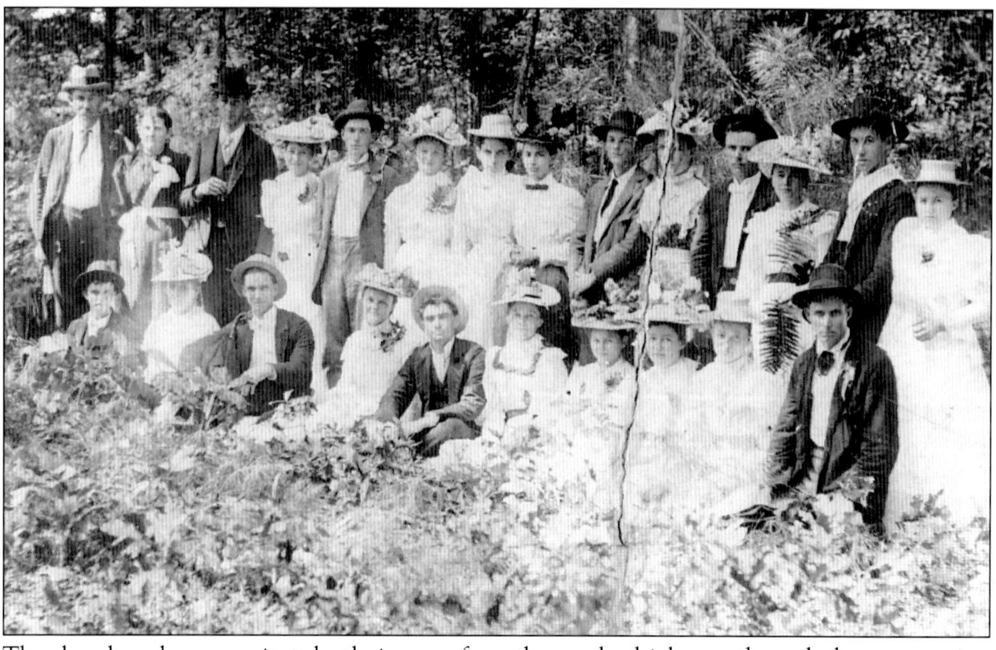

The church and community take their name from the creek which runs through the community. This picture, taken on September 6, 1898, has been identified as a baptism on Stave Creek. Mary Stringer and her husband, J.V. Stringer, are identified as the last two individuals standing on the right.

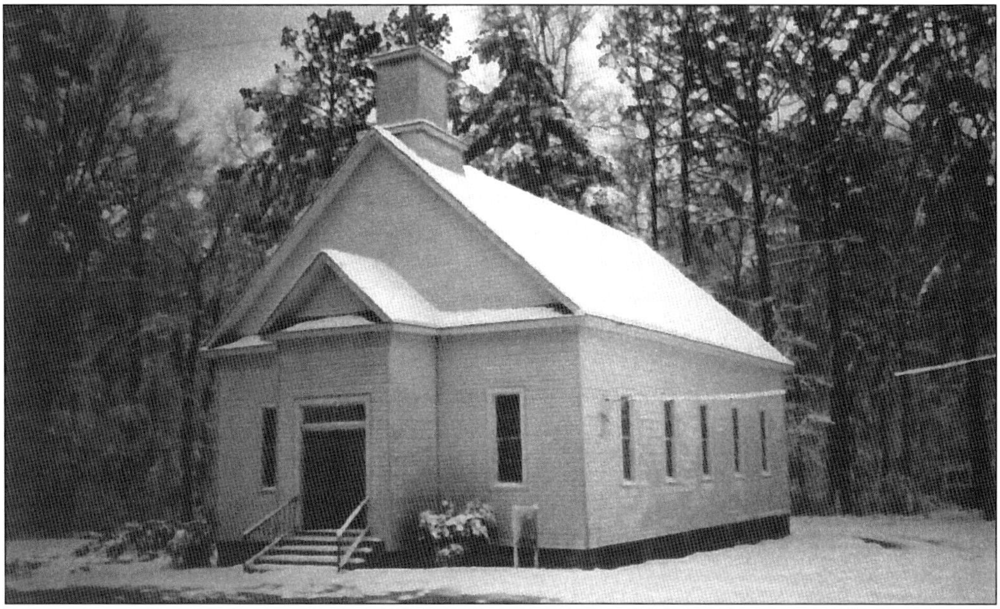

Cane Creek Church began in 1873. This building was erected in 1909 in Chance. When this photograph was taken, snow had fallen—a rarity in southern Alabama. The first trustees of the church were Howard C. Davis, Elbert Davis, E.D. King, and William Marvin Davis.

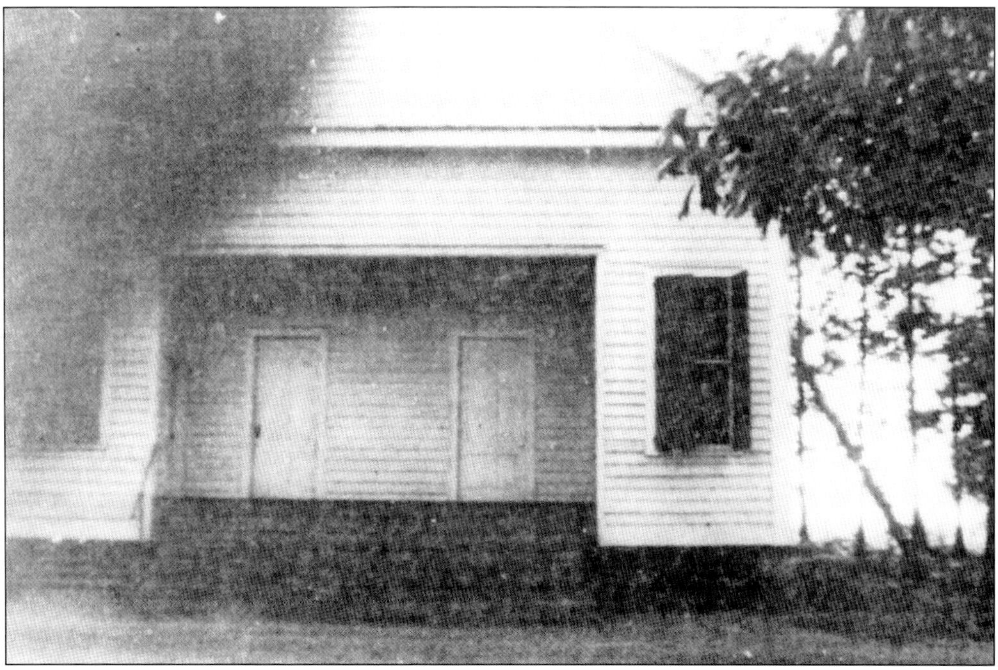

The earliest known photograph, seen here, of West Bend Baptist Church shows the wooden-frame building. The church was started by Jacob Parker and P.E. Kirven. Twenty-two churchgoers withdrew their membership from Ulcanush Baptist Church because they were tired of the distance involved in traveling to the Ulcanush services, and so joined the newly formed church. The new church was begun near West Bend Academy, and Rev. P.E. Kirven was the first pastor.

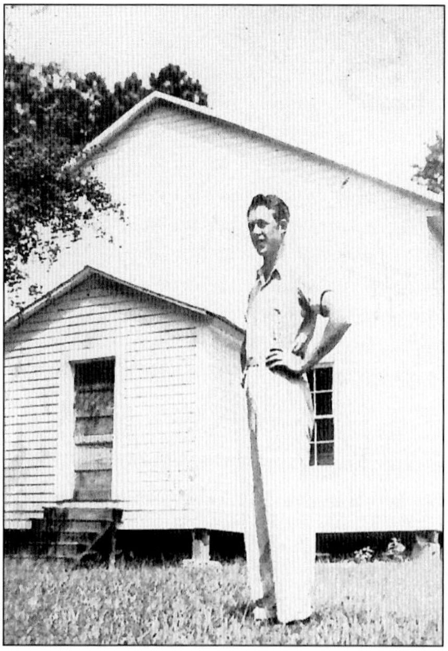

Chilton Baptist Church was organized in 1904 by some former members of Hopewell Baptist Church and Good Hope Baptist Church who were also tired of the distance involved in traveling to services. Warren Harrison had a sawmill, a gristmill, and a gin in the vicinity, and he sawed the lumber for the church building, which was to be built on the bank of Satilpa Creek, where the church remains today.

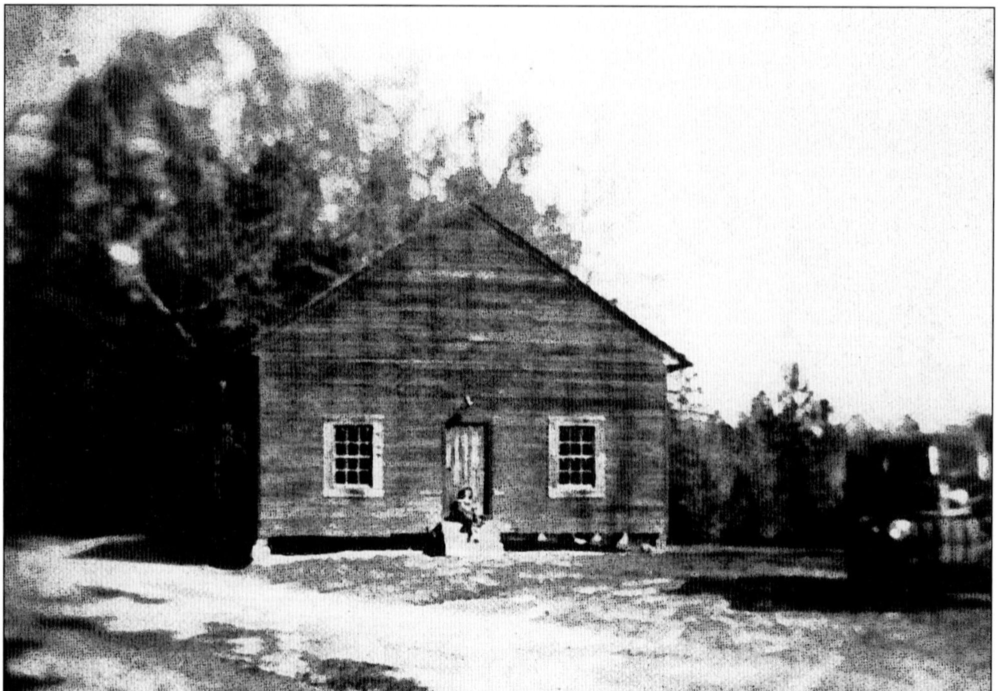

Hopewell Baptist Church was established in 1857 near the Jesse White house in Chilton. The first building was a log structure, which was moved between 1870 and 1872 just west of the present location of Hopewell. When the second building, shown here, was built in 1887, the log building served as a school and then was moved northward and became the home of Monroe and Clare McIntyre. In 1949, Hopewell moved to its present location, where the church was built under the urging hand of Rev. B.A. Lambert, the Baptist Associational missionary of Clarke County.

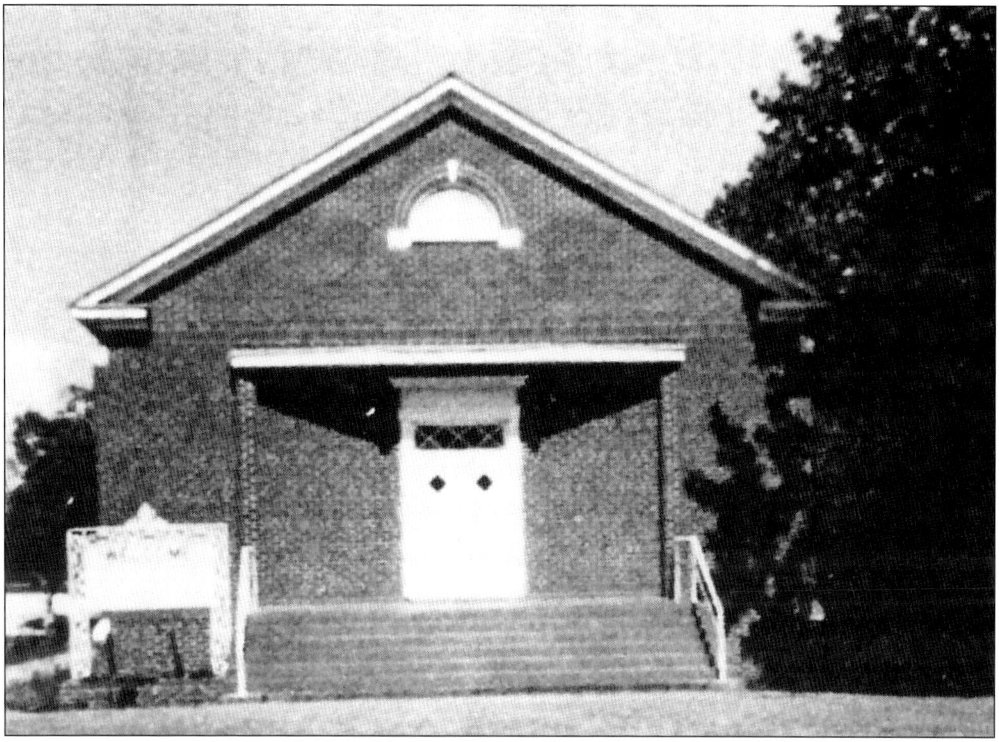

In 1904, a few members withdrew from Ulcanush to form a church in Coffeeville, which became the First Baptist Church of Coffeeville. E.T. Cave, John J. McCoy, Claude Dix, L.A. Fail, Heard E. Coate, Sister Lillie Dix, J.H. White, and E.T. Robinson organized themselves into a church. Rev. J.L. Tucker was the first pastor. The first church building was a one-room, wooden structure, costing $500 and located on the Masonic Lodge site in 1905. A two-story brick building was erected in 1946.

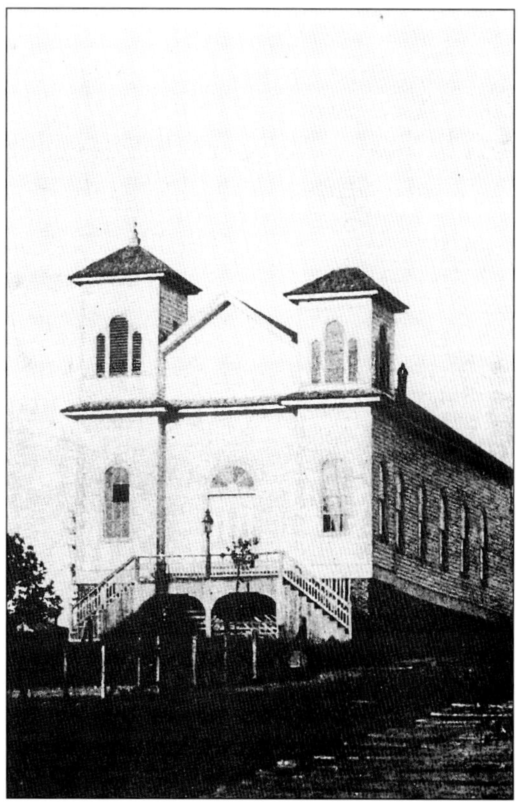

Thomasville Baptist Church was organized in 1890 by the Presbytery, which consisted of William A. Parker of Thomasville; W.B. Crumpton of Marion, Alabama; and I.A. White of McKinley, Alabama. W.A. Parker was the first pastor. The building was situated on Safford Avenue, facing east on the present church playground site.

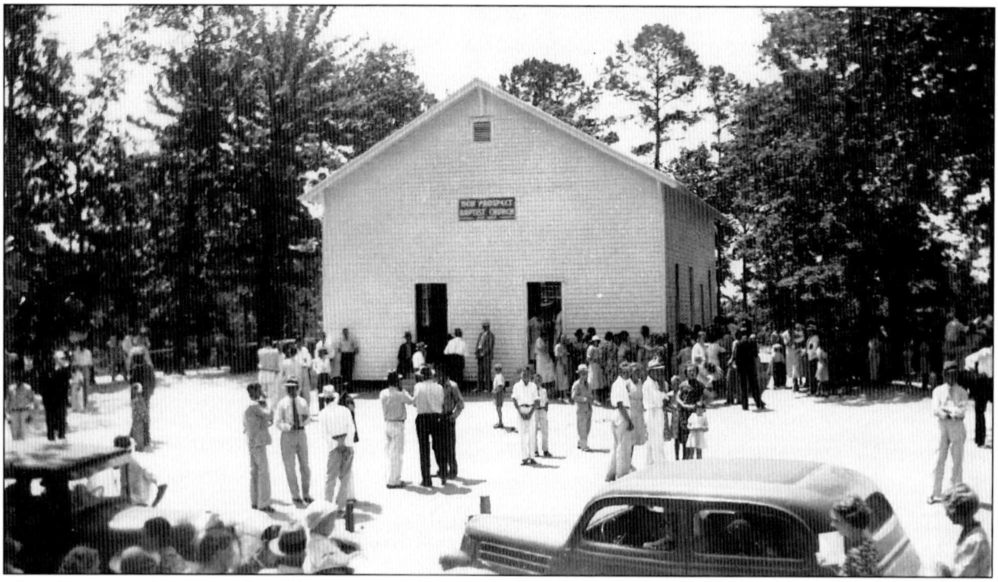

New Prospect Baptist Church was established in 1866. The first church was located about one-half mile in back of the present building. When the church was moved to its present location, a new cemetery was begun in front of the church. The first person was buried there in 1877. The church is located on Highway 154 in old Mitcham Beat, more accurately called McEntyre, but commonly called New Prospect because of the name of the church.

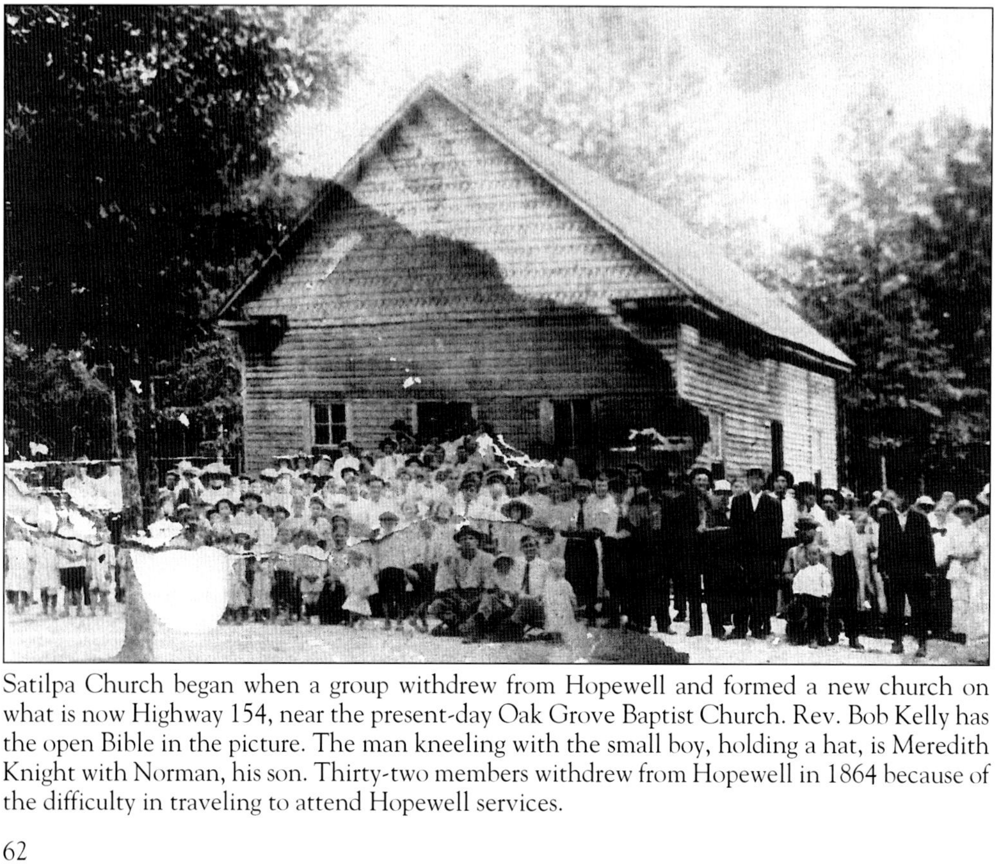

Satilpa Church began when a group withdrew from Hopewell and formed a new church on what is now Highway 154, near the present-day Oak Grove Baptist Church. Rev. Bob Kelly has the open Bible in the picture. The man kneeling with the small boy, holding a hat, is Meredith Knight with Norman, his son. Thirty-two members withdrew from Hopewell in 1864 because of the difficulty in traveling to attend Hopewell services.

Bethel Baptist Church was organized in 1901 and was located north of Coffeeville just off today's Highway 69. The photograph shows the front area of the structure that was first built. The children pictured here reveal that the church was often a social center as well as a place of worship for members of rural families.

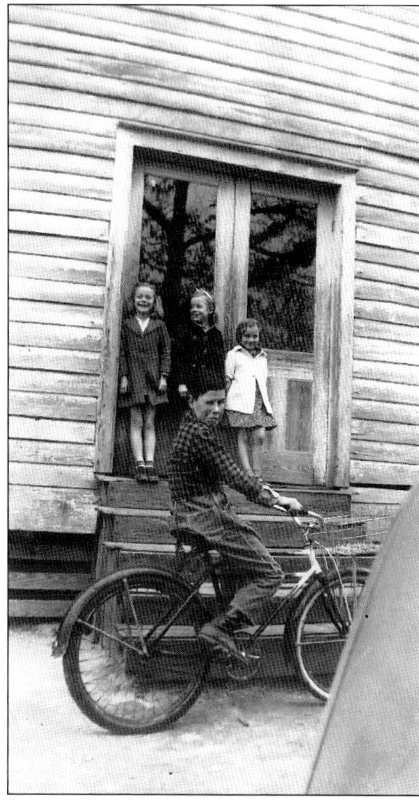

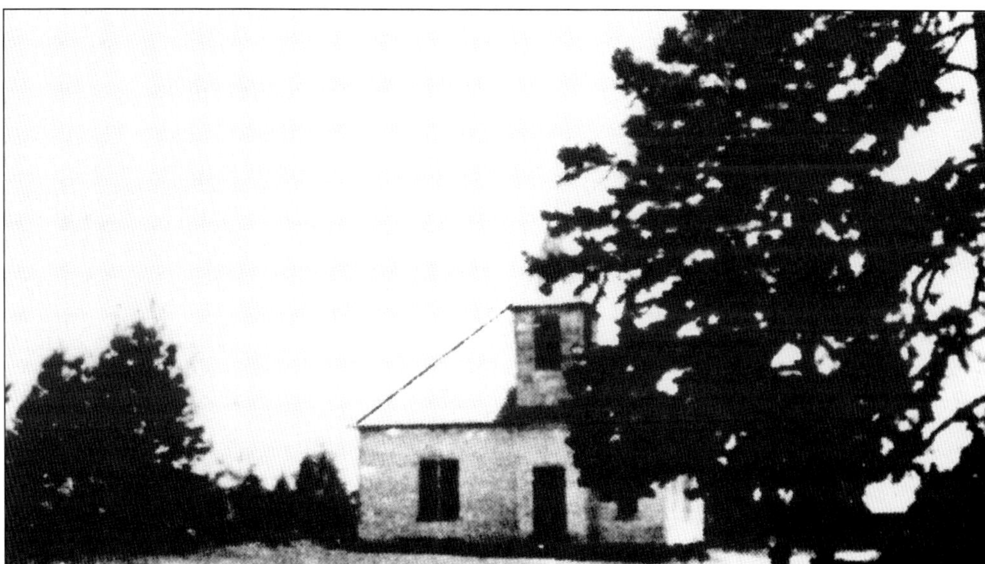

Salem Baptist Church was organized in 1832 by George D. and Stephen Williams. Rev. George Williams was the first pastor and there were 28 charter members. The first building was a log structure located on a site across from the old Salem Cemetery. Another church was built in 1889, another in 1907, and the present one in 1958.

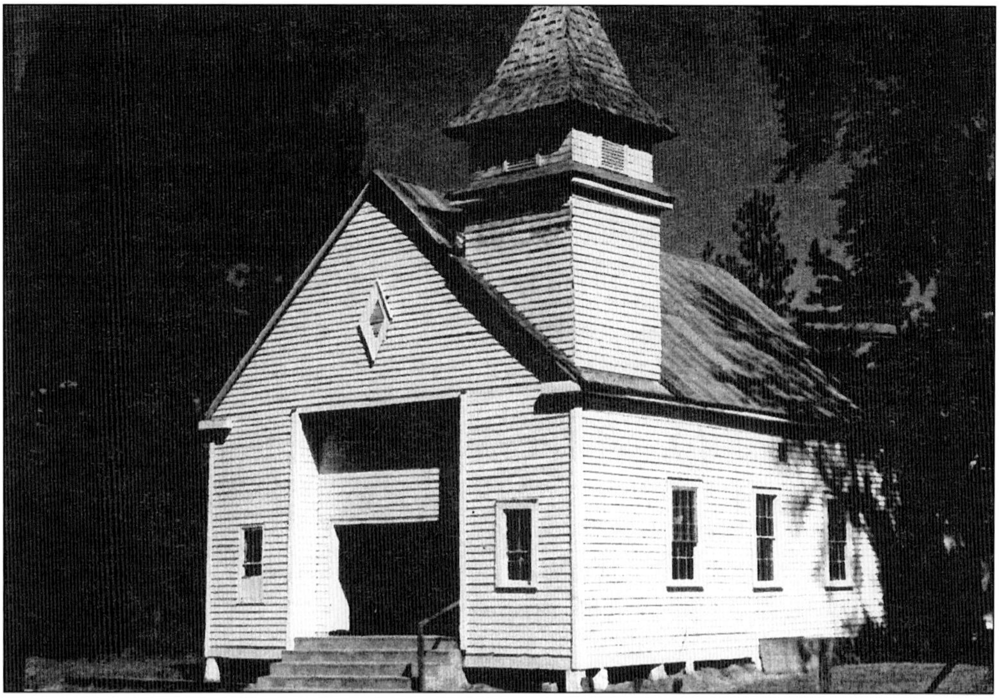

Mt. Nebo Church was located in the southernmost part of Clarke, down in the forks of the rivers. The origin of the church is uncertain, but it probably was started just after the Civil War. The first congregation met on a dirt floor. The present building was built between 1900 and 1910 and is shown in this photograph. The Mt. Nebo Cemetery is famous because death masks— an image of the person who had died—made by Ike Nettles are on some of the graves. Only a few of these remain. The church and cemetery are located near Hal's Lake Camp.

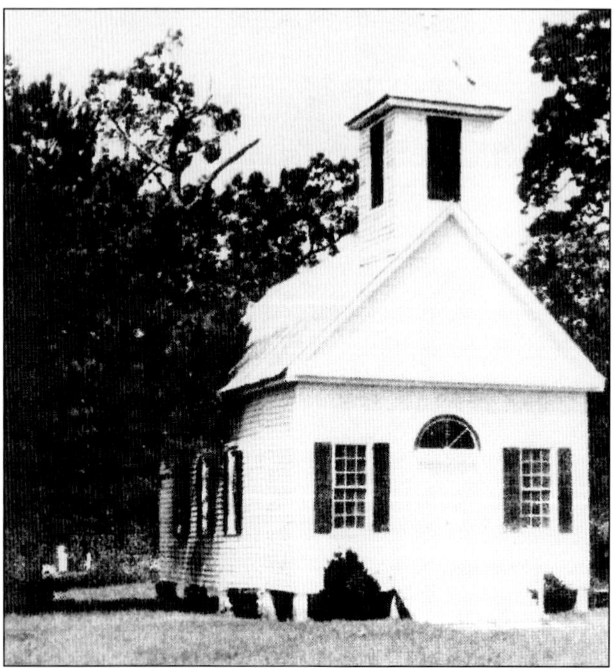

Gainestown Methodist Church began in a large two-story building in 1854 with the church on the lower floor and the Masonic lodge on the upper floor. One of the founders was Rev. Joshua Wilson, who settled in Clarke County in 1817. In 1911, a tornado damaged the building, and it was immediately rebuilt, using much of the original materials.

Friendship Baptist Church was organized in 1822 by Elders Anderson, Perkins, and Crumpton. Jonathan Anderson and Truehart Tucker were the first pastors.

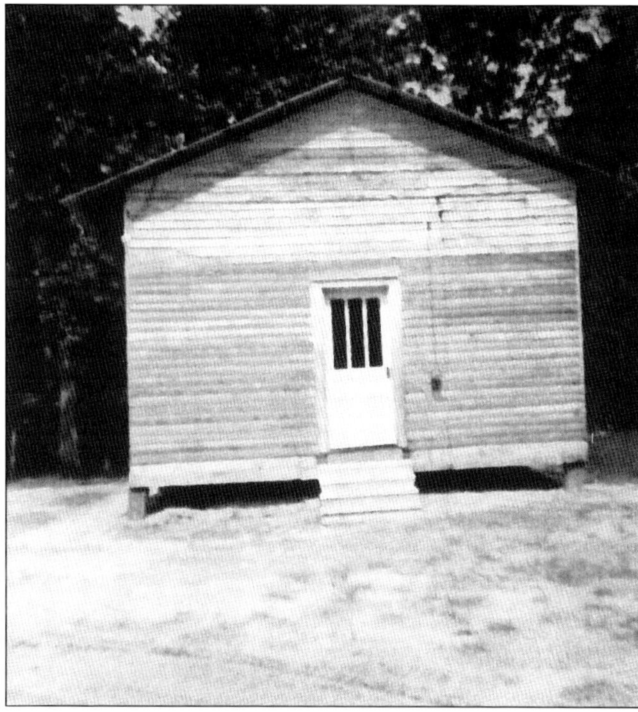

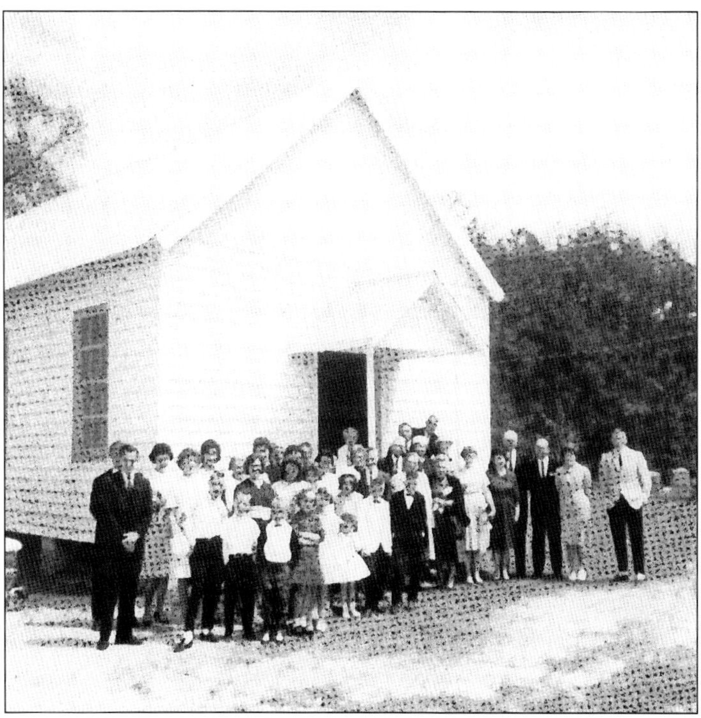

Rockville Baptist Church was established in 1879 by brethren P.E. Kirvin, R.J.W. Dewitt, and J.V. Stringer. Elder C.J. Miles was elected pastor. There were seven charter members who began this church 8 miles south of Jackson.

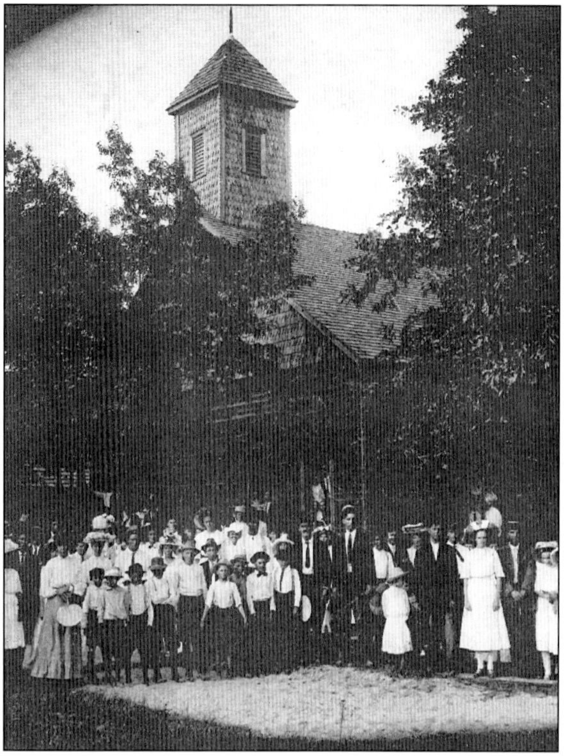

The first Methodist Protestant church in Sandflat, or Springfield, was founded by Rev. Memphis R. Evans in 1897. Evans Chapel United Methodist Church was later housed in a white-frame building which was constructed in 1951 across from the original structure.

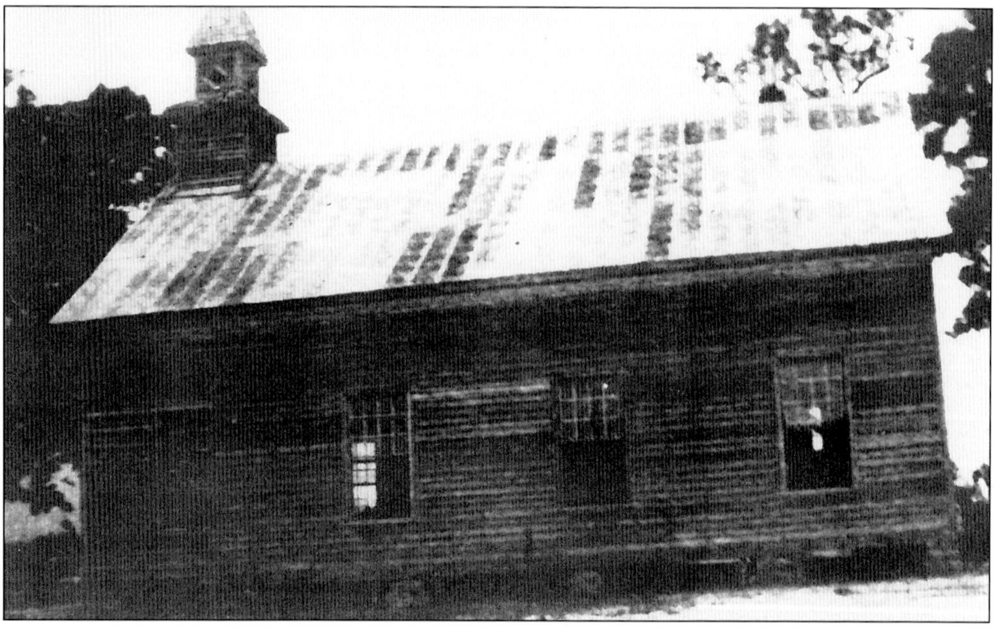

The oldest church in Clarke County in its original location is Ulcanush Baptist Church, located 2 miles north of Coffeeville on Highway 69. The church was established in 1816 after it grew out of a prayer meeting. Present at the meeting were John and Elizabeth Pace, William Stringer, William and Nancy Thornton, Rhoda Allen, Michael Miller, and Joseph Williams, who was also the first pastor.

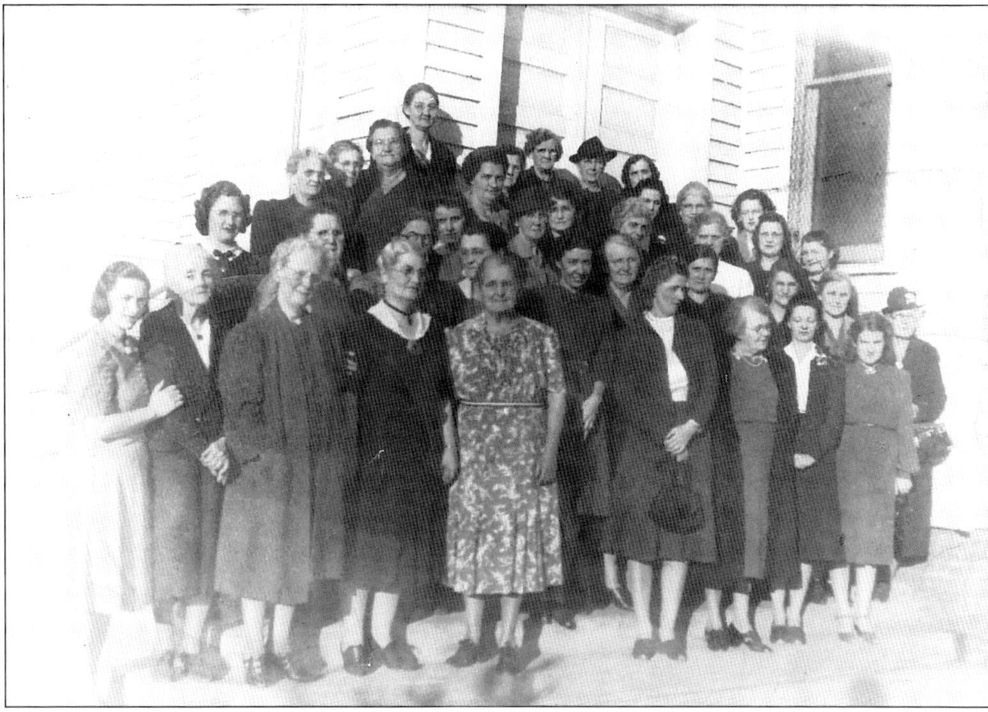

Sometimes known as "The Ladies' Aid," the Grove Hill Women's Missionary Society at Grove Hill Methodist Church was organized in 1890 before the first church was built on this site in 1910 under Rev. J.O. Lawrence.

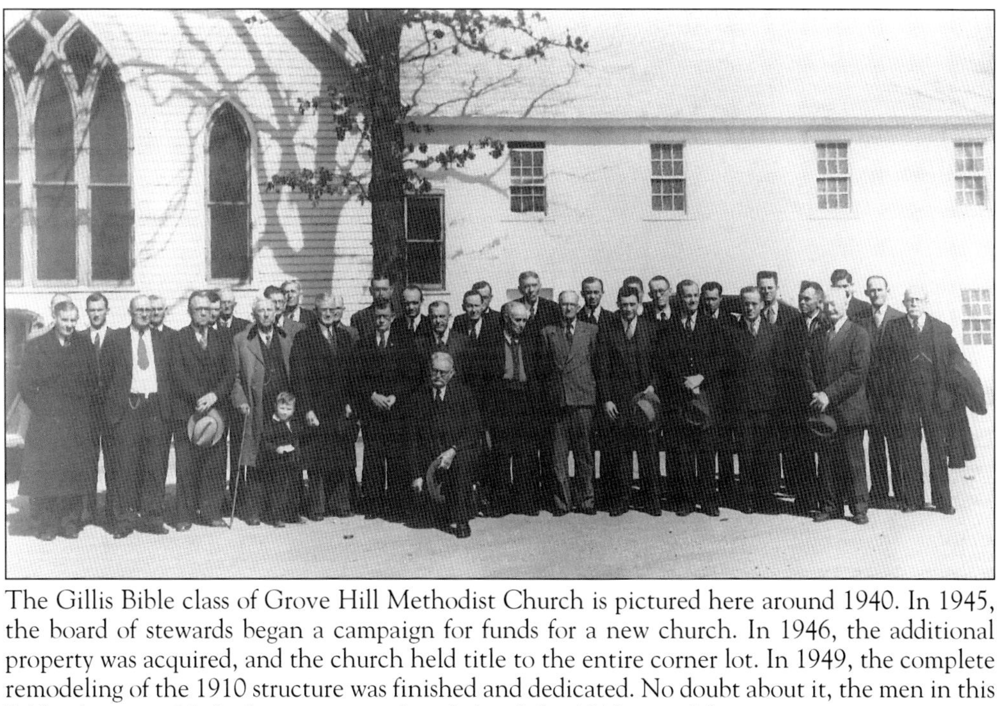

The Gillis Bible class of Grove Hill Methodist Church is pictured here around 1940. In 1945, the board of stewards began a campaign for funds for a new church. In 1946, the additional property was acquired, and the church held title to the entire corner lot. In 1949, the complete remodeling of the 1910 structure was finished and dedicated. No doubt about it, the men in this Bible class were likely the active members behind the 1949 remodeling.

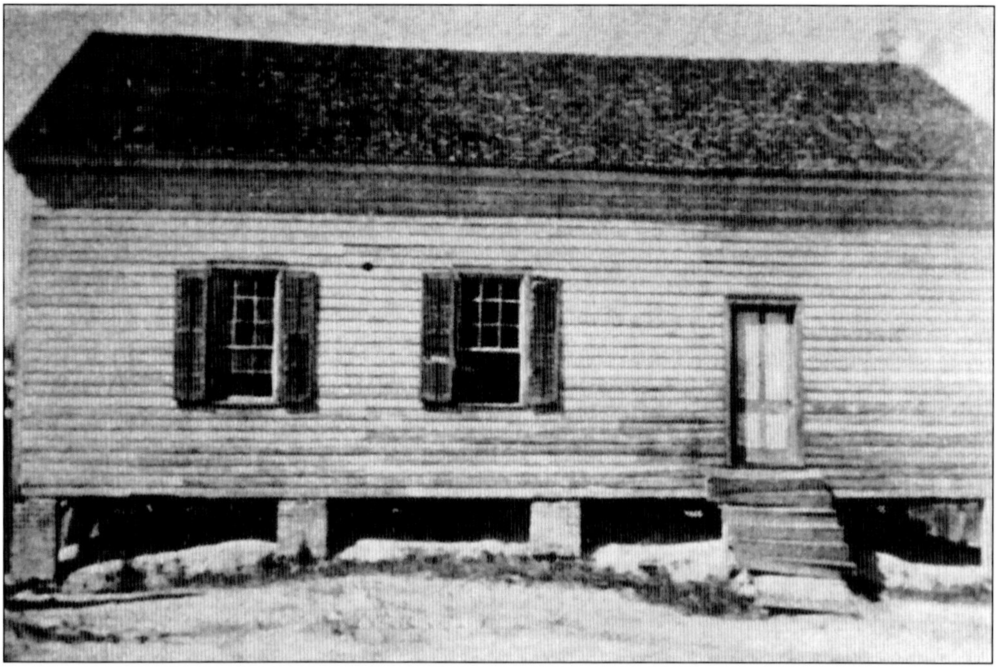

Elam Baptist Church was organized in 1834 at Choctaw Corner near the Indian Boundary Mound about 3 miles east of Bashi. In 1860, the church was moved to Bashi, and, then in 1875, it was moved to the present site.

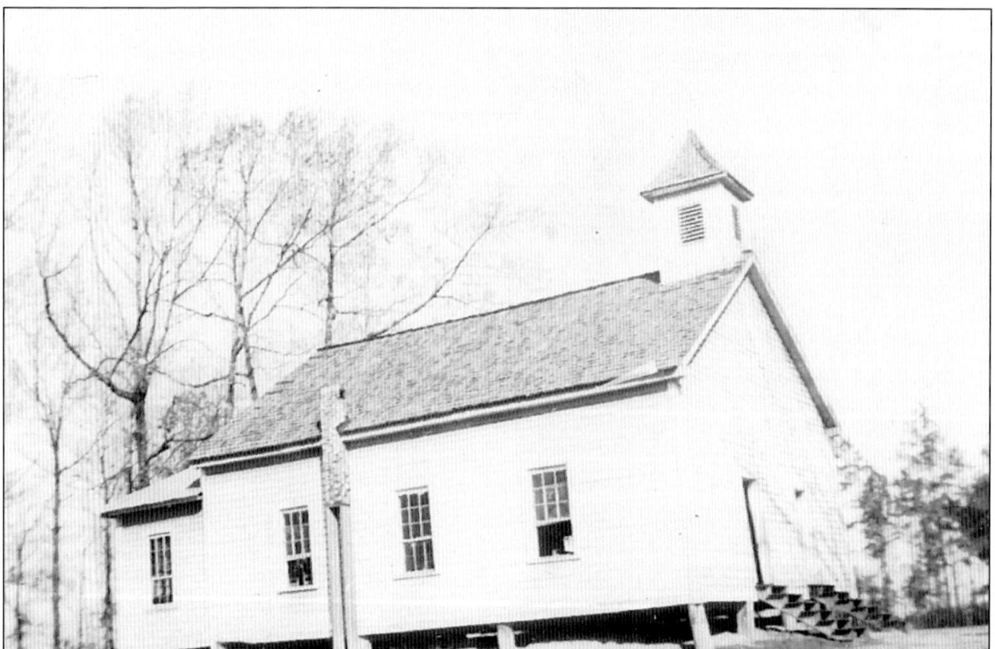

The first church in what was to become Clarke County was the old Bassetts Creek Church, founded in 1810. Elder Joseph Agee was the pastor, but the church finally disbanded. The New Bassetts Creek Church was formed in 1969.

Six

EDUCATION FOR ALL

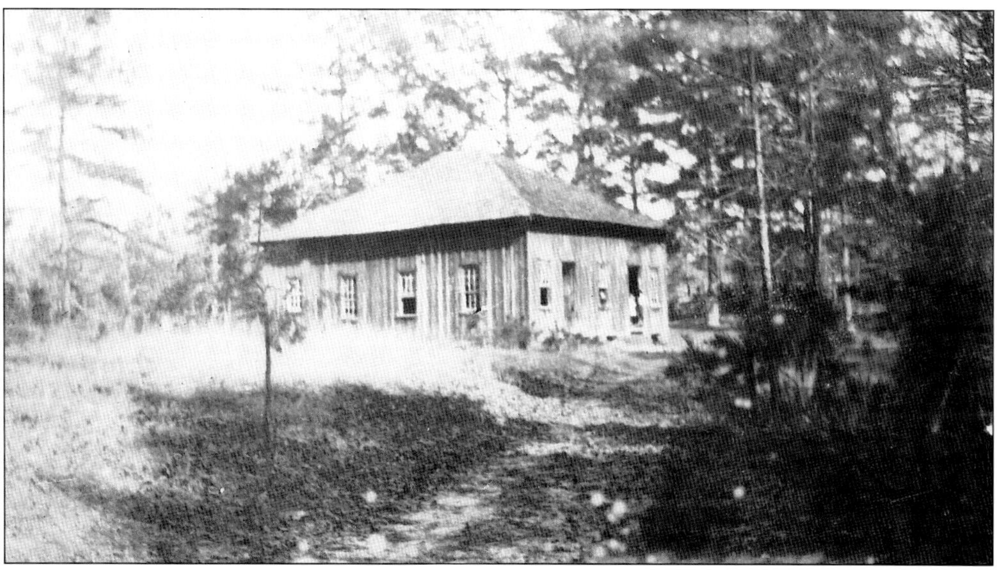

King Institute was built in 1880 and served the area 5 miles west of Grove Hill as a school and also a place for groups to meet for Sunday school until 1910. The school was consolidated with Zimco in 1913. Two versions as to why the school was called King Institute have survived over the years. Some say that an old black man whose name was King Tripp had lived on the spot, while others said it was named for the prominent Alabamian William Rufus King.

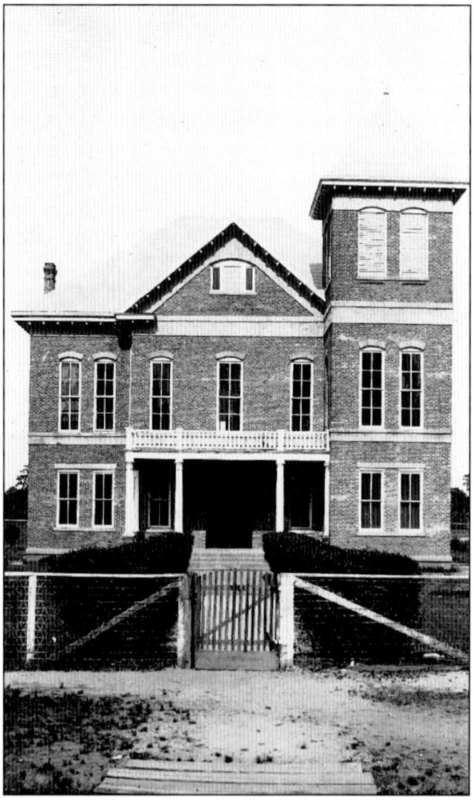

Clarke County High School, built in 1907 with money donated by the Sage Lumber Company, stood exactly where the present school campus is located on Church Street. Many students boarded in town so they could attend classes in this fine, brick building. An endowment for maintenance was set up in the state treasury in Montgomery that still pays $600 interest to the Clarke County Board of Education. This is interest on the maintenance endowment of $10,000, which will remain there forever. In 1907, $600 would have been more than enough to maintain the school, but now, it is almost unnoticed in the budgets of today that deal in millions.

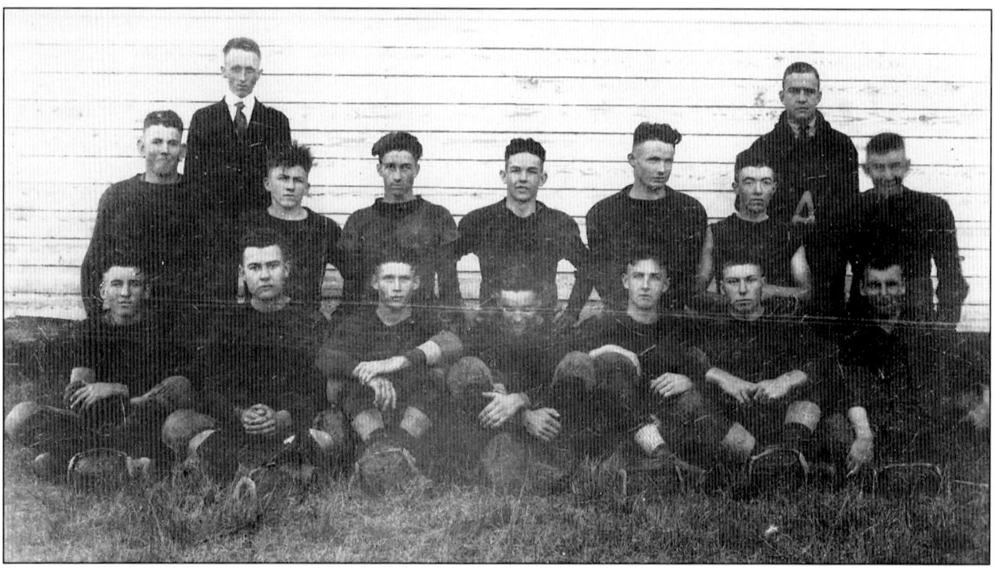

Clarke County High School had a state championship football team in 1920. From left to right, the team members are as follows: (front row) Eddie Pace, RE; Marvin Wells, LH; Emile "Red" Barnes, RH; Grant Gillis, QB and captain; Shelton Dunn, RT; Bill Coleman, FB; Ed Flinn, LE; (back row) Coach W.B. Stallard; Bennett Calhoun, LG; Yuilee Pace, sub.; Gerald Bradford, sub.; Herbert Bush, RG; A.D. Jordan, LT; Frank Bagby, sub.; Lucian Gillis, center; and Assistant Coach Andy Jaffe, a University of Alabama player who helped coach the team.

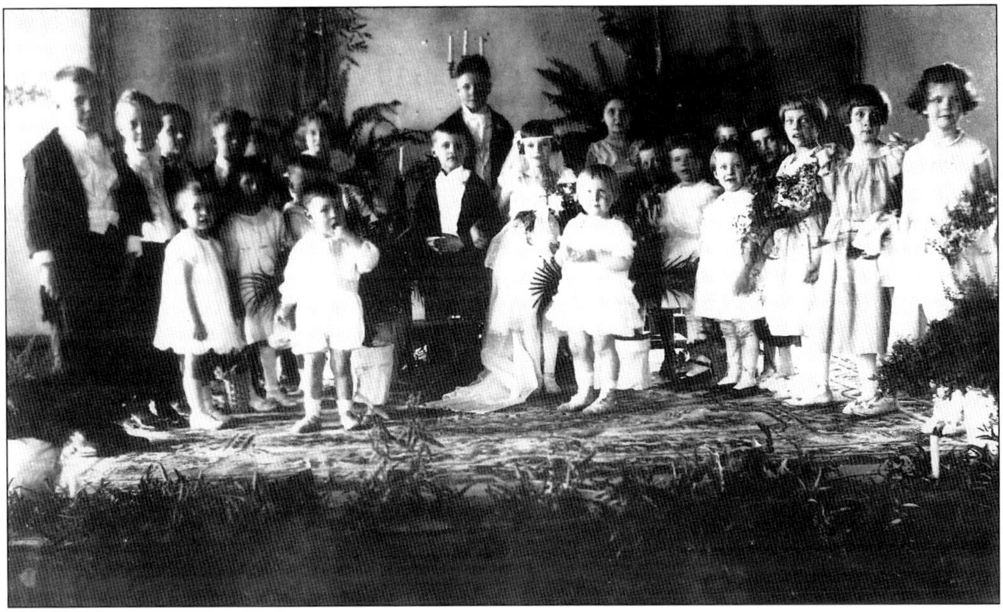

Tom Thumb weddings were popular in the 1920s, and this one was held in Grove Hill School during that decade. These events were usually performed as a fund-raiser, with children playing the parts in the wedding party. The bride is Ellie B. Dickinson and the groom is Broox Garrett. Some members of the cast are, though not in order, Tommy Tucker, Carlton Farrish, Willie Lee Tucker, Frances Plummer, Elizabeth Tucker, Roy Tucker, May Carter, Mildred Dickinson, Massey Bedsole, Clayton Dunn (preacher), Ora Cox, Virginia Guy, Edwina Burge, and Margaret Armistead.

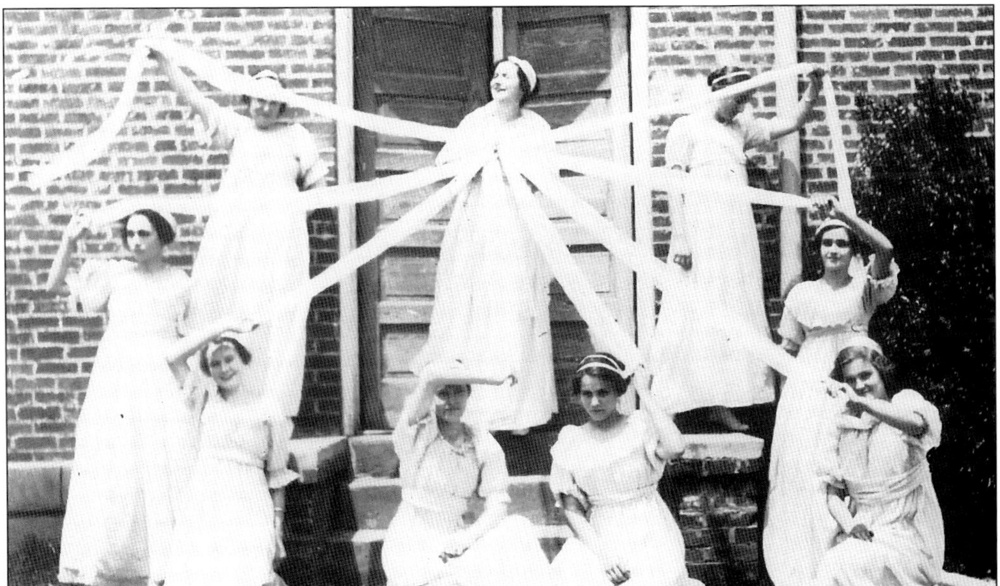

In the 1920s at Clarke County High School (CCHS), a class in elocution was required for boys and girls. This was a class in which the style of speaking and reading in public was addressed. Artistic expression was stressed, as can be seen in this photograph of CCHS young ladies.

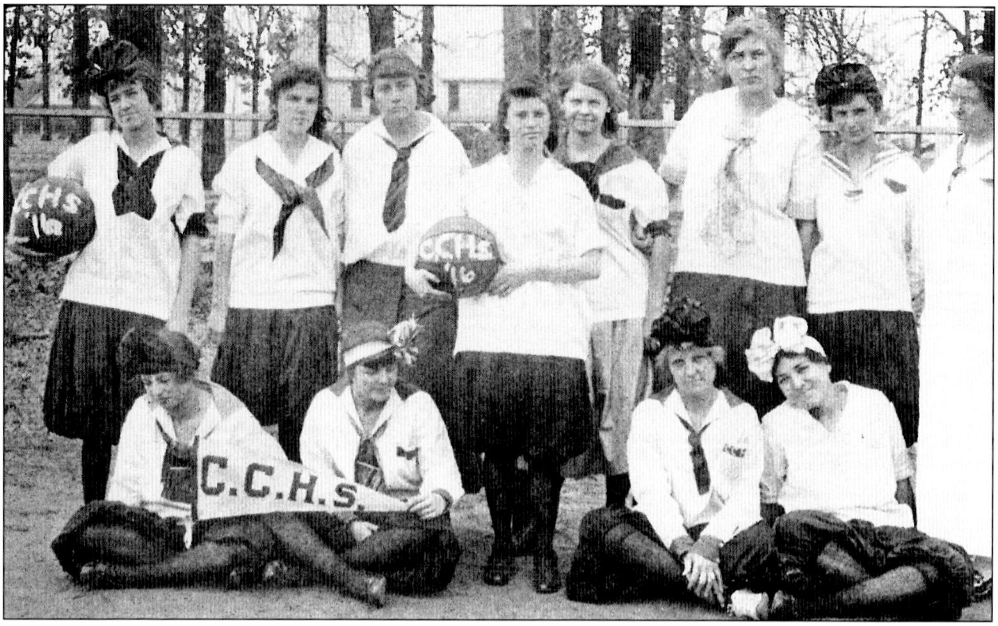

The girls' basketball team of 1916 is pictured here. The coach, Lillian Caldwell, was also the history and English teacher. The team included the following: Mary Lou Pugh, Mattie Lee Kimbrough (forwards); Rosalee Averitt (center); Ella Stringer, Leila Pugh (guards); Irvine Sims, Lucille Cobb, Effie Wiggins, Zeola Morgan, Mary Waite, Olive Mathews, and Lovey May Glenn (substitutes).

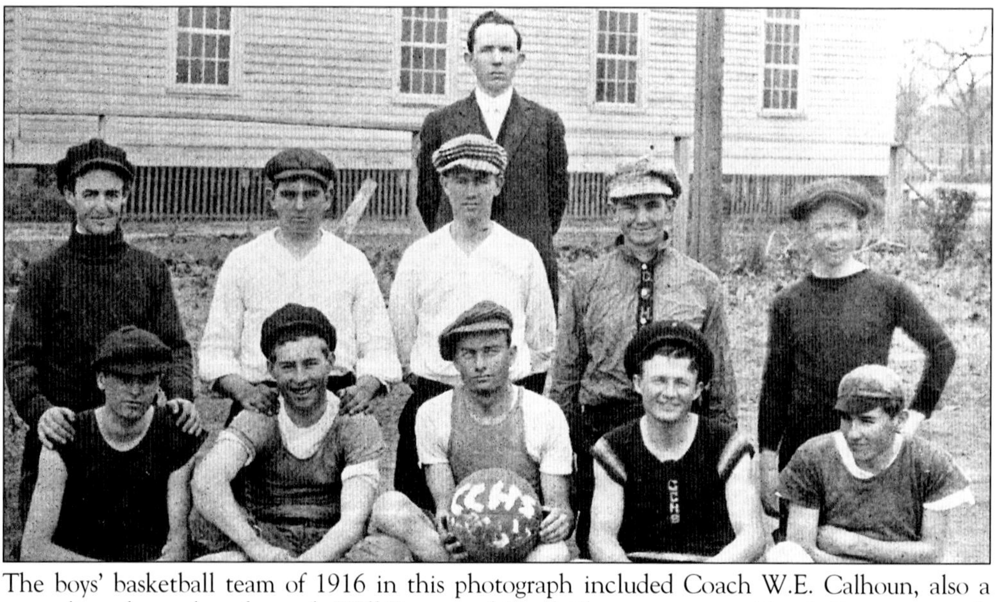

The boys' basketball team of 1916 in this photograph included Coach W.E. Calhoun, also a seventh grade teacher; forwards Will Evans and Cecil Chapman; center Travis Dungan; guards Gary Coleman and Alfonso Hill; and substitutes Milton McLeod, Astor Calhoun (guards), Raymond Hollingsworth, Clayton Foscue, Cory Calhoun (forwards), and Grady Allen (center).

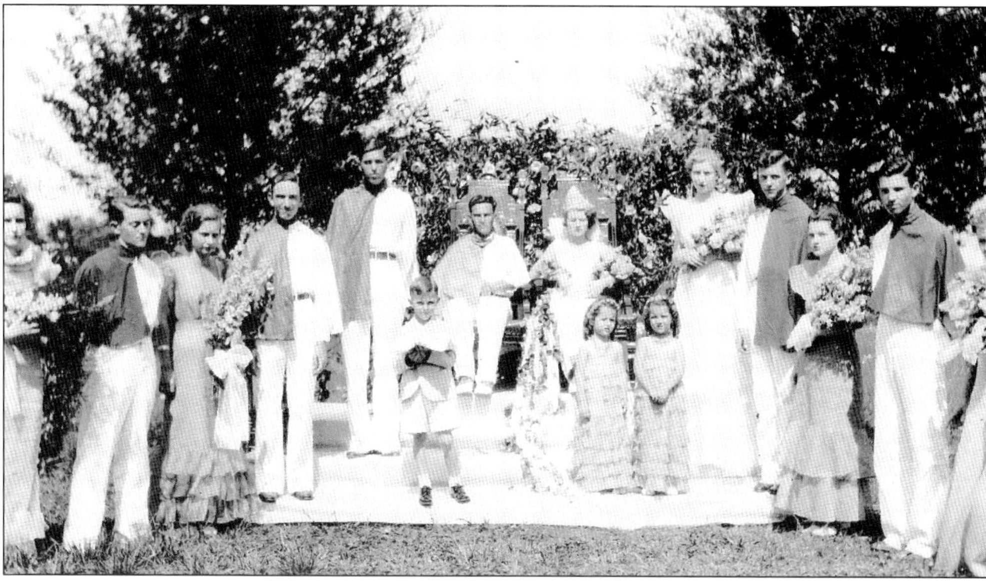

The May Day Court at Clarke County High School, *c.* 1934, featured Earl Pleasant as the king and Blonnie Hill as the queen. The small boy is Leonard Chapman, and the twins are Jo and Joy Chapman.

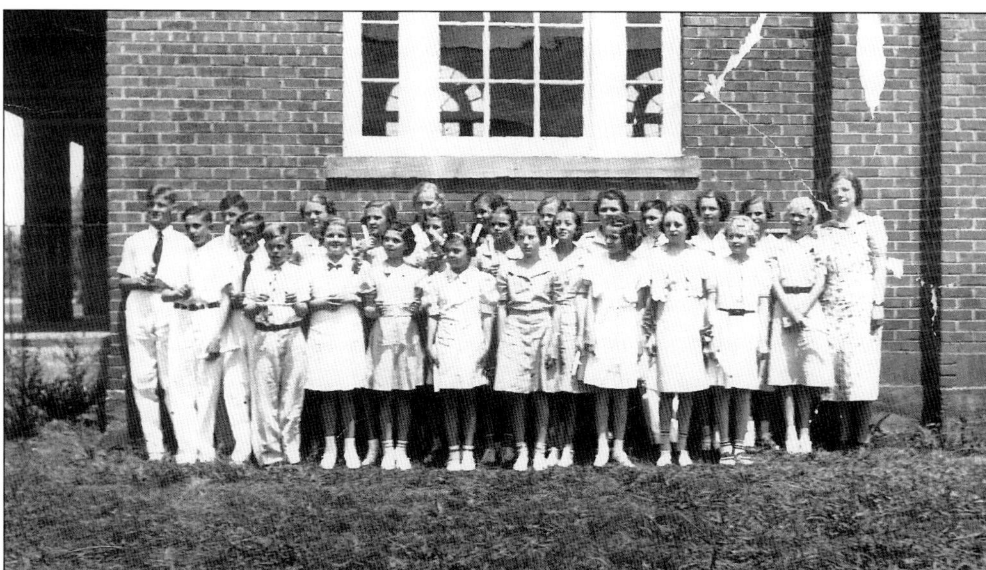

This is believed to be a picture of the sixth grade, in 1937, standing by the old Sage Auditorium, ready to enter high school at CCHS.

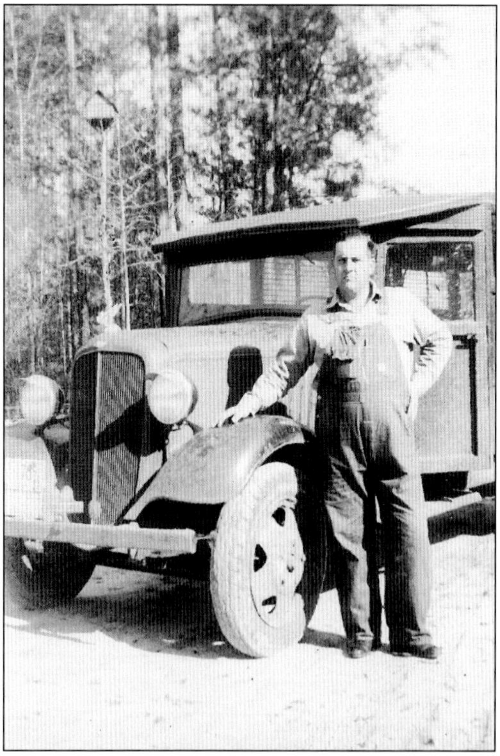

The early school buses which ran to Clarke County High School were privately owned. When the country schools were told to consolidate with the town schools in 1927 from the seventh grade and up, transportation had to be furnished for the children who did not live in town. Norman White of the Chilton community drove his "Blue Goose" on the Peacock Route, beginning sometime between 1930 and 1935. His first bus was a flatbed truck with a homemade body built on the back, complete with roll-up curtains.

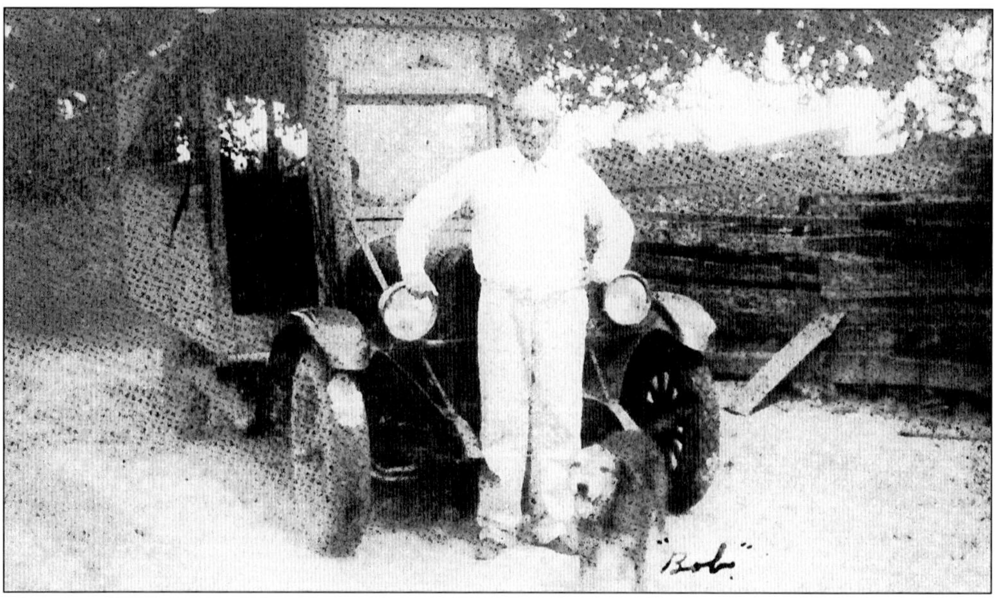

Charlie White, pictured here in 1934, bought a truck and had a body constructed on the back. He had the first bus in the Chilton area, and the bus also carried Peacock children until it became too crowded and Norman, White's nephew, got a truck. Charlie White never drove the bus. His son, Dovered White, then still school-aged, drove the bus and attended CCHS. Charlie's other son, Glover White, drove a bus to Coffeeville, dropping children at McEntyre School as well.

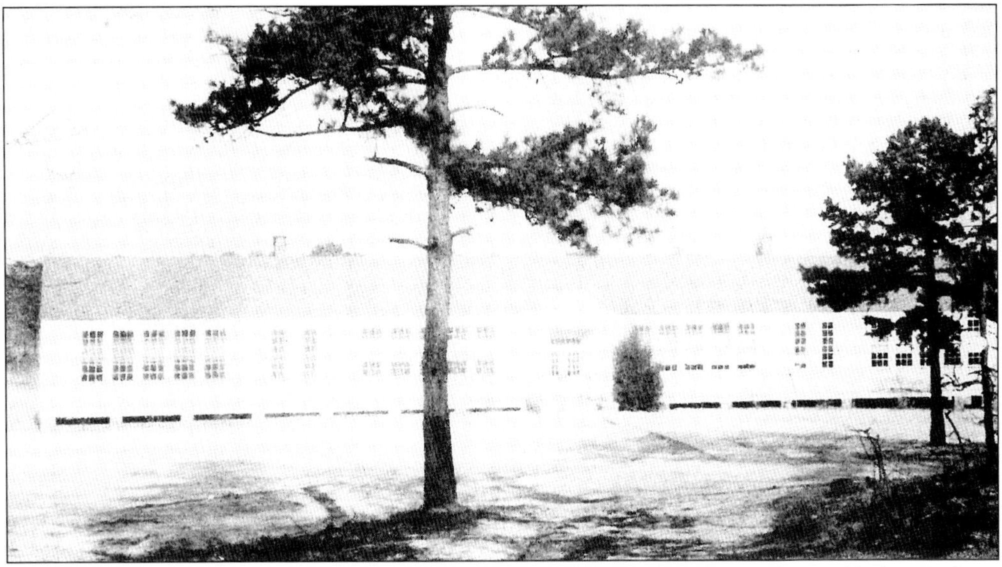

Thomasville Public High School, seen here between 1946 and 1947, was located behind where the old Solomon Bros. factory is today. This school for blacks served Thomasville and the surrounding areas.

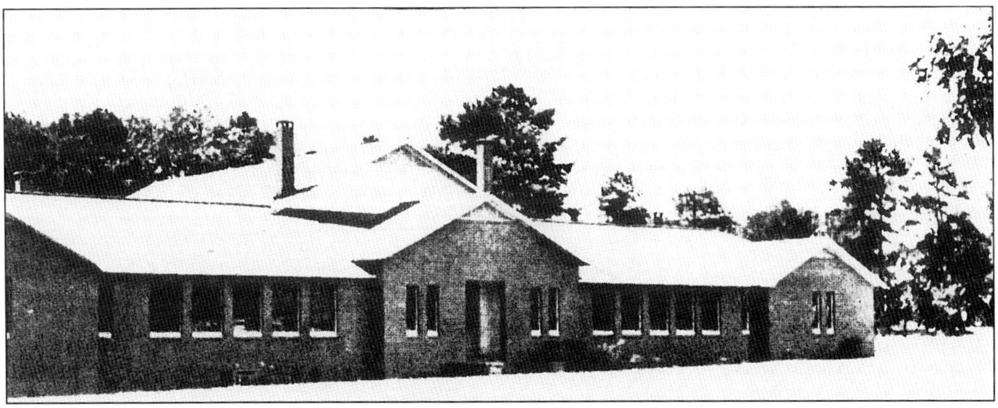

Wilson Hall School, Grove Hill, burned down in 1964. Built in 1949, this school is in the same area where, in the late 1860s, the African-American community established a church and a small, one-teacher school. Wilson Hall High School evolved from this one-teacher school in the early 1900s. The school was housed in the parsonage of the Wilson Chapel A.M.E. Church until, in 1915, the Rosenwald Foundation matched funds with local patrons and interested individuals and a separate building was constructed.

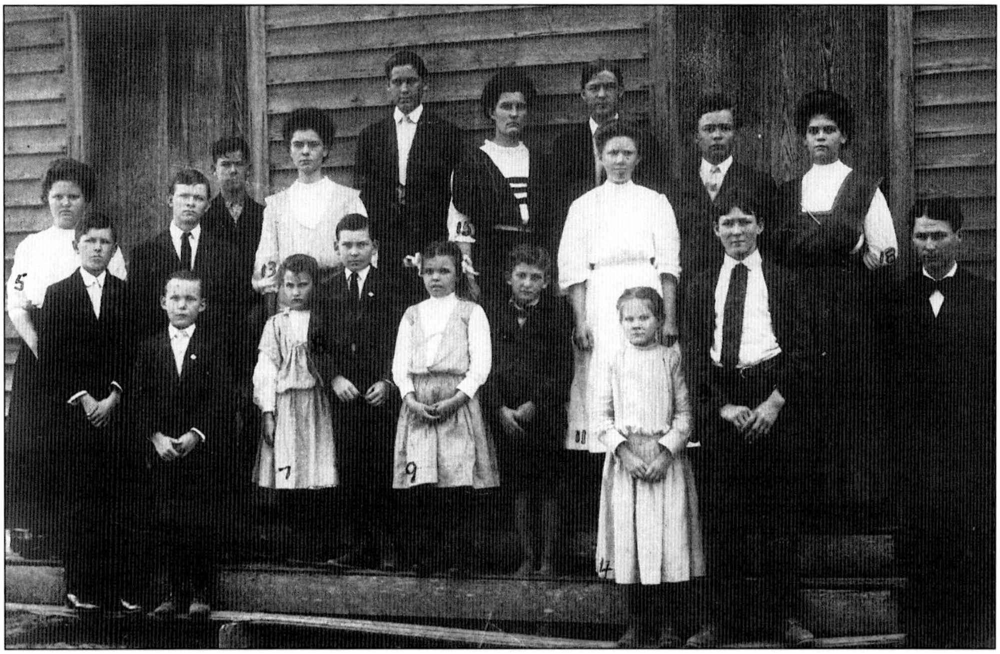

McEntyre School (New Prospect) is pictured here in 1909 with teacher Clarence Myrick. The students seen here are Cleveland Hare, Earl Etheridge, Henry Dennis, Nora Dennis, Pearlie Grimes, Adali Bell, Pearlie Harrison, Clarence Etheridge, Eva Huggins, Clarence Harrison, Loberta Hare, Dave Deas, Maude Etheridge, Otis Hare, Mabel Etheridge, Jim Deas, John Bell, and Lillie Gilmore. The school was located in the vicinity of today's New Prospect Church and Cemetery.

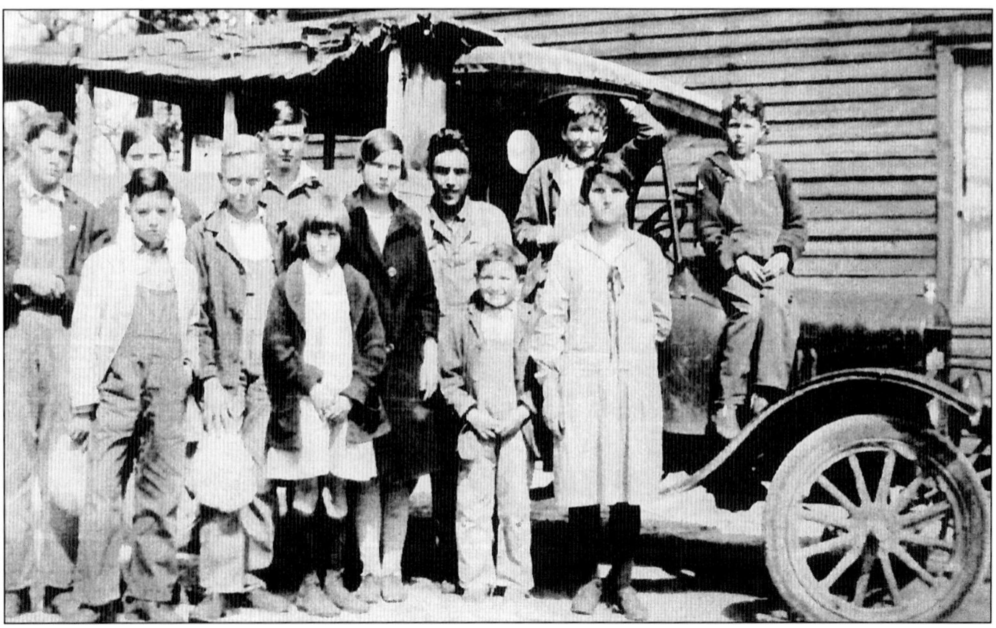

Seen here in the late 1920s, an early school bus, at McEntyre (New Prospect) School in McEntyre (Mitcham Beat), is pictured with roll-up curtains and a homemade body on a flat-bed truck. The owner was possibly Glover White.

Cane Creek School, Chance, was constructed in the late 1800s. After it burned in the early 1920s, the school was rebuilt in 1923 across from Cane Creek Methodist Church. Classes were held in the church until the new school was ready. When the school closed in 1942, students were transported to Thomasville schools.

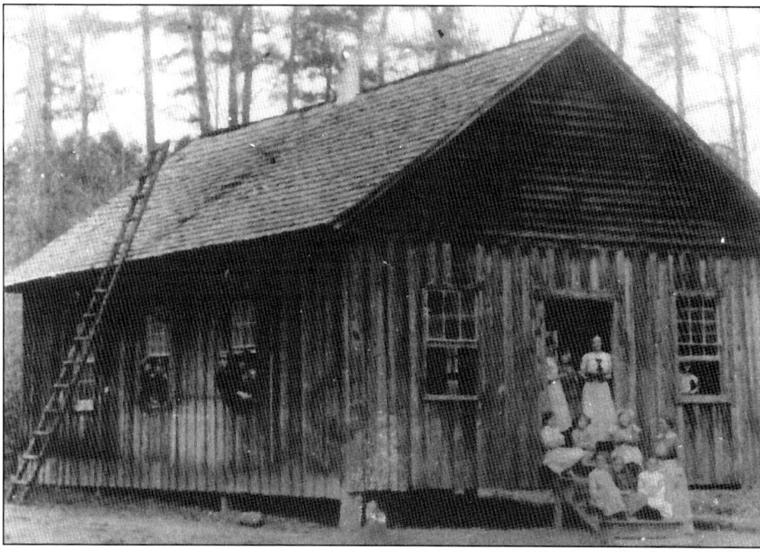

Wilson's Mill Pond School was located near the gristmill and pond that belonged to Alex Wilson, who lived nearby. The school pictured here was built before 1910. Robbie Chapman Faile was the school's teacher, a young woman, when this picture was taken.

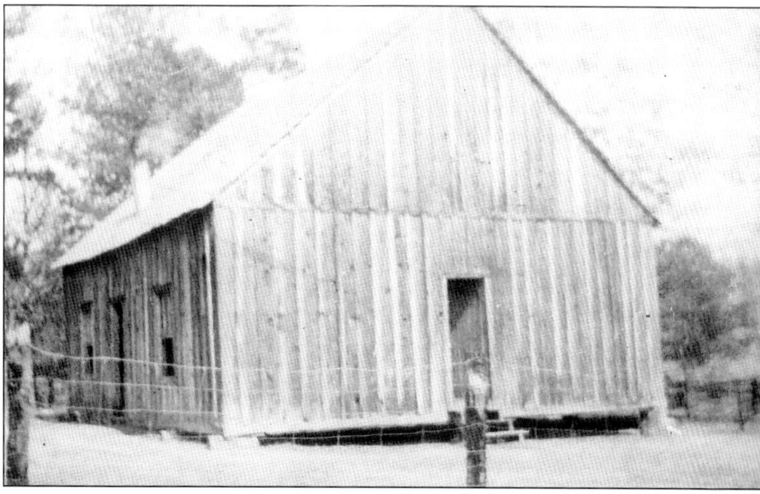

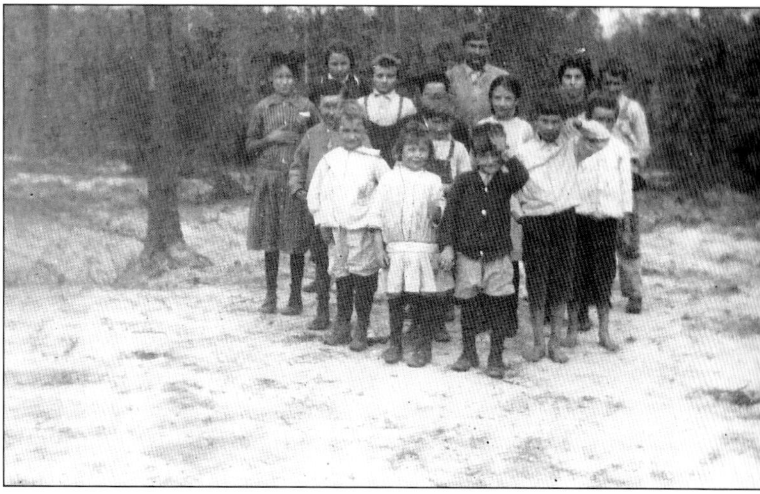

This photograph shows students at Wilson's Mill Pond School. The school was located on the road just beyond the pond, on the hill. After it was no longer used for a school, it was converted into a residence.

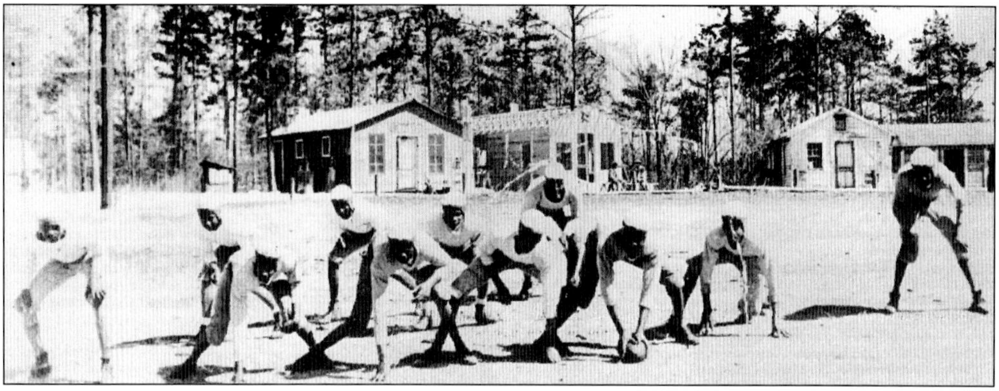

Wilson Hall High School's first football team is pictured here in 1948. Team members were Peevy Smith, RE; Elbridge Eans Daffin, RT; Johnny C. Horn, C; James Mitchell, RG; George L. Callier, RT; Willie Calhoun Jr., RG; Woody Pugh, LE; Hollis L. Horn, FB; Leland Burroughs, QB; Levon Chapman, RHB; and Ronald Burroughs, LHB. James O'Neal Pogue, Willie James Wright, James Pendleton, and Gillis Dickinson were also on the team. Woodrow McCorvey was principal and coach.

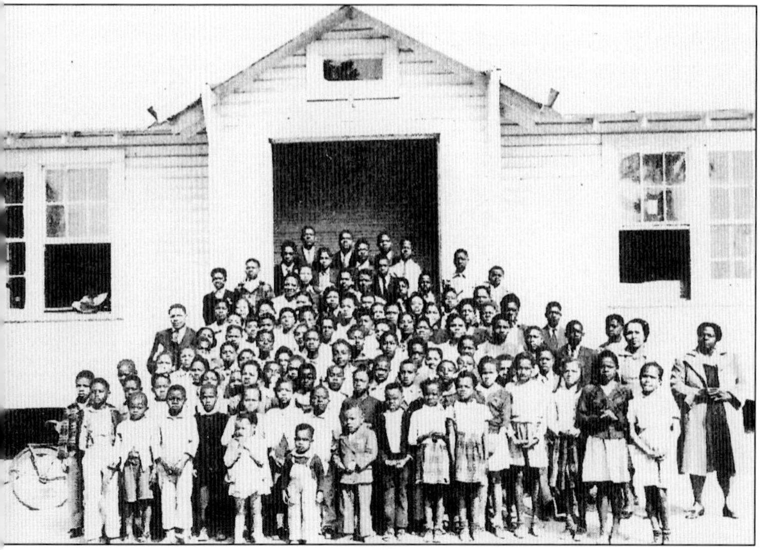

The student body of Indian Ridge Junior High School in 1946 is pictured here during the tenure of Principal F.O. Ball.

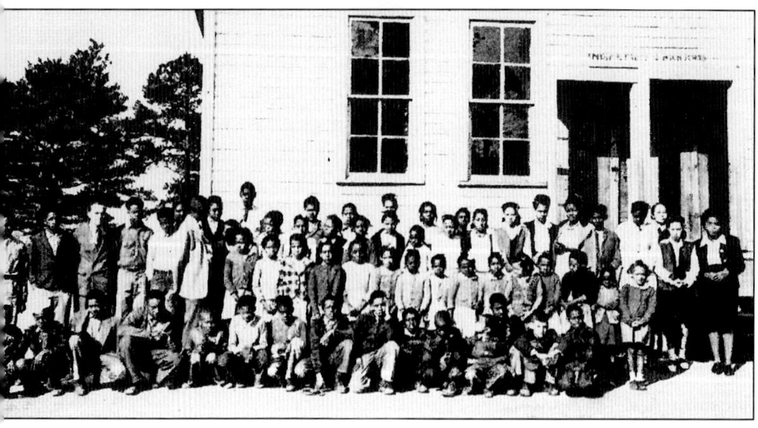

This picture is of the student body of Mackey Branch Junior High School in 1946. C.M. Willis was principal of the school.

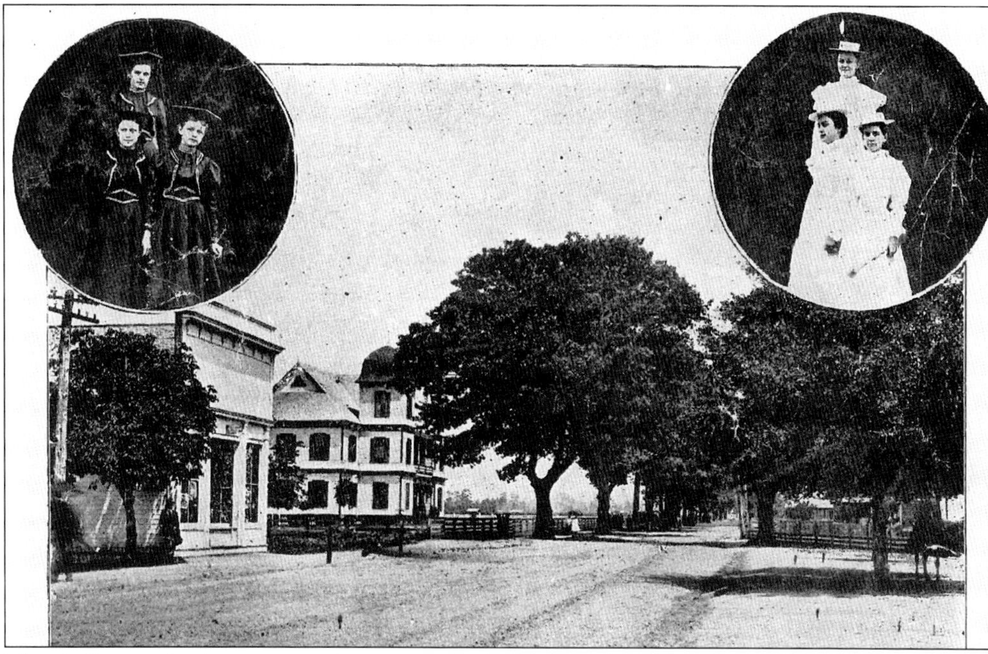

The College in Jackson is seen here around 1916. This school was located on the street which took its name from the school, College Avenue. The college, whose proper name was the Jackson Agricultural College, was built in 1896. Agricultural schools were authorized in 1891, and one was to be established in each congressional district.

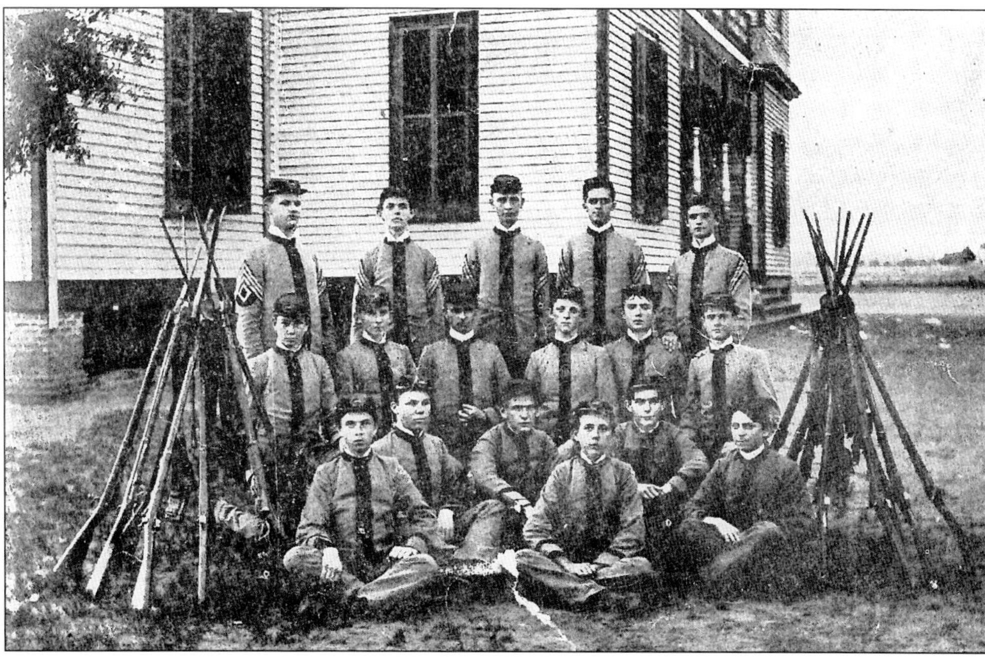

For a few years, students at the Agricultural College wore uniforms. The boys wore uniforms and had regular drill practice as late as 1910. The girls wore white uniforms in warm weather and dark blue uniforms in winter. By 1904, the school was no longer a college, but was named the First District Agricultural School.

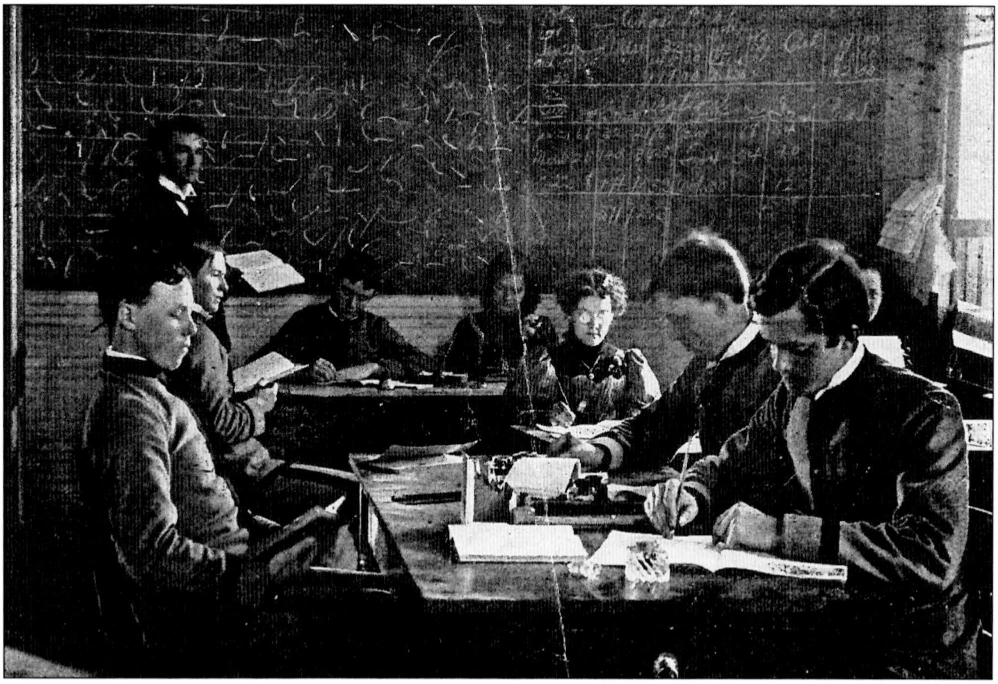

This view of the Business Department at the College shows a class most likely run by a business college graduate, who taught bookkeeping, banking, shorthand, typing, and penmanship. The cost for these courses was $3 a month.

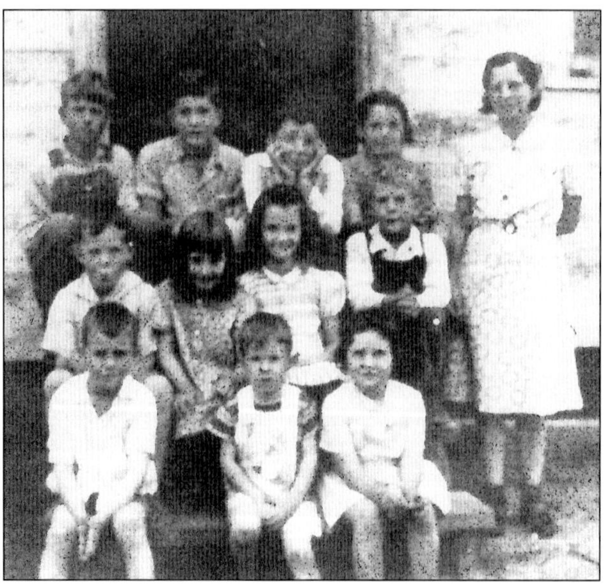

The first school in Gainestown was established by J.A. Lambard in 1840. The school here was built around 1900 about half a mile north of the Methodist church. The teacher was Bertha Agee Norris. In this picture, from left to right, are as follows: (front row) Calvin Syphrit, Charles Norris, and Priscilla Campbell; (middle row) Billie Syphrit, Anna Watson, Annette Syphrit, and Clay Myers; (back row) Charles Blackman, Malton Flinn, Dan Campbell, and Annie Laurie Campbell. The date of this picture is between 1942 and 1943.

In Thomasville, Alabama College was founded by Williams Temple, C.M.E. Church, to provide education for the black community. The college was located on the hill that rises from the railroad tracks to Old Highway 5 and consisted of eight or nine large, white buildings. The date of deeds and acquisition of the property is 1903; however, two earlier dates, 1889 and 1898 are possible for the acquisition of some of the property. The school was later named Miles Memorial College and was moved to Birmingham.

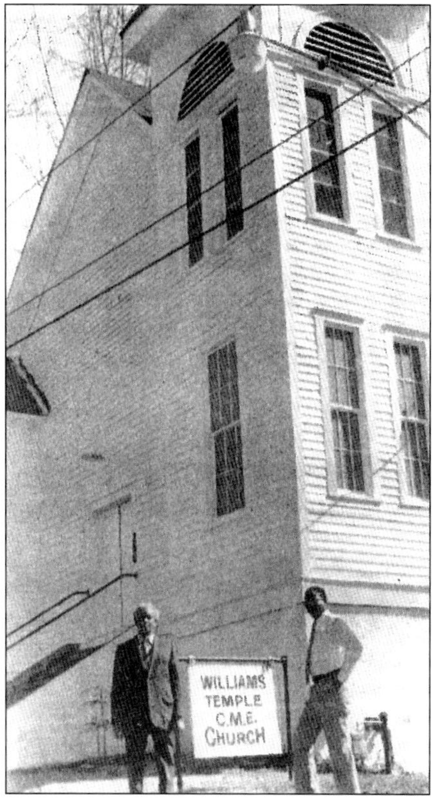

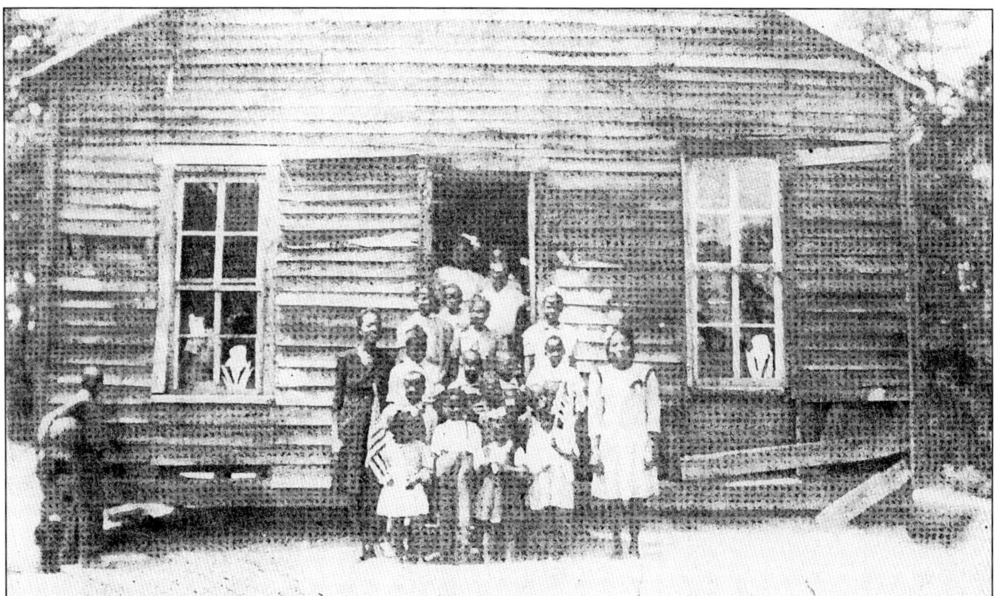

This school picture from 1945 is of the black school in Choctaw Corner, a town that was thriving before Thomasville was founded.

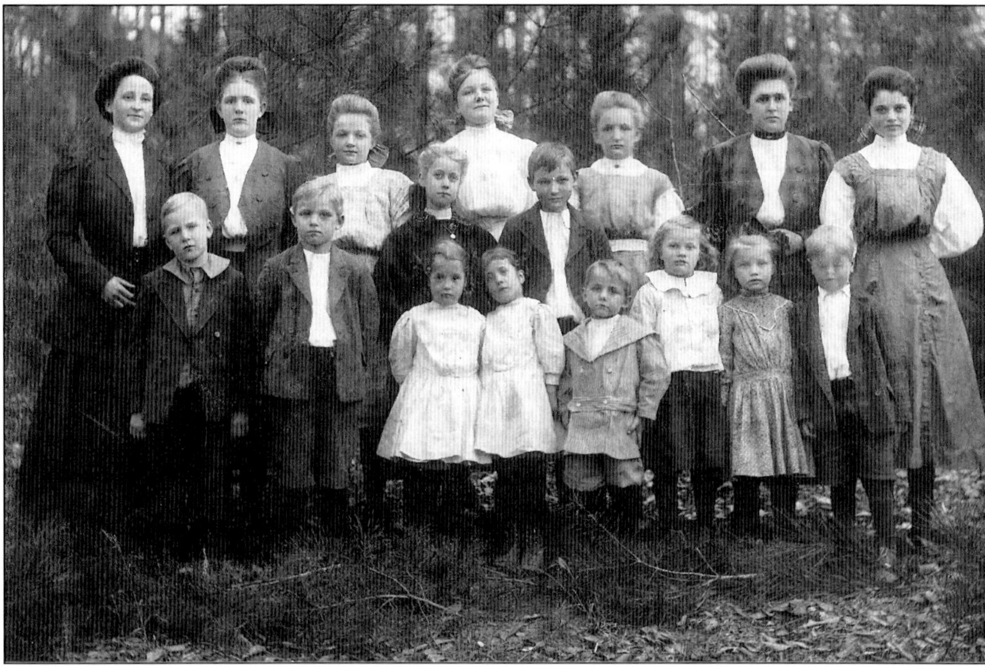

A school picture in 1909 shows the St. David School, west of Thomasville, when Miss Ola Beverly was the teacher.

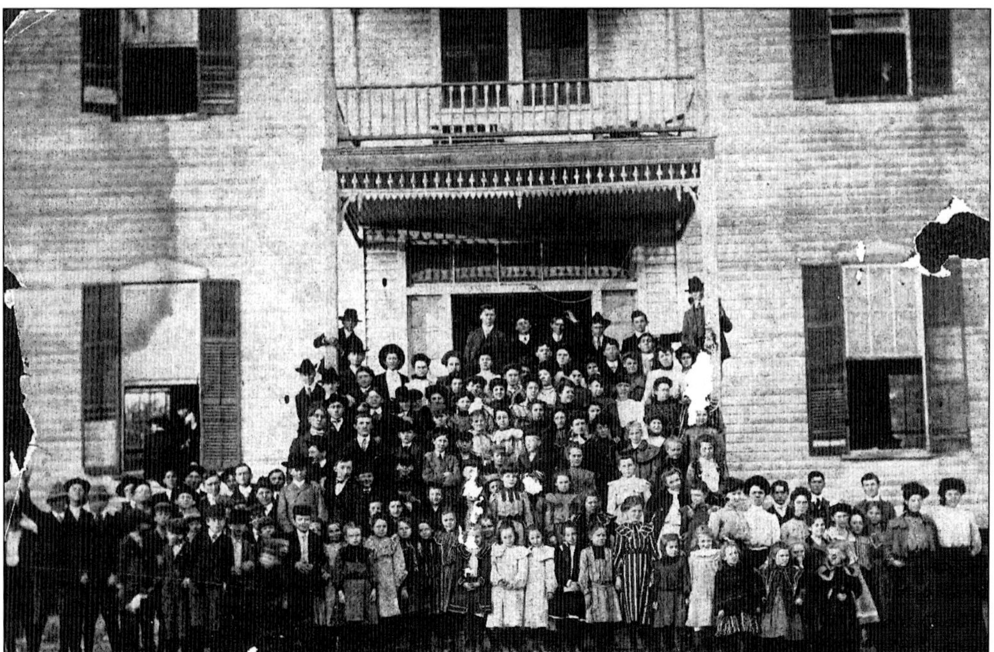

This two-story school, the South Alabama Institute, was constructed as Thomasville grew. This is the school that area students attended until the 1920s, when it was destroyed by fire. There were rooms for 11 grades. School began each morning with the principal reading the Bible and leading a prayer, and then announcements were made. This was called chapel exercises. A brick auditorium was where they met each day.

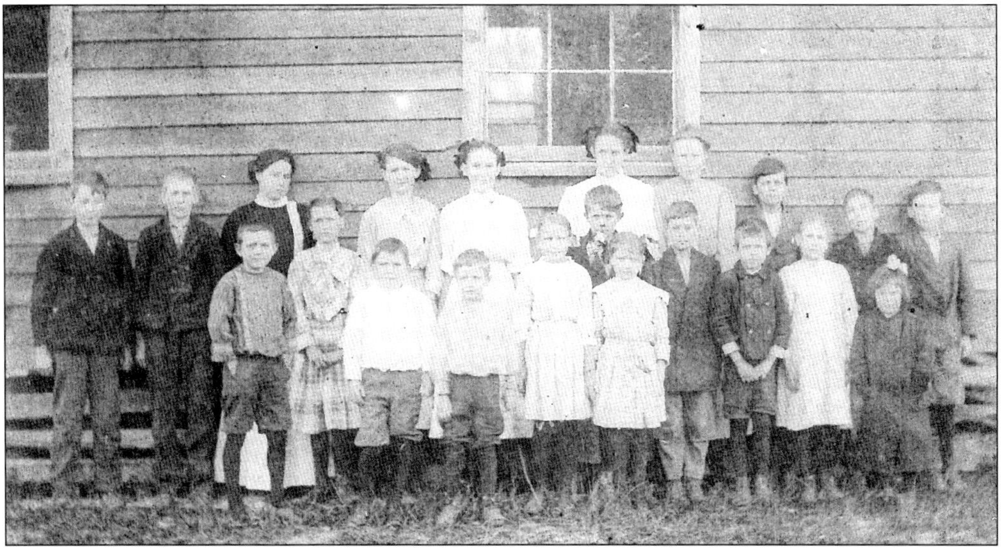

This school group picture was taken at Chilton Baptist Church between 1905 and 1910. Chilton Church was built in 1905, and Chilton School began in 1915. From left to right are as follows: (front row) Earl Trawick, Albertia McIntyre, ? Ratcliff, Fannie Hare, Trever Griffin, ? Ratcliff, Sibyl Branton, Gordon Griffin, Flossie Smith, and Tommie Lee Griffin; (back row) Albert Smith, Ollie Smith, Mrs. Florence Furr (teacher), Aliene McIntyre, Katie Hare, Ada Hare, Ellen Smith, Bertram Griffin, Tommie Smith, and I.J. Griffin.

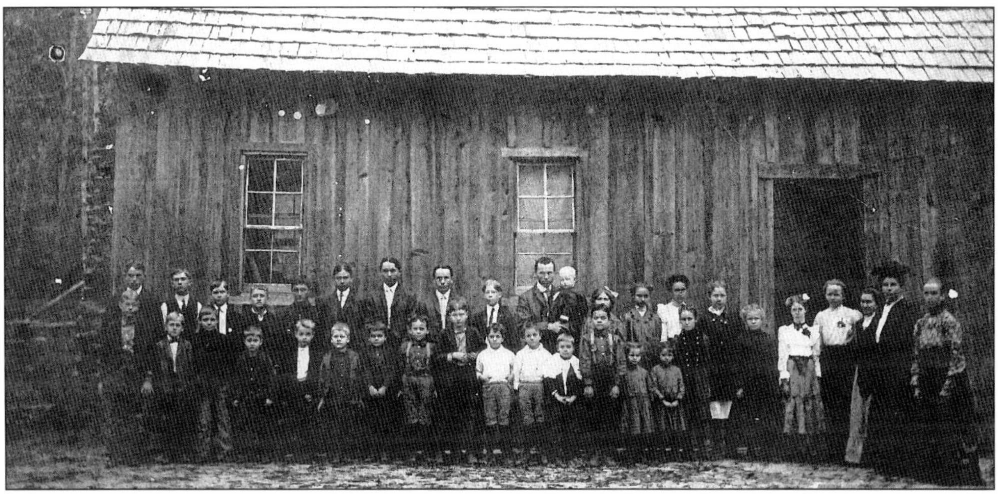

This is a rare photograph from 1907 of the school on Cotton Patch Branch in Chilton, across from J.B. Gaddy's house today. Children on the east end of the community attended classes here. Children on the west end of the community were attending Hopewell School. The students are identified, from left to right, as follows: (front row) Volney Andrews, Ollie Smith, Lee Branton, Lonnie Andrews, Albert Smith, Henry Andrews, Trevor Griffin, I.J. Griffin, Presley Andrews, Freddie Jones, Leslie Jones (twins), Sibyl Branton, Bertram Griffin, Mamie Jones, Gracie Jones, and Katie Hare; (back row) Connie Smith, Robert Sheffield, Sidney Smith, Bell Harrison, Sam Branton, Willie Smith, Claude Smith, Wesley Smith, Artimus Sheffield, George Smith, Eugene Smith (baby), Ellen Smith, Alma Branton, Ada Hare, Annie Smith, Annie Andrews, Leona Sheffield, Ola Smith, Mrs. Mary Branton, Miss Margret Cook (teacher), and Mrs. Mirtie Smith.

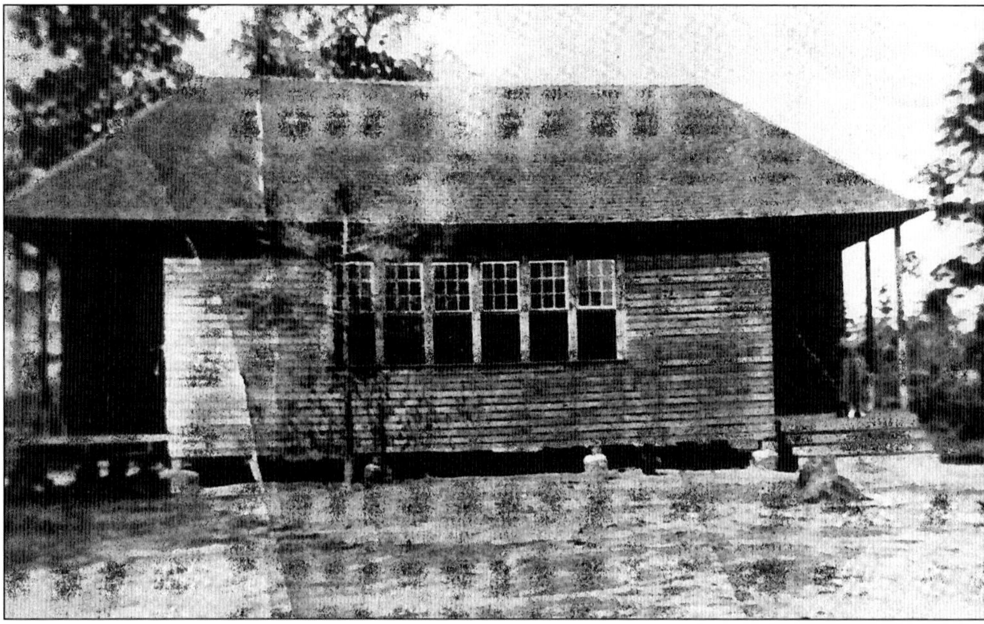

Chilton School was begun in this building in 1915. This structure consolidated the two schools on the east and west ends of the community—the Smith School, as it was sometimes called, and the Hopewell School.

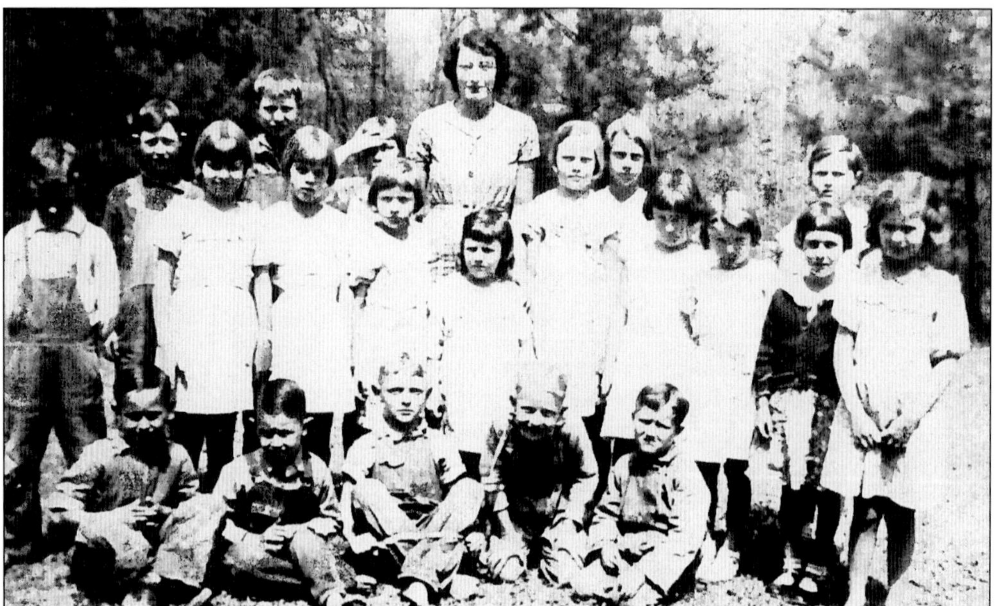

Grades one, two, and three, during the 1934–1935 school year, are shown at Chilton School. The students, from left to right, are as follows: (sitting) Junior Goodman, Bootsie Goodman, Junior Harrison, Buster Sheffield, and Ocie McIntyre; (first row, standing) Edward Bedsole, Lavinia Roberts, Laura Mae Gibbs, Willie Mae White, Susie Bedsole, Lallie Sheffield, Faneeda Hall, Juanita Harrison, Margaret Hall, Vernie Roberts; (second row, standing) Massey Goodman, Jesse McIntyre, Bama Harrison, Lucille Smith (teacher), Dora Sheffield, and Vera McIntyre.

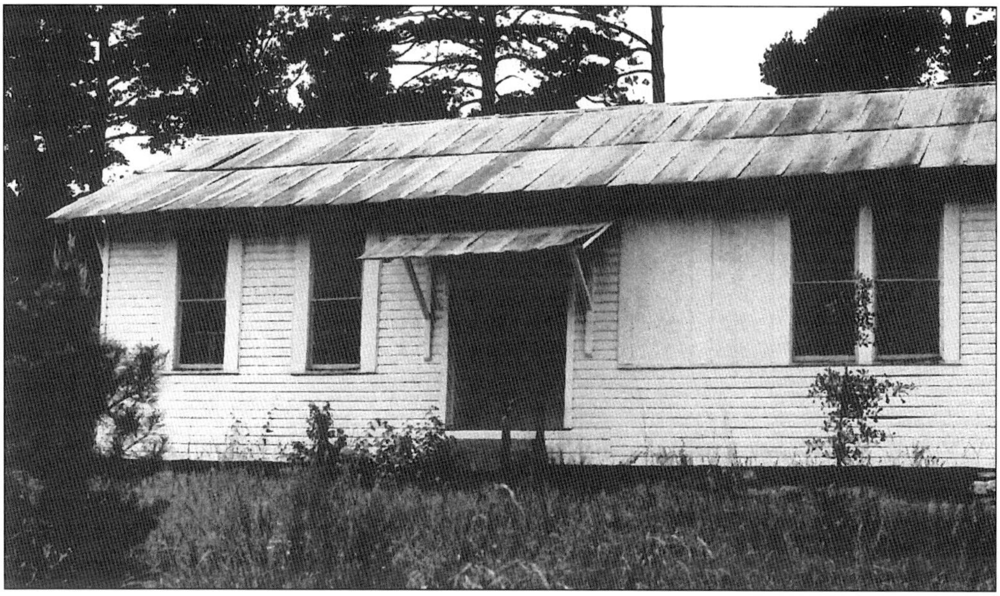

The original McEntyre School was established before 1895. Classes were held in the old Methodist church located where this school building is now. The area, commonly known as New Prospect, is more correctly called McEntyre.

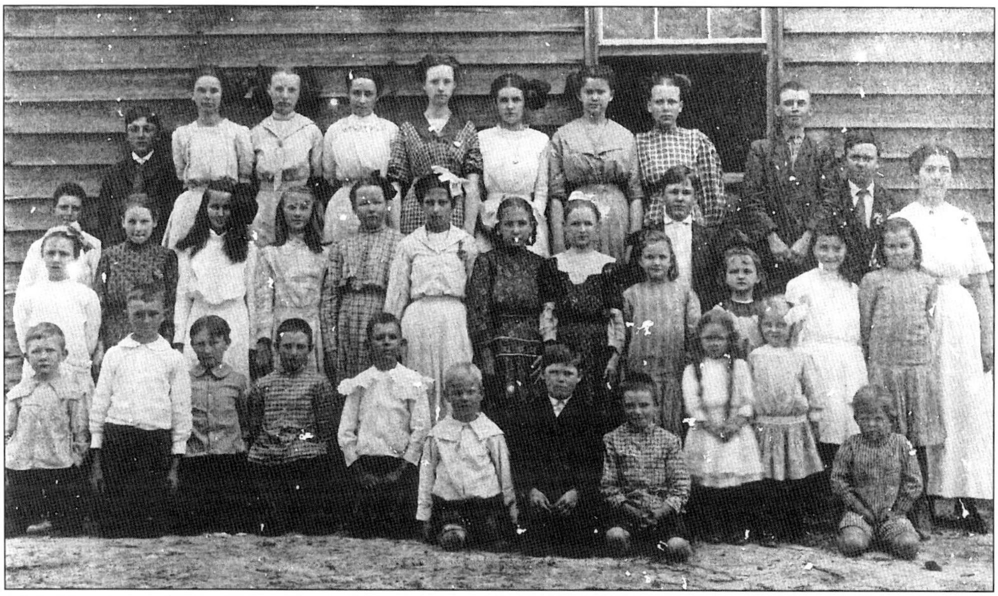

The first through the seventh grades are pictured in this 1911–1912 photograph made at Bassetts Creek School. The students are, from left to right, as follows: (front row) Hattie Baugh, Ossie Newton, Jim Munn, Jerry Fendley, Warren Fendley, Tommy Williamson, Nathan Baugh, Robert Baugh, Walter Fendley, Love D. Phillips, Annie Mae Daniels, and Coma Harrell; (middle row) Earl DeWitt, Mary Jane Lowe, Helen Clark, Dale Fendley, Ellen Walker, Betty Williams, Annie Williamson, Mattie Lowe, Johnny Baugh, Blanche Harrell, Mittie Grey Munn, Claude Hall, and Clee Harrell; (back row) Luther Hale, Edna Munn, D. Fendley, Pauline Clarke, Catherine Fendley, Corrine De Witt, Clyde Harrell, Stella Williamson, and Will Munn. The teacher is Ida Corley Henley.

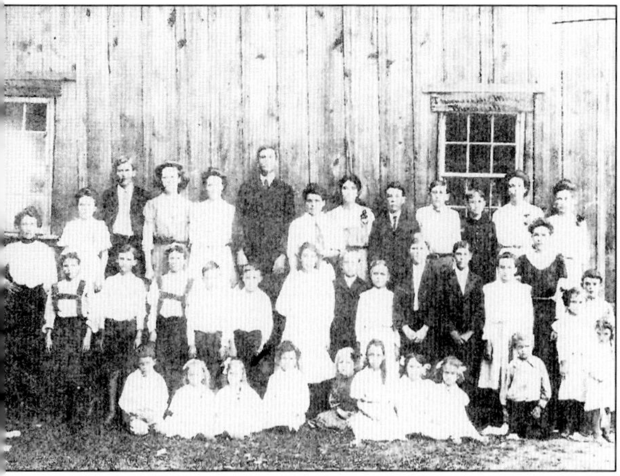

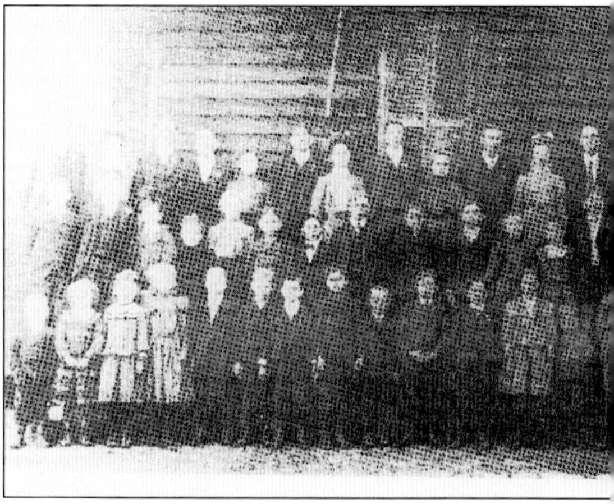

Left: This is Old Tallahatta School around the turn of the century. The students are, from left to right, as follows: (front row) Earnest Cassity, Eula and Zula Goodman, Dollie Cassity Gibbs, Princess Eva Hill Jackson, Ethel Hudson, Mollie Wilkerson, A. Jordan, Josephine Wilkerson Gates, unidentified, and Clayton Hudson; (middle row) Annie Horton Norwood, Lomie Cassity Goodman, Eva Wilkerson, Horrie Norwood, Bessie Wilkerson Hurt, Robert Cassity, Curtis Wilkerson, Etta Hudson Lee, Moses Hill, Avelle Hill Norwood, Acie Hill, Lige Wilkerson, Flossie Wilkerson Cassity, Nettie Norwood Cassity, Alice Wilkerson Cassity, and Travis Hudson; (back row) Cora Cassity Smith, Leslie Hill, Alberta Hill Huggins, Ethel Hill Cloud, Cleveland Hill, Ruth Cook, Lula Hudson Cassity (teacher), Jim Cassity, Tom Huggins, Coleman Wilkerson, Cora Hudson Griffin, and Lula Cassity Smith.
Right: This picture of the old Morvin School was taken around 1905. From left to right are as follows: (front row) Tom McClinton, unidentified, Annie May Day, Pete McNider, Christopher Crenshaw, Fred Pugh, Ben McNider, Ellis McNider, ? Todd, ? Todd, Lilla ?, Will Todd, and Lawrence Armistead; (middle row) Tom Armistead, Cleveland Crenshaw, Grady Armistead, Sue Willie Digmon, Essie Armistead, Grady Smith, Will Armistead, Vernon Perry, Irby McNider, unidentified, Arie Mae Armistead, Emily McClinton, Oscar, unidentified, and unidentified; (back row) Houston McNider (teacher), Wilson McNider, unidentified, unidentified, Henry Crenshaw, Bertha Smith, Oscar Hearn, Hattie McNider, Walter Perry, Dora Crenshaw, unidentified, and Bette Crenshaw.

Seven

Life in General

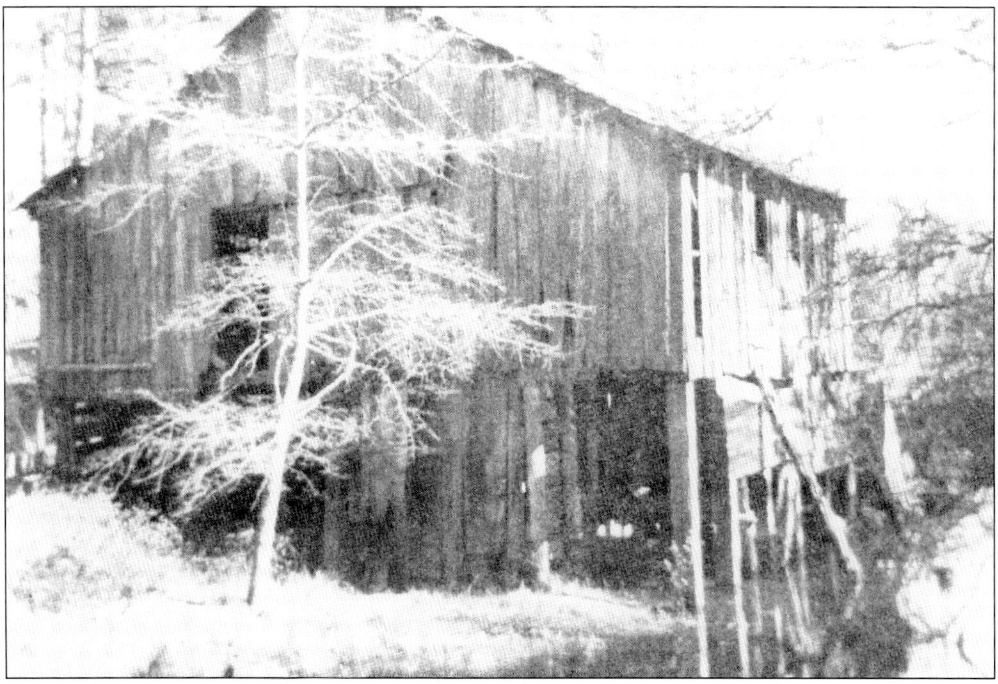

Much of rural activity in the community centered around the gristmill, where corn was ground into meal, one of the staples of the country diet in the South. The gristmill and the cotton gin, which at one time was located at Alex Wilson's mill pond, drew people for obvious reasons. However, once a year on July 4th, a flat rock resembling a cement slab provided a hard surface for dancing and frolicking. The traditional event featured a picnic and dance every year. Wilson's Mill Pond is located not far from the Watt Smith place. The mill was built between 1868 and 1872 and served the area well into the 1940s. All is silent now except the water. The mill, as a landmark, is sorely missed.

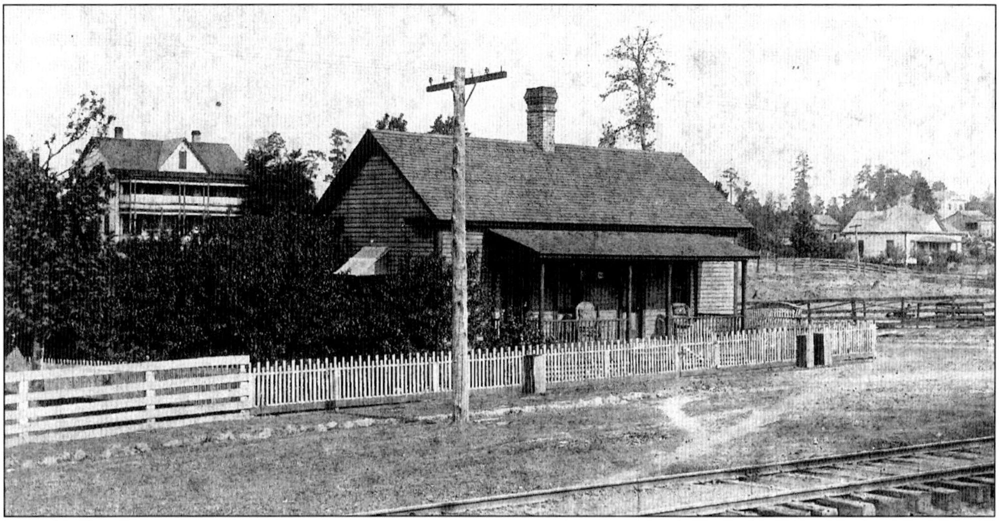

This rare photograph reveals yet another view of Thomasville, looking west toward the area around the former United Security Bank building on a corner downtown. The dwelling next to the railroad has not been identified. It is assumed that the picture was taken around the turn of the century.

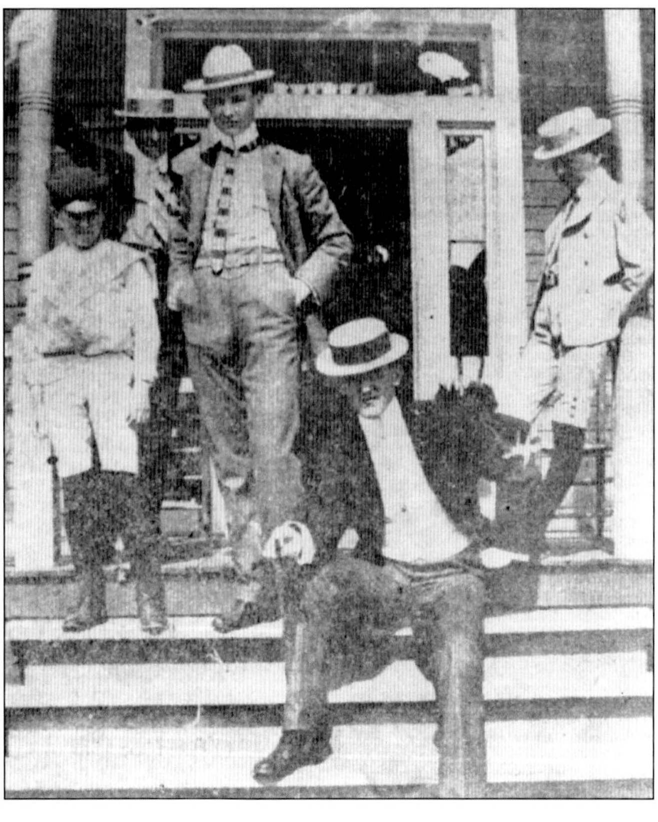

Here we see a fashion statement on Easter Sunday, 1902, in Thomasville, made by the "Bedsole Boys." In the picture are J. Linyer, Ocie A., T. Jesse, James G., and Massey P. Bedsole. This family's contribution to the development of early Clarke County, especially in the Thomasville area, was one of distinction.

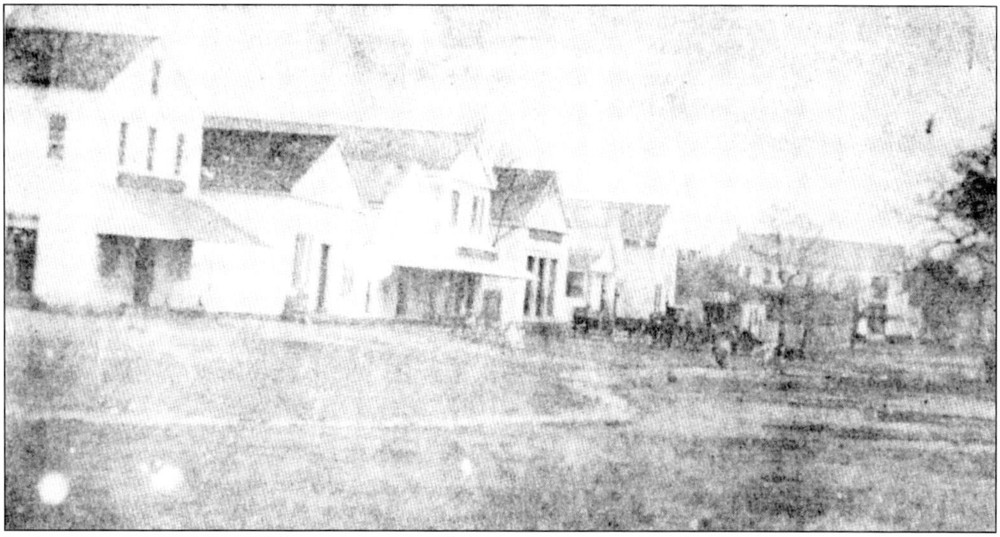

Robert Gamble of the Alabama Historical Commission provided us with a rare glimpse of old Claiborne in the 1850s. This picture shows a number of businesses in Claiborne, which was listed as a principal town of Alabama along with Montgomery and Mobile in 1820.

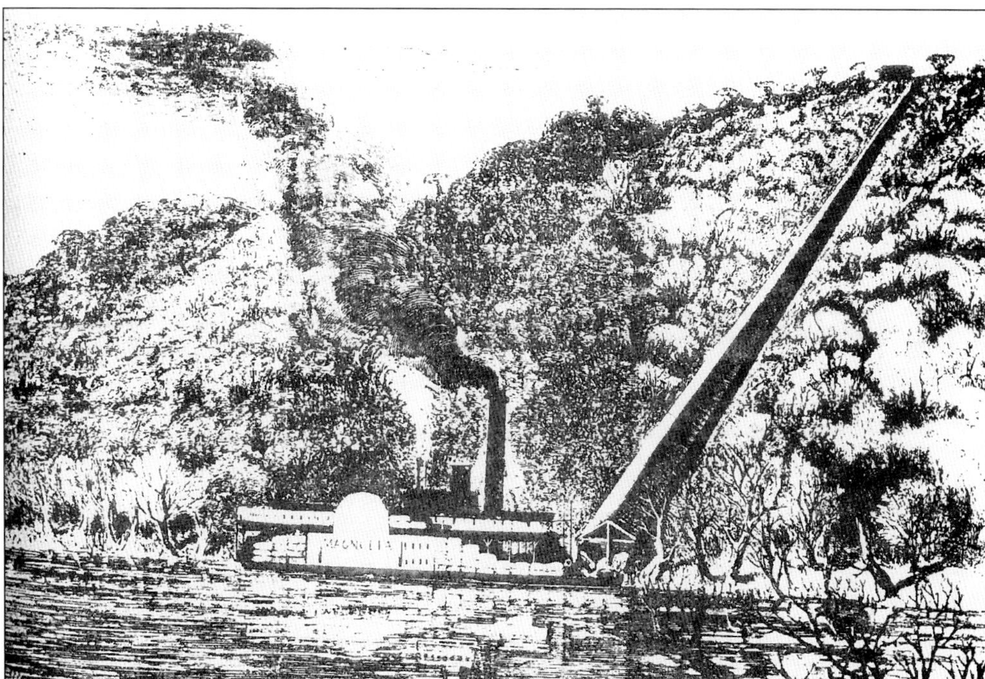

Claiborne Landing had a covered tramway and 300 steps which provided a way for steamboat passengers to reach the busy town of Claiborne high above the river. Goods delivered to the Alabama River town were winched up the bluff to the warehouse by mule power.

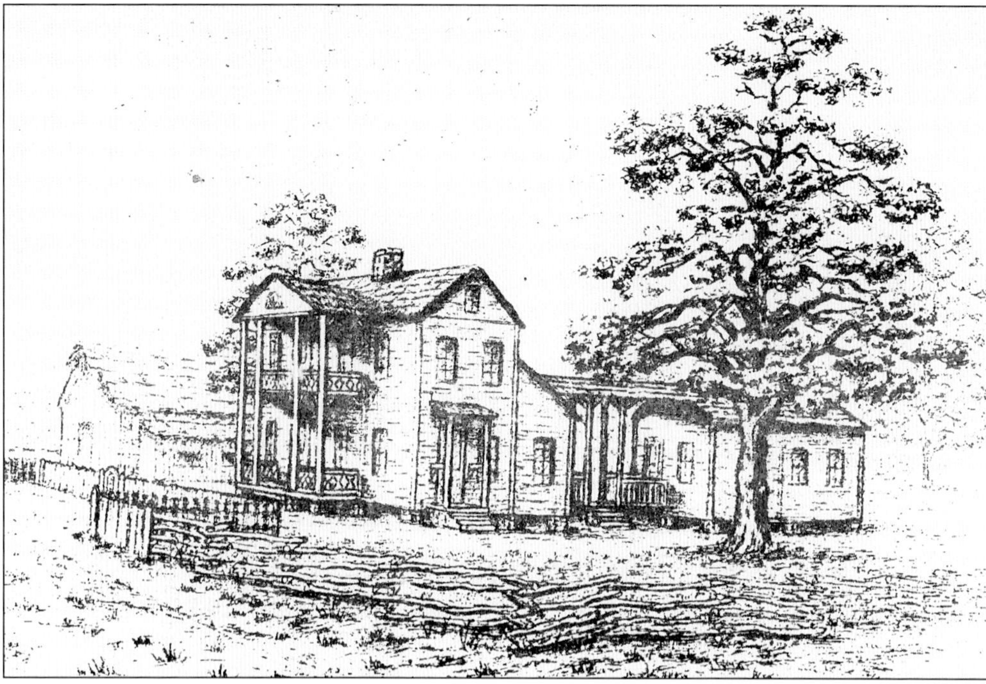

Built before 1832, Hickory Hall was a stagecoach way station between Mobile and Selma. It was located in the Fort Madison-Manila community. This drawing was done by Mrs. James Dealy.

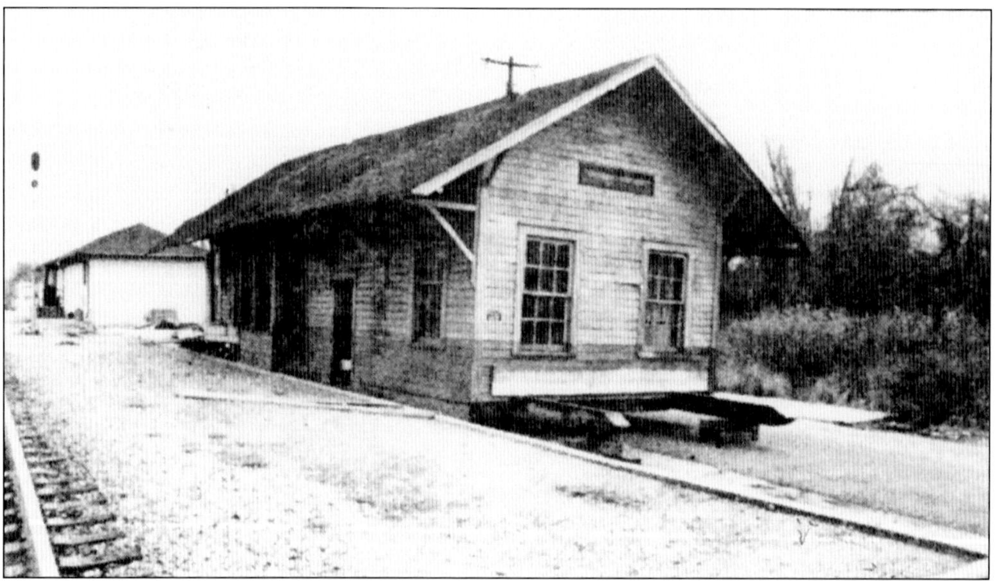

The Jackson Depot was completed in 1888. In early 1984, the Southern Railway Company built a new depot at Jackson. Mr. and Mrs. J.P. McKee purchased the old depot and moved it intact to their property at Carlton about 12 miles south of Jackson. It has been restored and preserved and celebrates its 100th birthday this year.

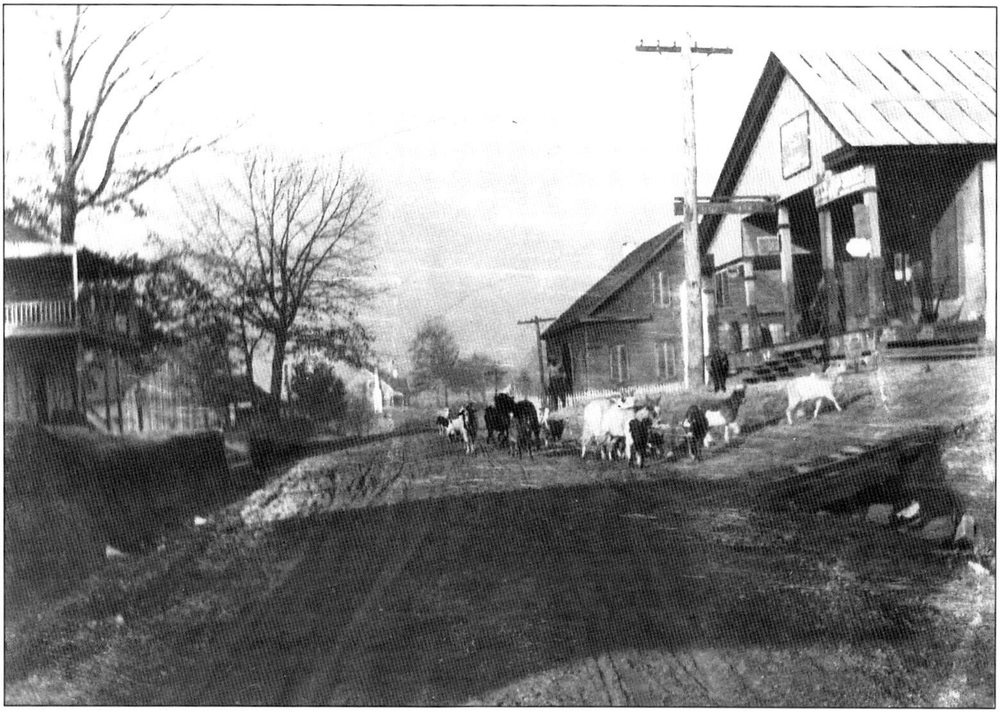

On the left in this photograph and on the left of the street in Whatley are Jeffrey's Store, the Alex Whatley house, and the Bob Chamberlain house. These goats were near the Coleman Store in 1912 when this shot was taken. On the right of the street, beyond Coleman's Store, is the I.L. Chamberlain house.

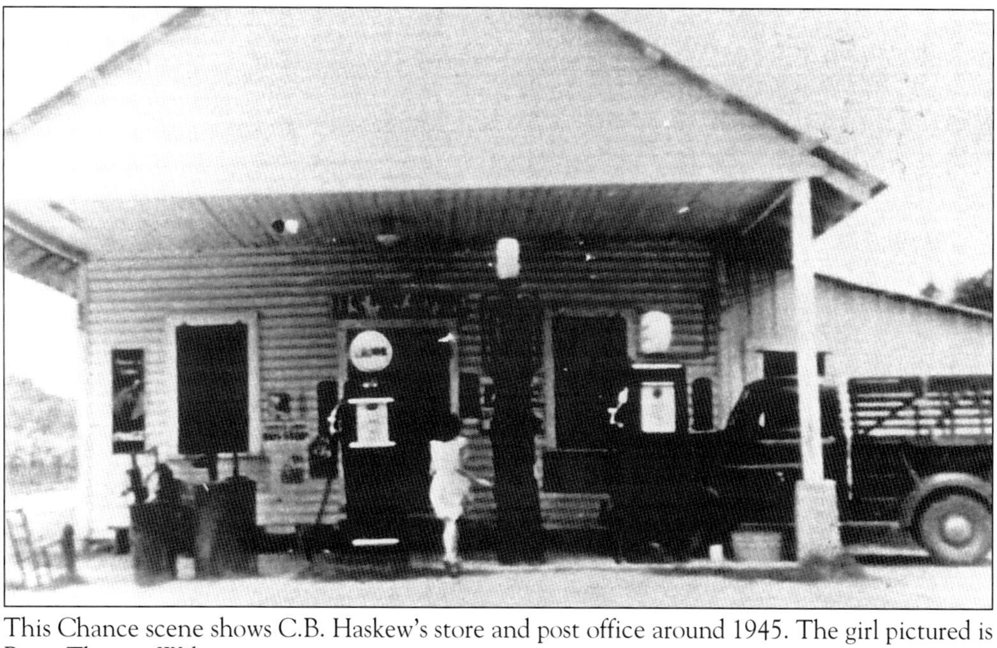

This Chance scene shows C.B. Haskew's store and post office around 1945. The girl pictured is Betty Thomas Wilson.

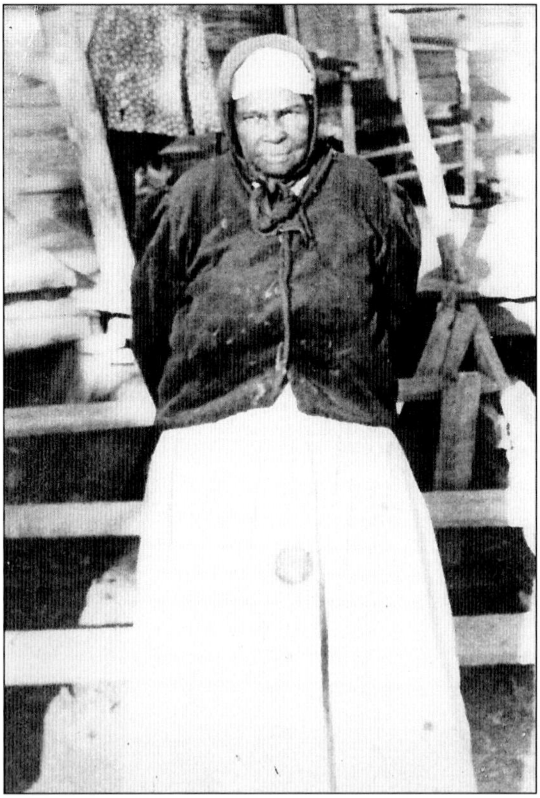

Eliza Reasor Holt, the wife of Nathan Holt, must have spent her life in service to others. In her young life in Bashi, she was a slave. In her later life, she was a mid-wife. Mrs. Holt was born in 1836 and died in 1940. Remembering the long life (104 years) of Mrs. Holt allows us a brief glimpse into the past and deepens our appreciation for the progress made since her time.

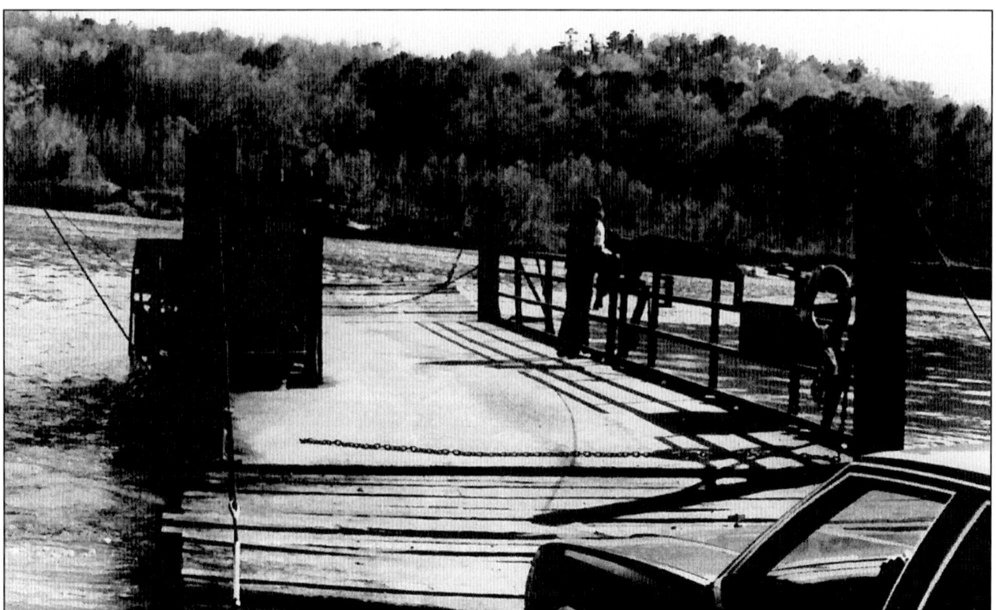

This ferry at Packer's Bend on the Alabama River makes it possible, even today, for travelers to cross the river from Clarke County to Wilcox County. Once, ferry travel was the only way to leave Clarke County's southern-most half, for two rivers form the county's southern boundary.

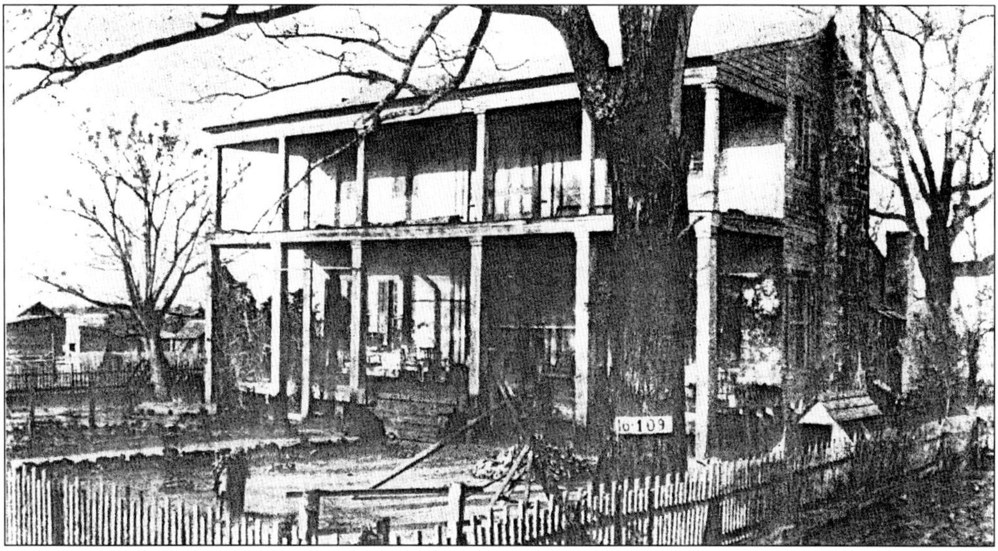

The Albert Wilson House was built in Suggsville between 1850 and 1860. In 1982, Isaac Grant stated in an editorial in the *Clarke County Democrat* that "The following prominent citizens have died since that time: . . . Jere Austill . . . I. Kimbell . . . Dr. Neal Smith . . . Albert Wilson . . ." The "time" spoken of here was 1856, when Grant began the publication of the *Democrat*. Suggsville, like Claiborne and Gainstown, was a prominent town in Clarke County's early history.

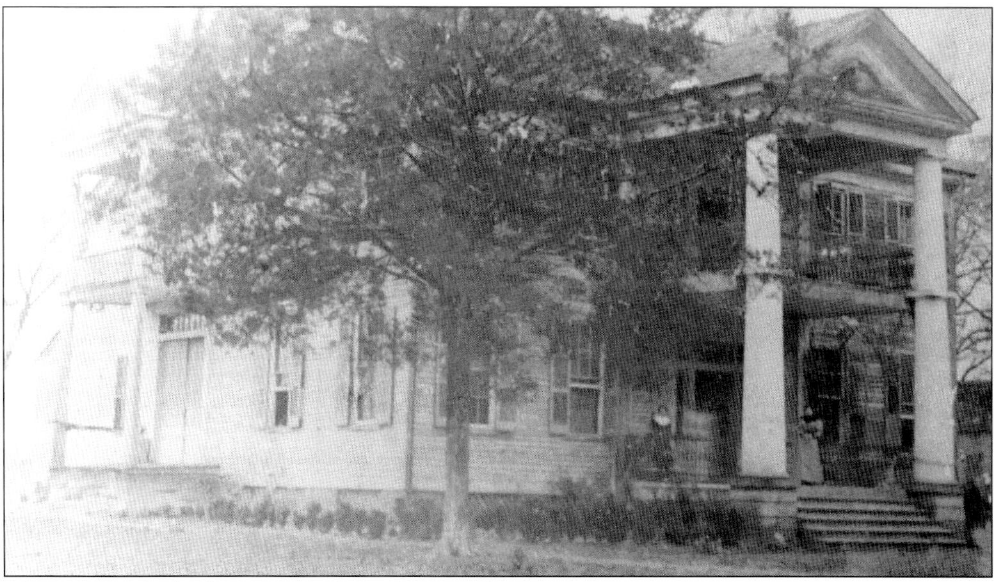

Shown as it looked in 1890, the Wilson-Finlay house was built between 1846 and 1851 in Gainestown. Dr. Joshua Sanford Wilson, "planter, physician, politician, protector and guardian of orphan children," left much for us to appreciate in the life that he lived. The *Clarke County Journal* on April 9, 1863, stated that ". . . Dr. Wilson was a good man . . . a most worthy citizen." The house, itself, deserves notice since Dr. Wilson hired Isaac Fuller of Maine to build it. Records showed that the stonemason who built the foundations and the limestone columns came over from England to do this work. The stone came from the Gainestown quarry, a short distance away on the Alabama River. Mr. and Mrs. Louis M. Finlay Jr. own the house now.

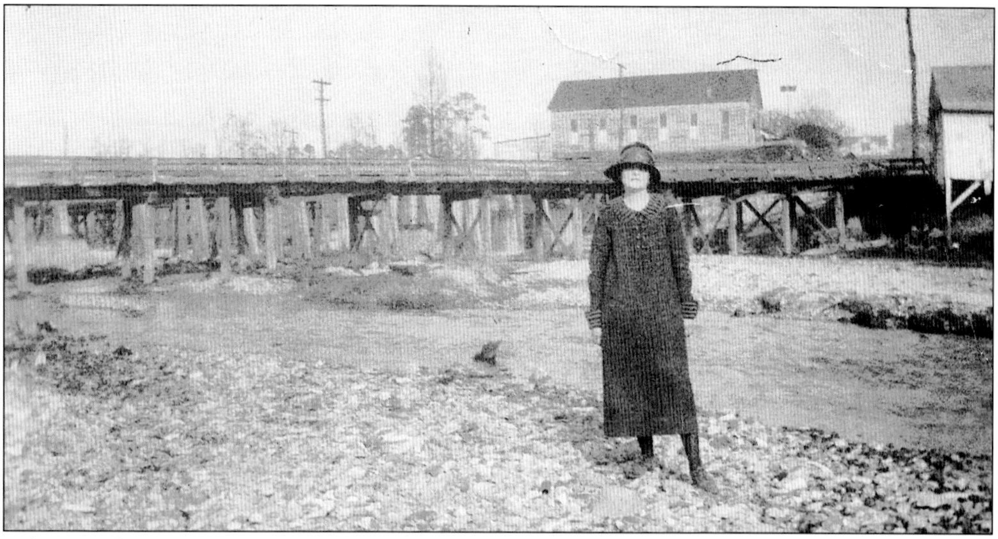

Fulton in the 1920s proved to be an interesting place. Contrary to most of the other residents of Clarke County, the people in Fulton had more amenities, such as a movie theater called the Airdome, which sat up on the hill to the left after one passed the mill on the right and crossed the railroad tracks near the entrance to the present-day plywood mill. The floor was even slanted like theaters today, the seats were theater seats, and silent movies were shown with such stars as Tom Mix, Douglas Fairbanks, and Mary Pickford. On June 5, 1920, *The Forbidden Woman* was showing. Sound was provided by a foot-pedaled player-piano, and the projector was a hand-cranked machine that provided only a picture and no sound. Admission was 25¢.

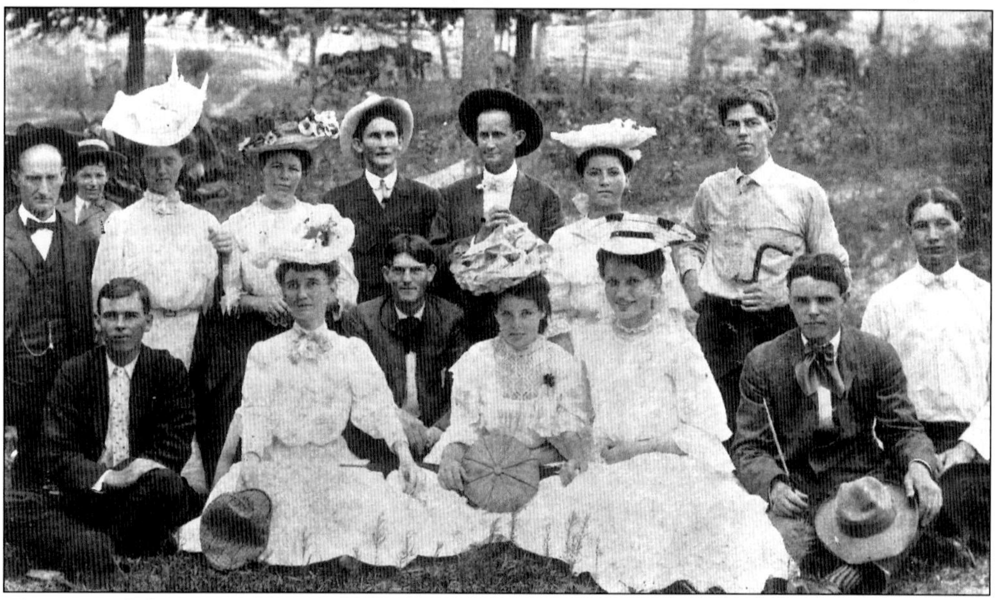

This turn-of-the-century picture was taken somewhere in Peacock, the area sometimes called Good Hope, between Chilton and Grove Hill, just off Highway 17. Identified here are, from left to right, (front row, seated): unidentified, unidentified, Dee Council, unidentified, unidentified, Grover Cleveland Fendley, and unidentified; (back row) Alex Clark, unidentified, Bertha Fendley, Colon Henley, unidentified, Forrest Clark, unidentified, and Therman Henley.

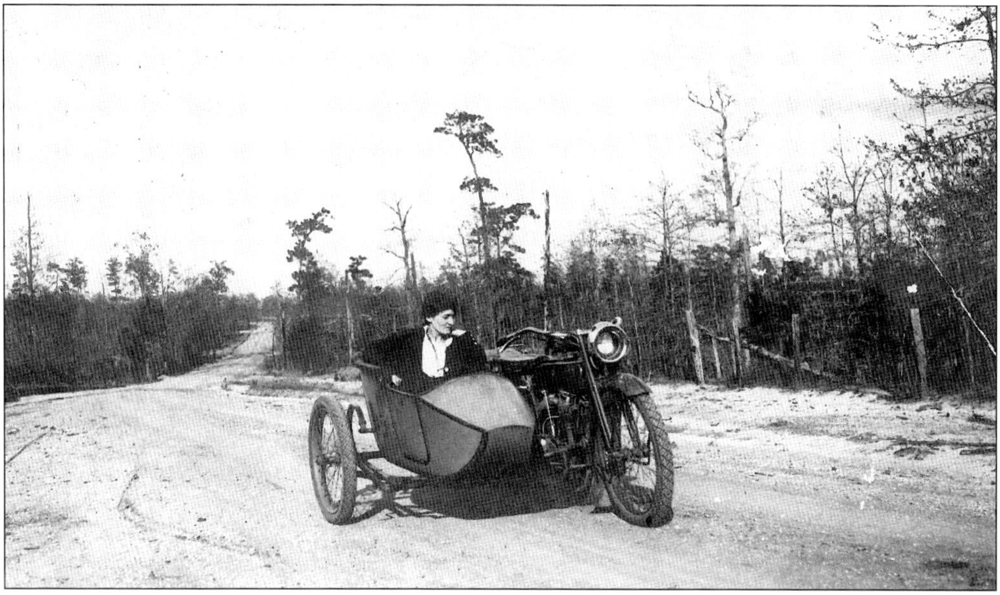

Transportation has taken a new turn by 1918 when Irene Garrett Chapman posed in a side-car while the driver took this shot.

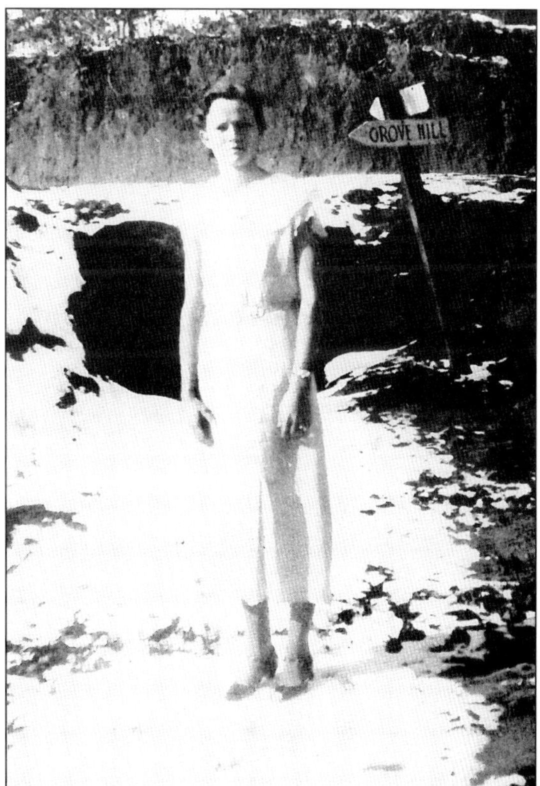

Travel became more frequent and easier after road signs giving directions to towns, such as the county seat of Grove Hill, were put in place. As evidenced by this photograph of Jessie A. Hudson, taken in the heart of McEntyre near Prospect Church, perhaps a Ford Model T will drive by any minute now.

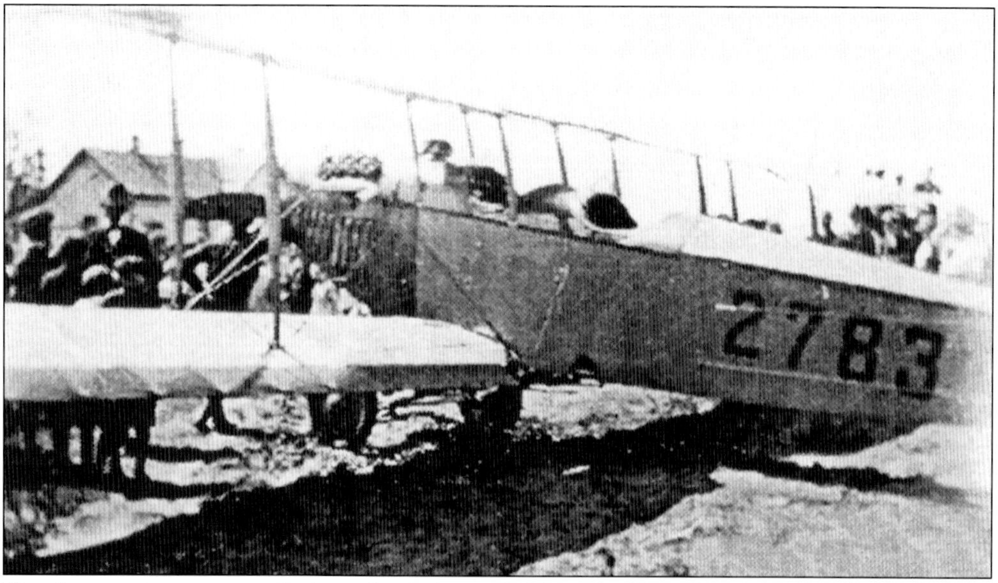

The first airplane to visit Jackson landed in a field at the First District Agricultural College Farm, in the vicinity of Fairview Circle, sometime between 1918 and 1920. The house in the background is the home of William Hardy Fluker.

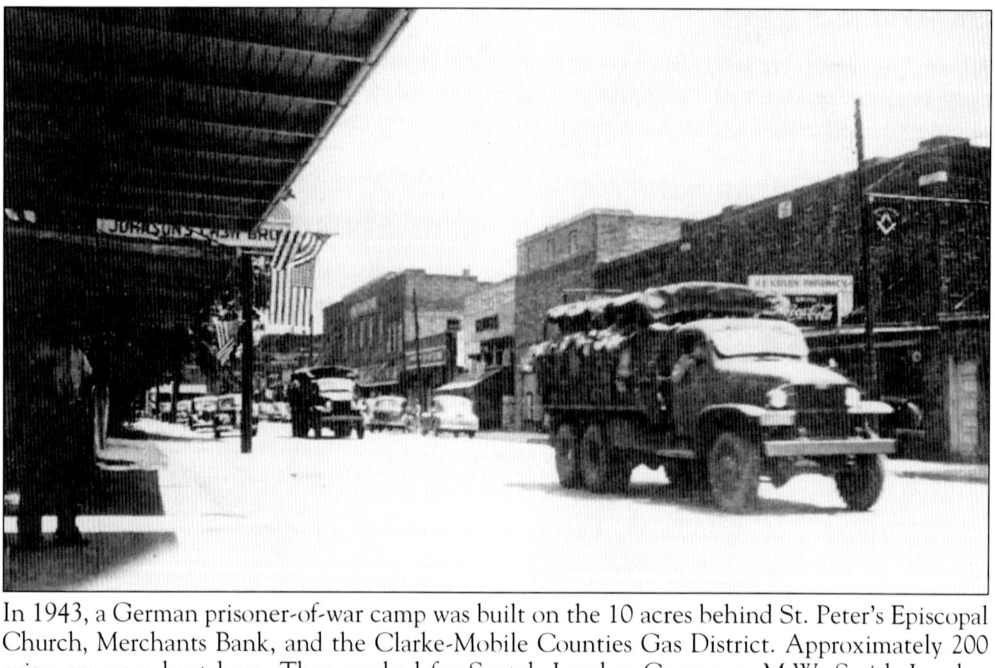

In 1943, a German prisoner-of-war camp was built on the 10 acres behind St. Peter's Episcopal Church, Merchants Bank, and the Clarke-Mobile Counties Gas District. Approximately 200 prisoners were kept here. They worked for Scotch Lumber Company, M.W. Smith Lumber Company, and International Paper Company. The prisoners remained in Jackson until the end of the war.

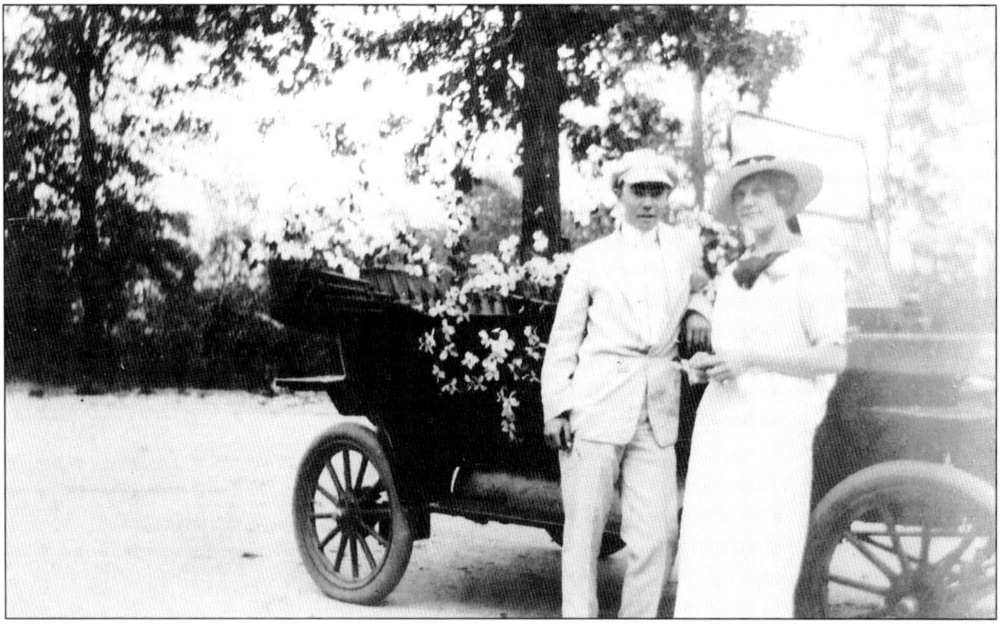

Sunday afternoon "sparkin'," or courting, near Grove Hill is seen here. The car, laden with dogwood blossoms, suggests spring, youth, and love. Identified here are S.P. and Zeola Chapman.

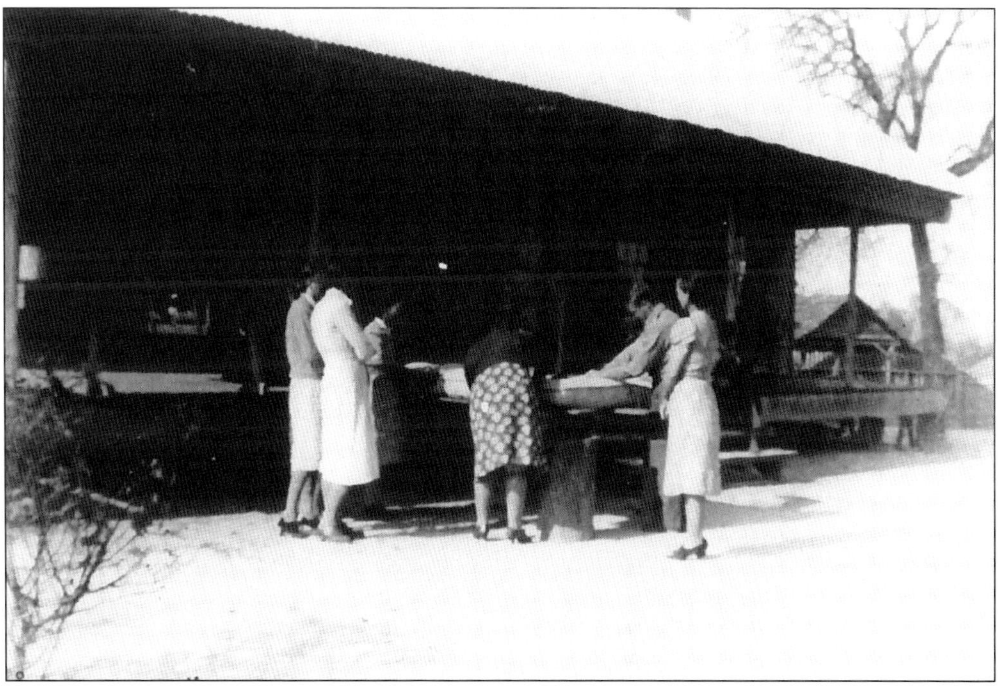

At the Ben Huggins place in the Bethel community, north of Coffeeville, in December of 1940, a bed-making was held for the area ladies as a service to country citizens. Wallace Wise brought materials and helped the women learn to make mattresses. Ladies gathered from the neighborhood to watch and learn this skill.

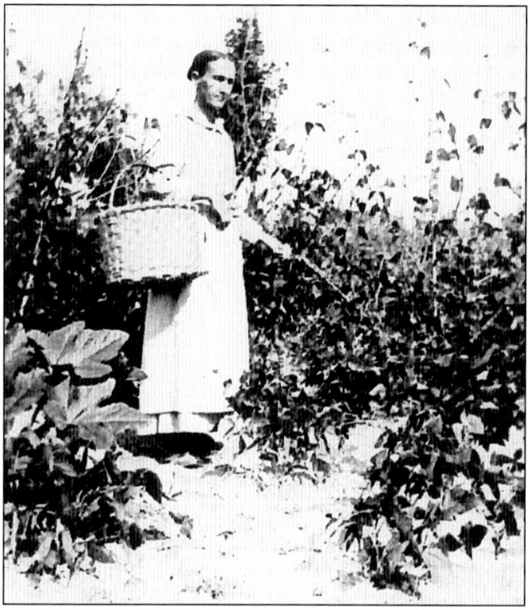

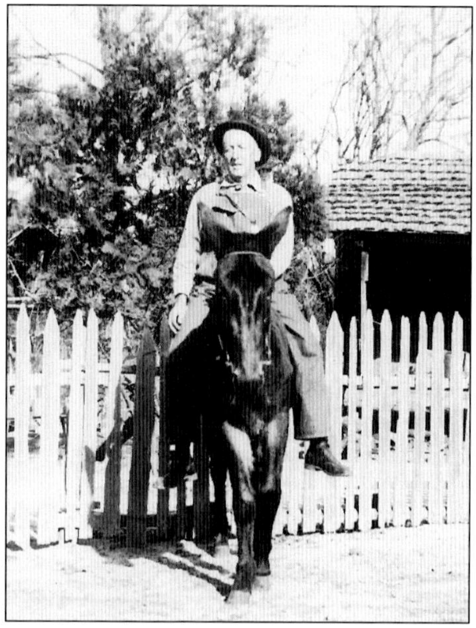

Left: Country women like Mrs. Emma Smith, seen here in her garden in the early 1900s, often worked to raise food for their families. Even the container, in which she will place her vegetables after they are picked, is homemade. The hand-woven basket is made of white-oak strips after the green wood has been split using a froe and a mallet.
Right: Country farmers in the 1920s rode mules, wore overalls, farmed the land, raised all their own food, kept the fence mended, handrove boards on the roofs, and kept hay in the barn. Identified here is Alex White on his mule, Nell.

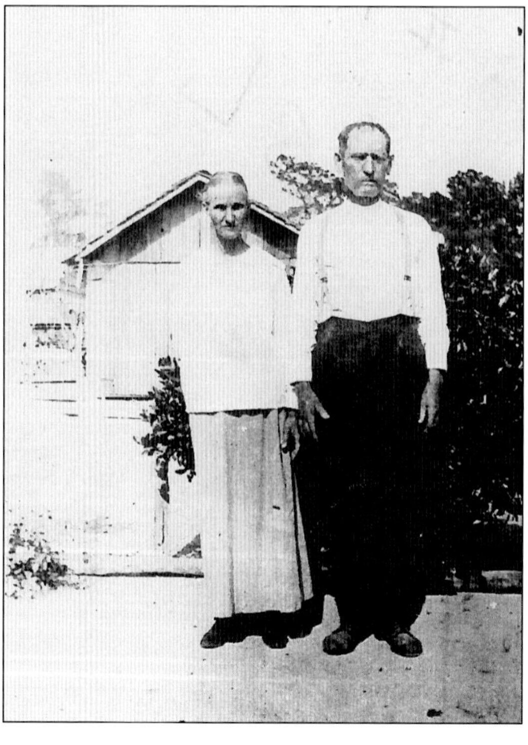

Country preachers like Rev. Wash Etheridge, who pastored at 13 different locations, moved from church to church. Reverend Etheridge married his first couple on December 8, 1889, and his last couple in 1932 or 1933. His baptismal record is outstanding in that he baptized 691 people at these 13 churches over a period of about 50 years. He preached 210 funerals. His life and ministry ended in 1933. He was the preacher who was at New Prospect Church preaching a "protracted meeting" when Lev James was killed on the way home, during the Mitcham War, in 1893.

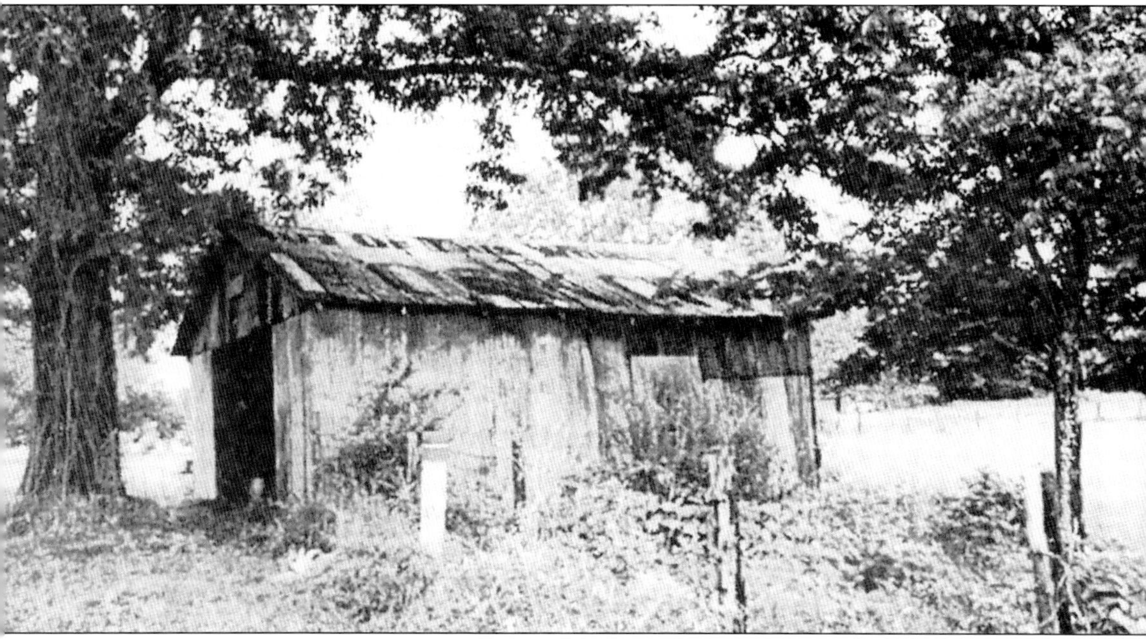

On May 24, 1997, the *Mobile Register* carried this picture of a wooden structure in Clarke County. On its roof was painted the following message: "Top of the World, Rock City." In 1936, the owner of Rock City, Garnet Carter, hired Clark Byers to paint advertising slogans about the attraction on barns, homes, and other roadside structures. Clarke County's Rock City artwork is on the property of Johnnie Newton, on U.S. Highway 43, south of Grove Hill.

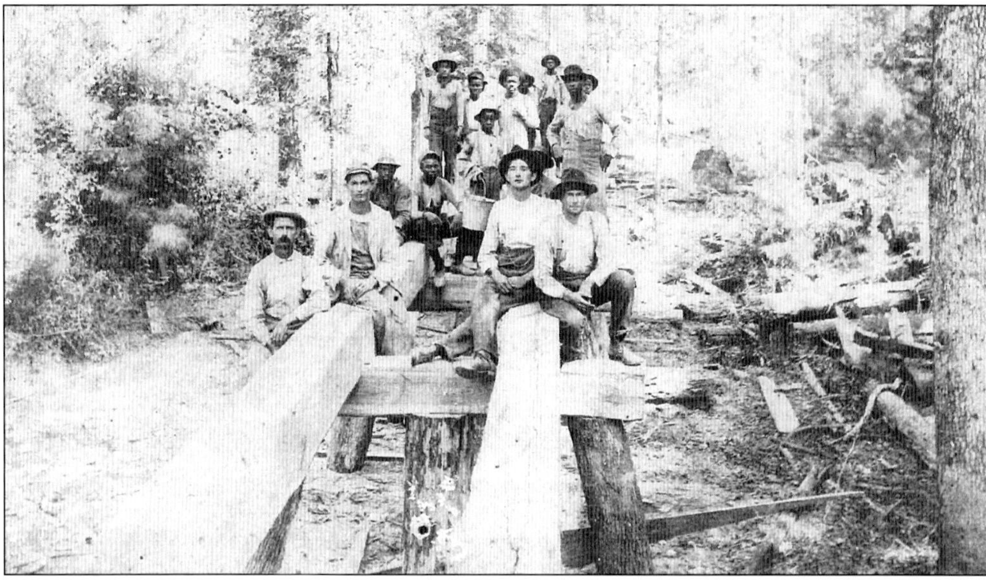

The Mobile and Birmingham Railway selected the route that their train would travel in June 1887. This picture shows one of the crews that put down the tracks through Thomasville in 1887. The first train pulled out from the station in February 1888. In 1899, the railway's name was changed to the Southern Railroad. This first passenger train was operating on February 14, 1888, carrying passengers from Thomasville to Mobile and Mardi Gras. The train left at 5:30 a.m. and arrived in Mobile at 10:25 a.m. at a cost of $3.75 in fare.

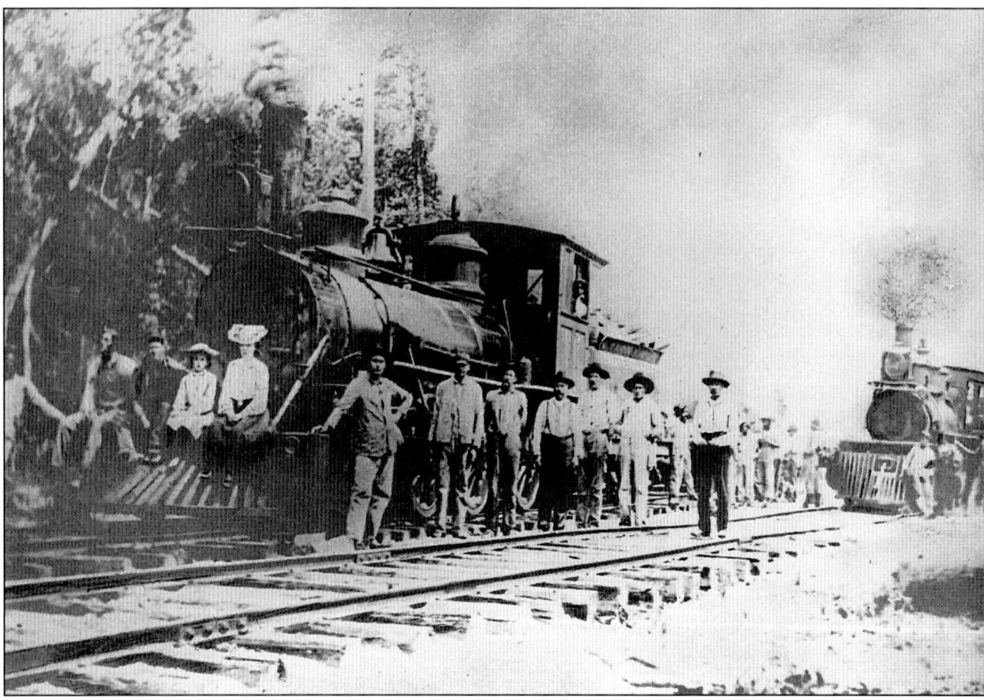

The big #4 locomotive, called "Jumbo," the small #3 Spot, railway employees, and farmers who lived near the railroad line at Hebron Switch on the Zimmerman Railroad are pictured in this shot taken in April or May 1907. The Hebron Switch was just across Jackson Creek.

Eight

Clarke at Work

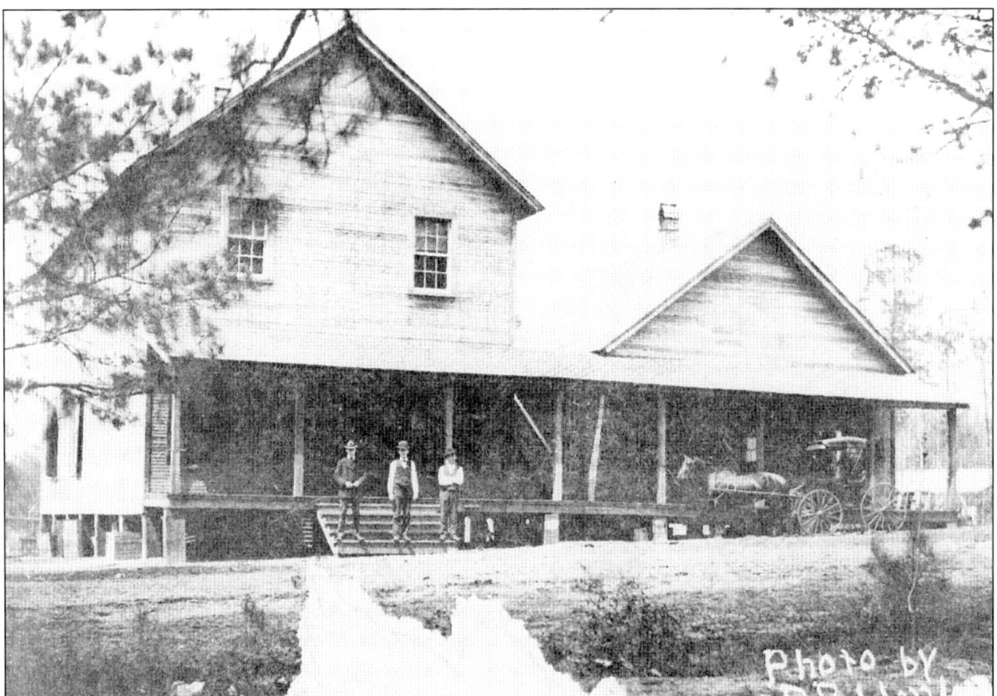

Seen here is the commissary of C.W. Zimmerman Manufacturing Company of Jackson. It was called the "lower commissary" since a woods commissary operated closer to the workers. C.W. Zimmerman and his nephew, C.L. Warner, established Zimmerman Manufacturing Company in 1898. Collie Moore ran the commissary at Jackson in 1907. Chess McCorquodale also ran the lower commissary for a period. Bass Porter ran the commissary in town around 1914.

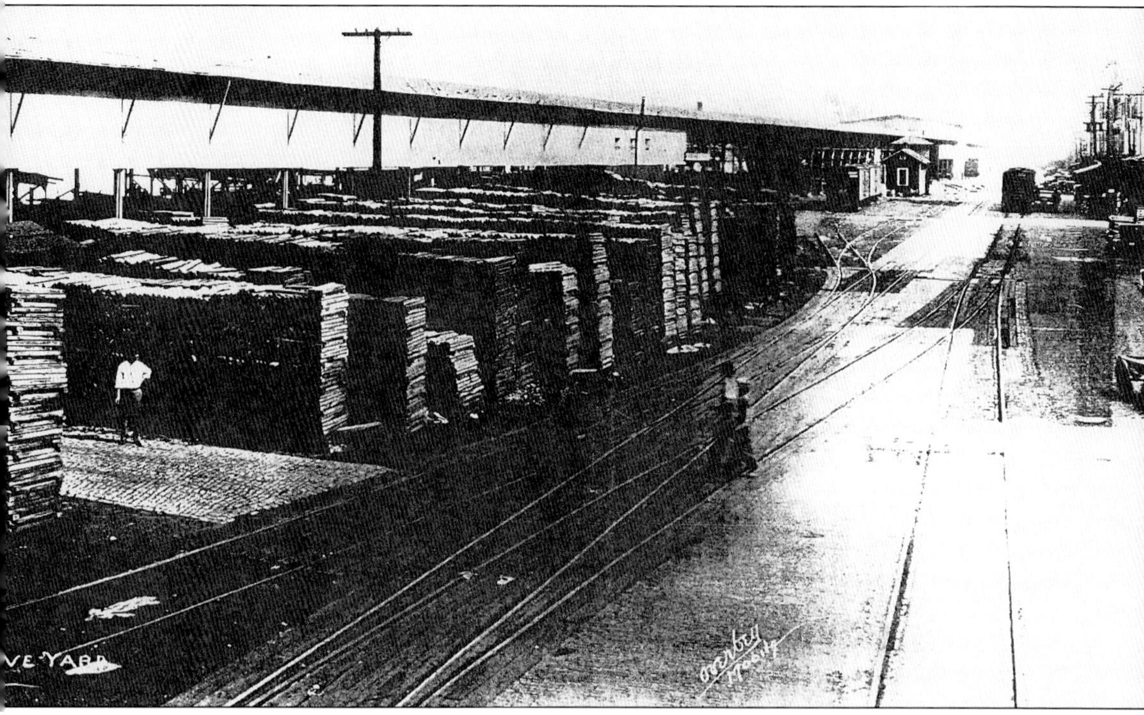

Stavemaking in Clarke County was an industry that turned large, white oak trees into the rough, raw material for finishing the staves once they were shipped to their final destination, usually France or Italy. Staves were made using hand tools, such as the broad axe, a drawing knife, a froe, etc. Stavemakers from the "old country," modern-day Croatia, came and worked in many places, including Clarke County and other sites in Alabama, from the 1890s to about 1914. What we know about these stavemakers comes from those who came and stayed in America. Many of these immigrant men married local women; these families include the Pezents, Klepacs, Erzens, Turks, and Pongerayters. Others came, but returned home when the stavemaking business slowed due to the rumors of the beginning of WW I. Scenes like the one in this picture of staves on the dock in Mobile waiting shipment grew rare. Shipment of the staves was almost impossible because ships were being used for war preparation and operation. Approximately a dozen stave mills had been set up all over Clarke County doing the same work described above, though doing it mostly with machinery. They met with the same wartime difficulties.

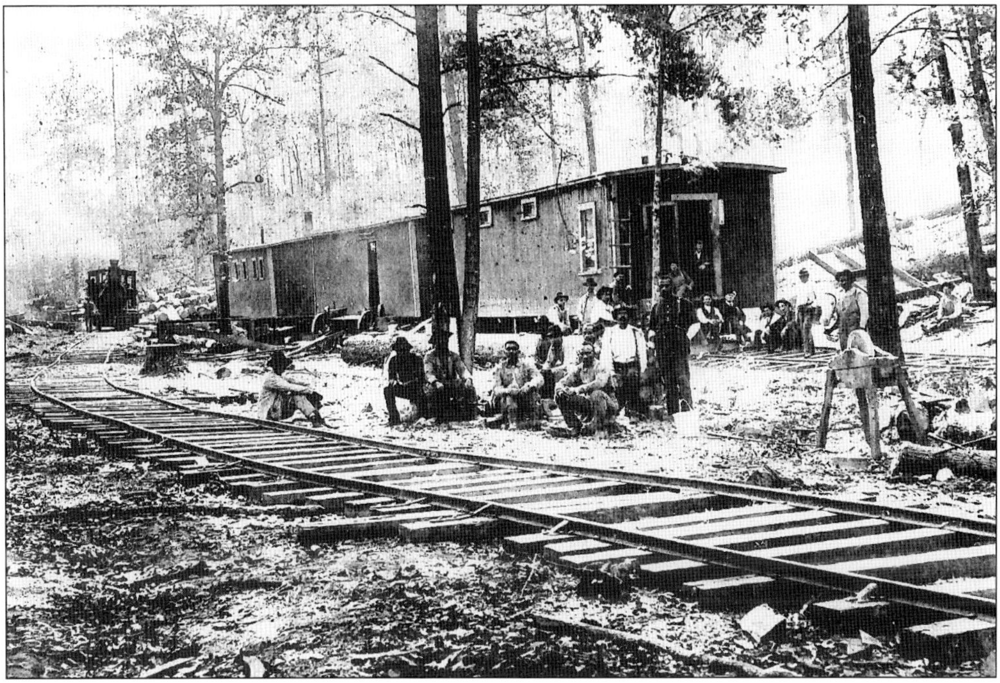

The scene here is of a Zimmerman logging camp near Zimco in the early 1900s. Zimco was the hub of the logging operation. It was already a thriving community with a school, post office, and stores. The Camp Five community was so named because 5 or 6 miles north of Zimco was where one camp was located.

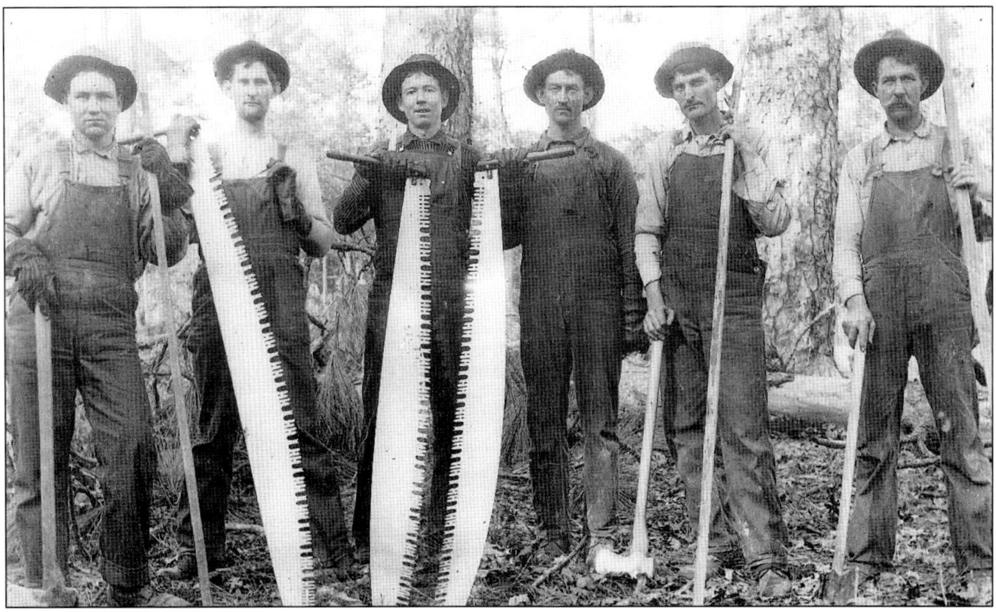

The wage hands pictured here were a saw crew for Zimmerman Manufacturing Company. The main line ended at a place called Sally Gap, near Tallahatta Springs. Zimmerman had a camp near Bedsole's Store in Mitcham Beat, and these men are from that area.

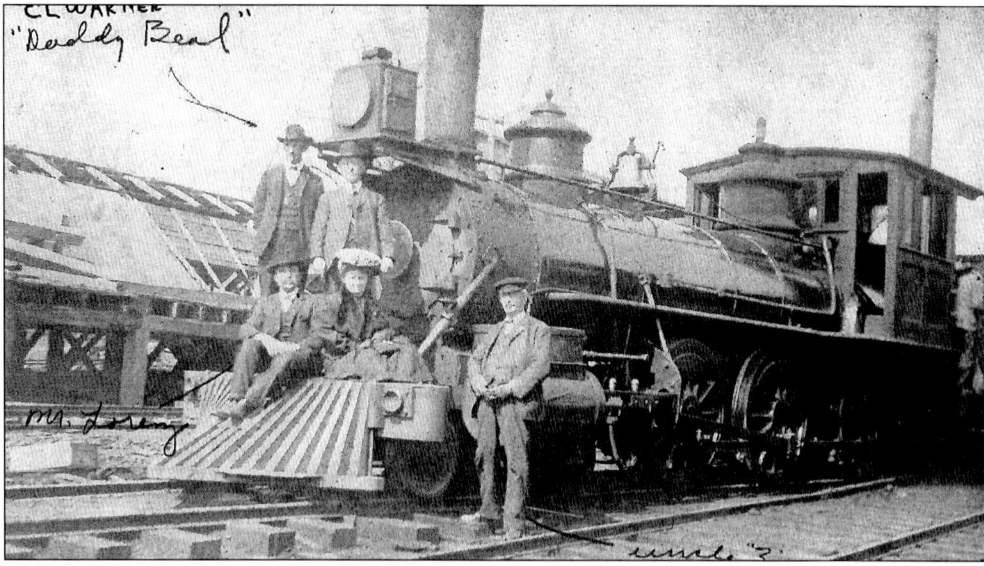

One of the five locomotives used by Zimmerman Manufacturing Company is pictured here. Forty logging cars could be pulled by the locomotives. The railroad was 40 miles long and headed toward Linden from the Jackson area. In 1916, Zimmerman was the largest single enterprise in Jackson. Their camps, built upon railroad car framing, included such buildings as offices, commissaries, boardinghouses for laborers, feed houses, and camp cars for employees. The company's payroll was $125,000 a year, and the company owned 35,000 acres.

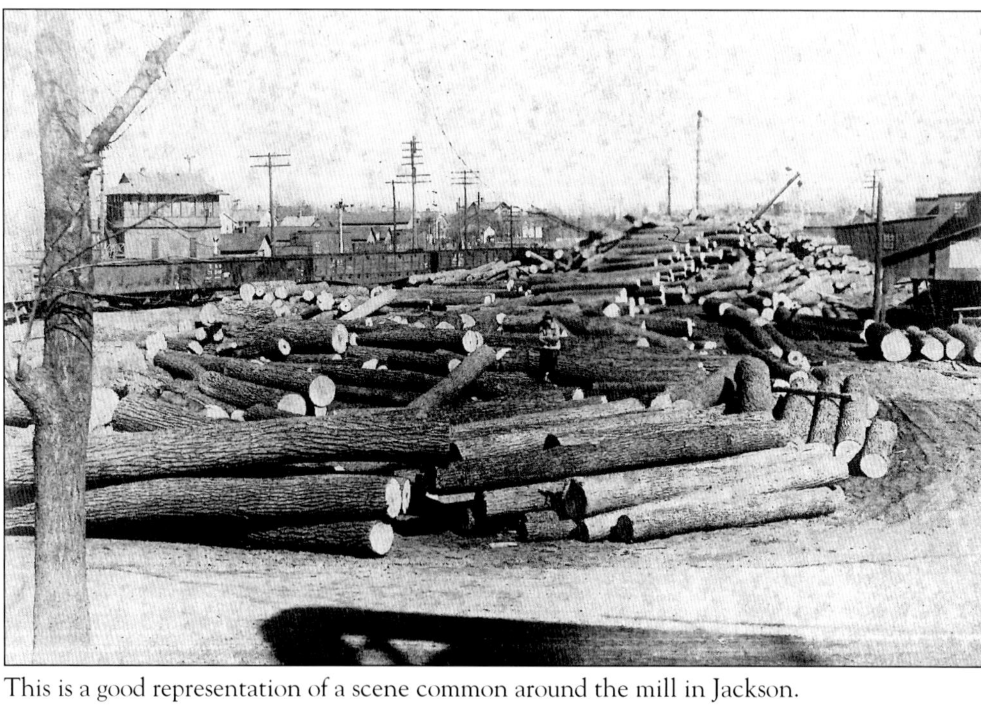

This is a good representation of a scene common around the mill in Jackson.

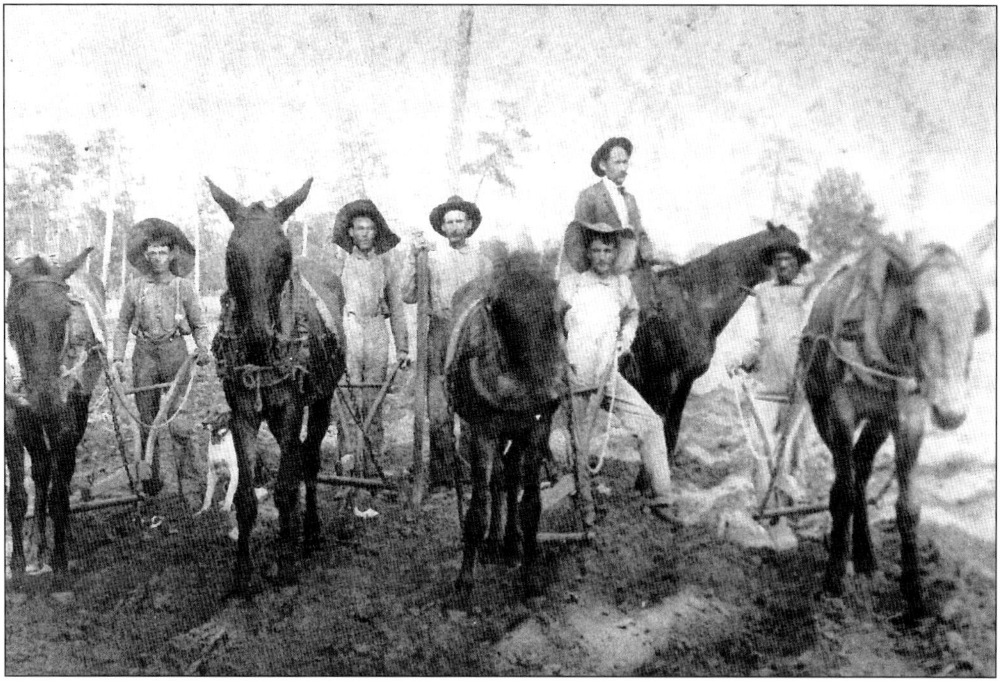

Howard Kennedy and Strother Eddie Kennedy, the first two men at the plows from the left, are helping to clear new ground around 1901 on family property in the Chance area.

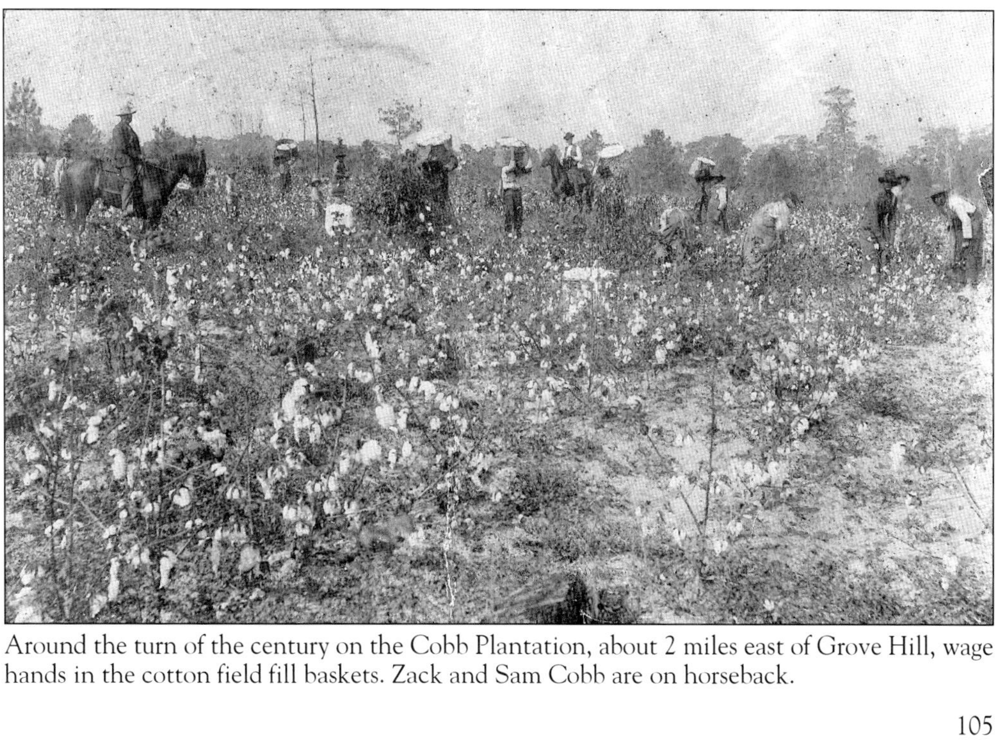

Around the turn of the century on the Cobb Plantation, about 2 miles east of Grove Hill, wage hands in the cotton field fill baskets. Zack and Sam Cobb are on horseback.

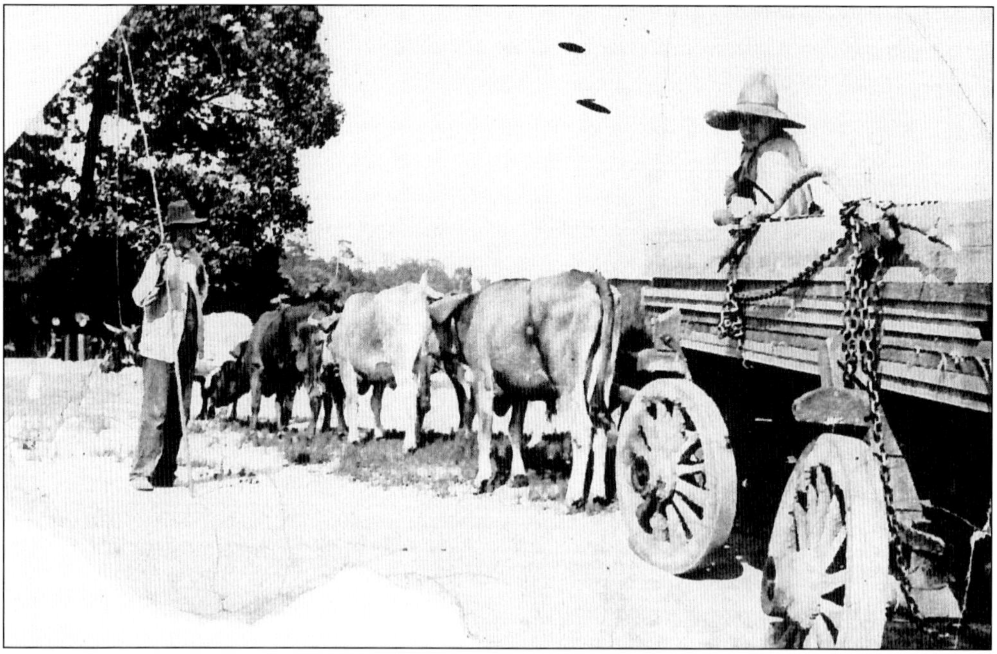

In the early 1900s, R.A. Bumpers owned a sawmill in Allen. He can be seen in this picture driving the oxen that are pulling the wagon loaded with sawed lumber from his mill.

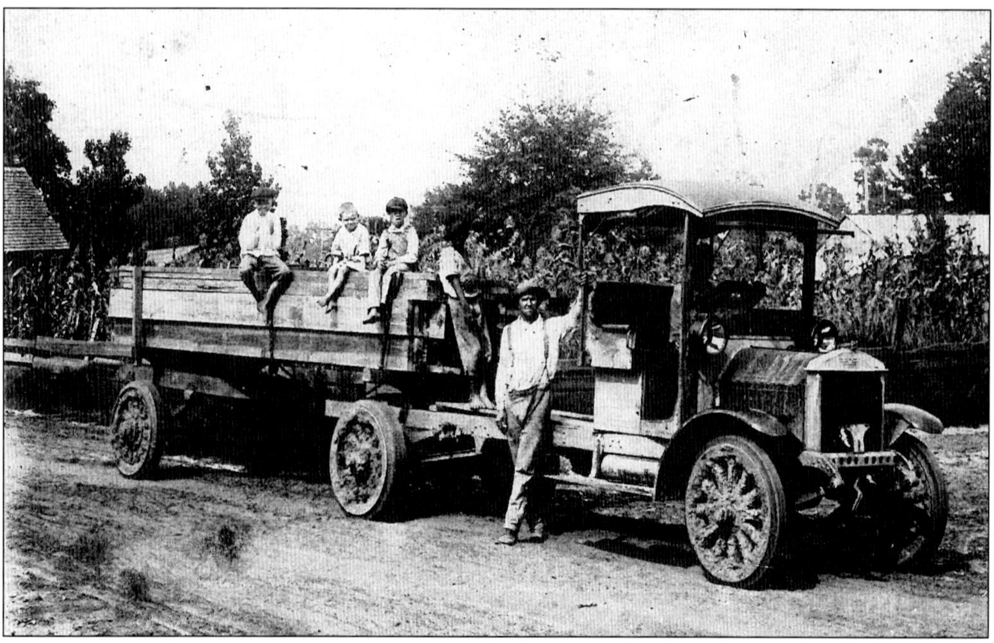

William W. Williams purchased one of the first log trucks in the area around 1921 to 1923. The truck was manufactured by the Federal Truck Company in Detroit. Identified are Strother "Bo Diddle" Morris (standing on truck), Williams (standing on ground), Wilbur and Doyle Williams (boys on the truck), Byrd Doyle (driver), and unknown (in overalls).

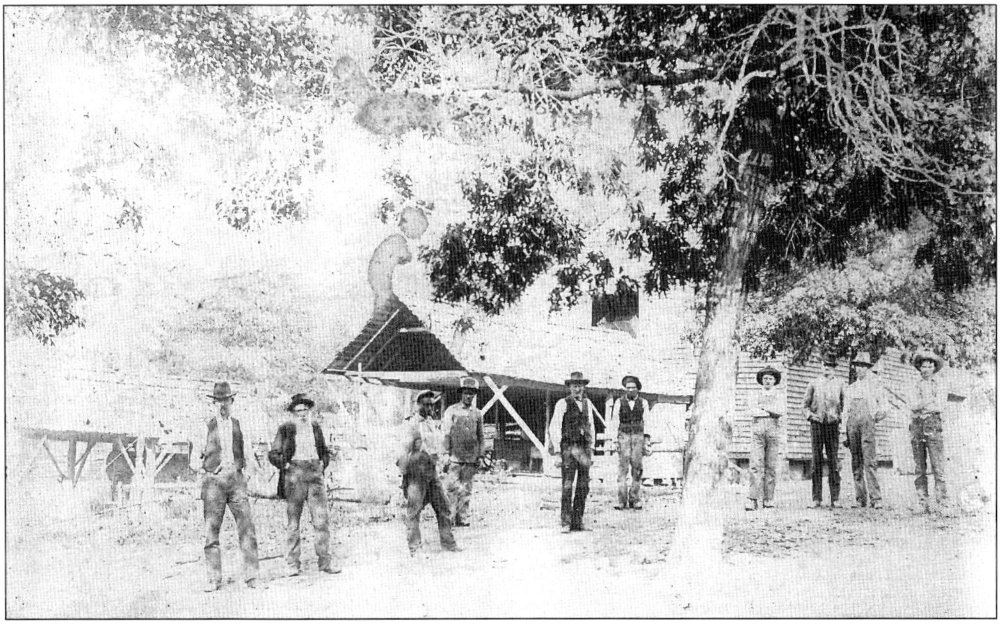

This picture is of the sawmill, gristmill, and cotton gin owned by George Thomas Reid in Tallahatta Springs sometime in the early 1900s.

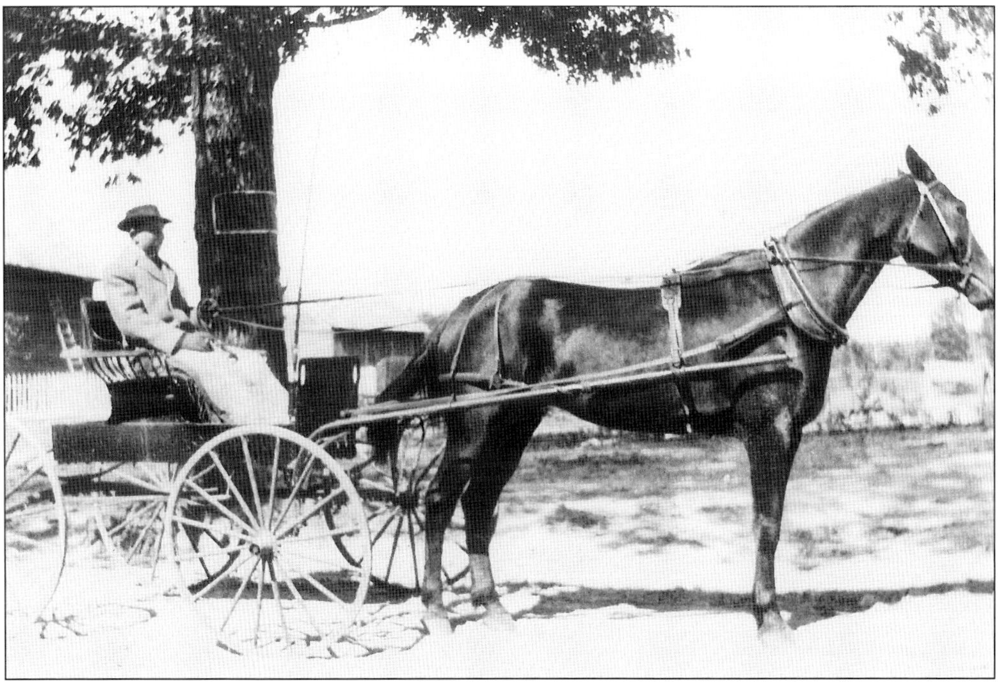

Dr. John Cooper Godbold Jr. was a respected figure in Whatley from 1912, when he arrived in Whatley, until his death in 1952. He was a professional who provided medical care to a large area around Whatley. After his marriage to Birdie Coleman in 1914, they stayed and gave much of themselves to the community. Beginning his career in 1912 meant horse-and-buggy transportation, bad roads, house calls miles from the office, and limited facilities in a rural town. Yet, he gave a lifetime to his oath to help his fellow man.

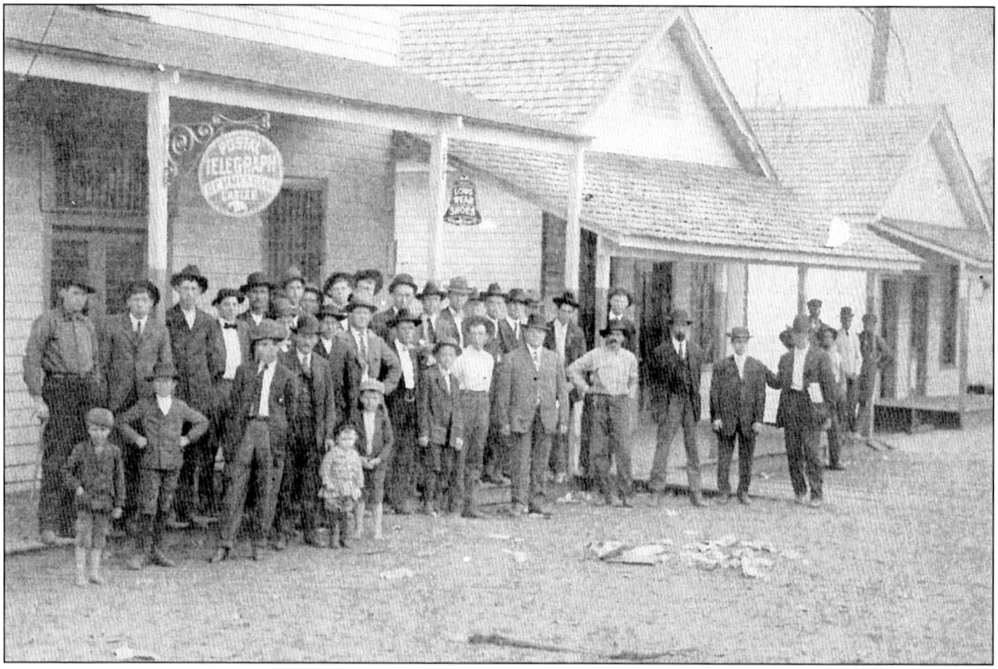

The Scotch Lumber Company offices in Fulton, complete with telegraph lines, were photographed between 1900 and 1912.

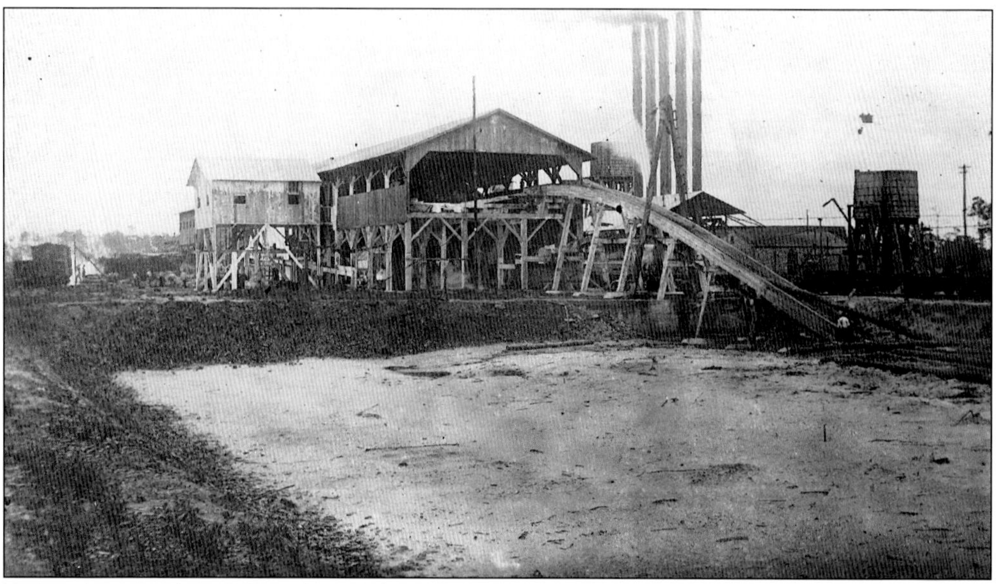

Early photographs of Scotch Lumber Company were taken by Erik Overbey, a Mobile photographer hired by Mr. Billy Harrigan, whose collection is housed today at the USA Photo Archives. This picture was made around 1912.

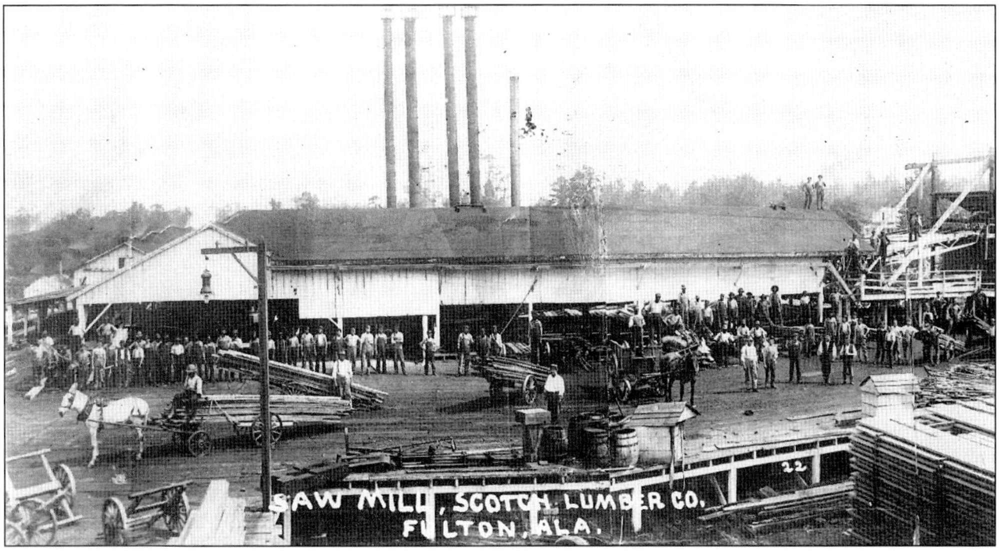

A planned layout for this picture, taken by a professional photographer, dates this one around 1912. This is an early sawmill with wage hands and wagons and mules for moving.

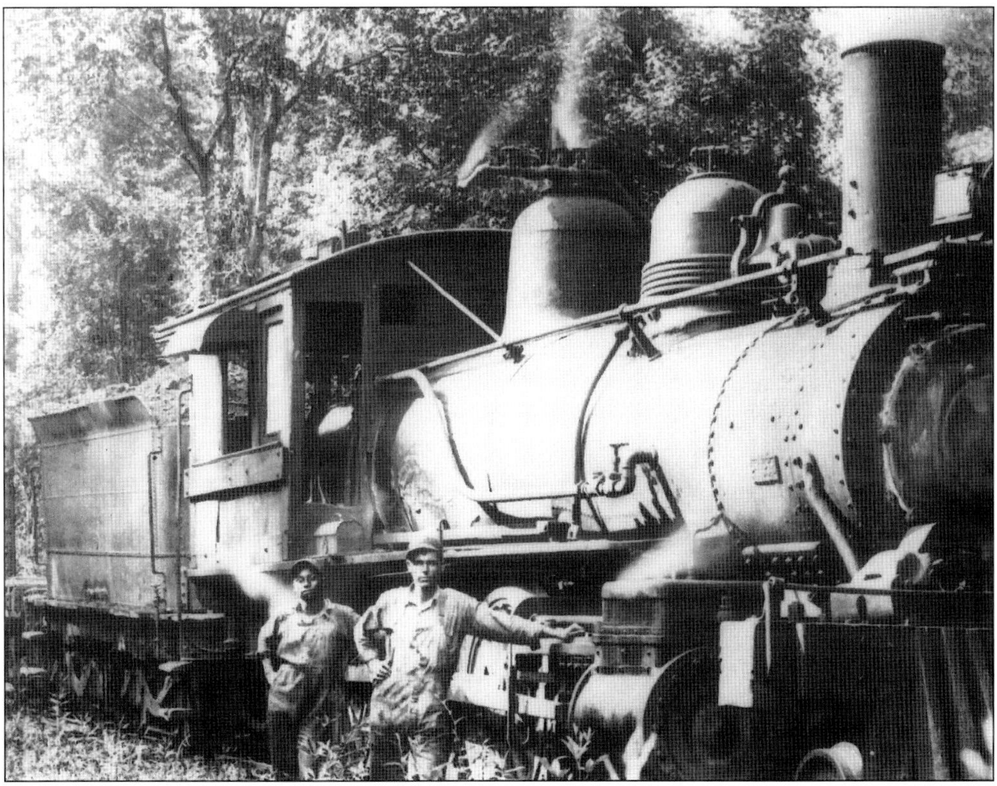

The #12 Spot, Scotch's main line rod engine and their most prestigious engine, was engineered by Tom Holloway (a near-Casey Jones type engineer), who is standing to the right in the picture. Holloway was a folk hero to the people associated with Scotch. The #12 Spot was used to transport the log train to Fulton where the sawmill was located. The man standing next to Holloway was probably his fireman.

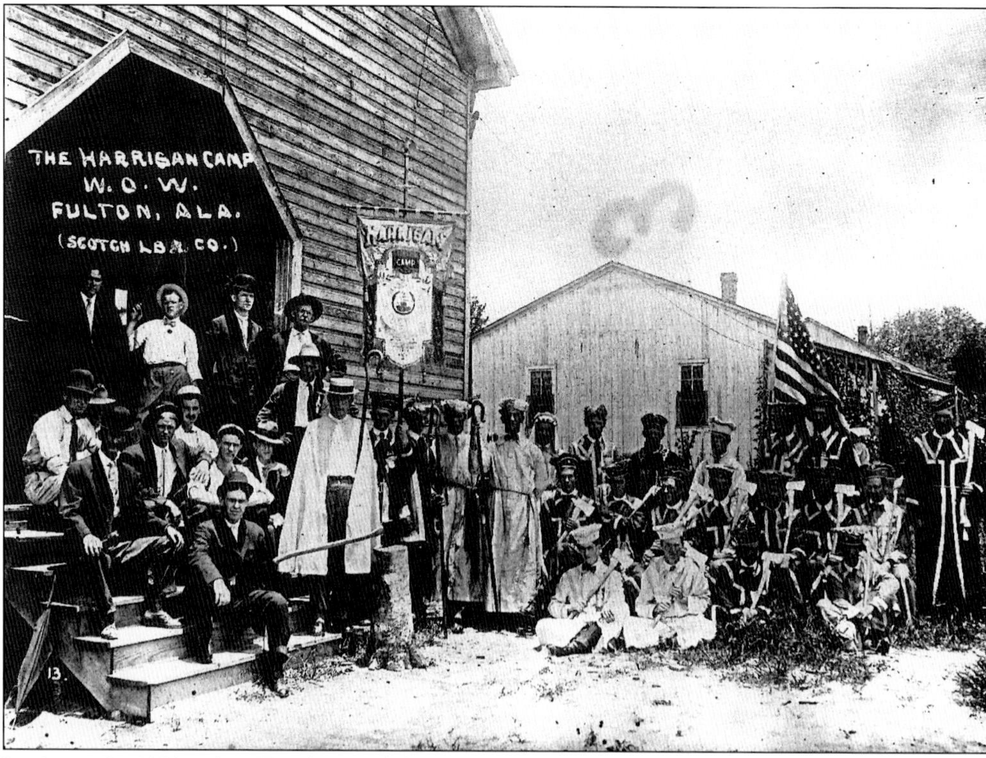

In the early 1920s, the Woodmen of the World established a lodge, Harrigan Camp No. 484, in Fulton. Gus Hermanson did the book work for the group, which furnished services such as insurance disability and retirement benefits as well as financial assistance for doctor bills and payment for artificial limbs, which were not unusual in the early sawmill towns.

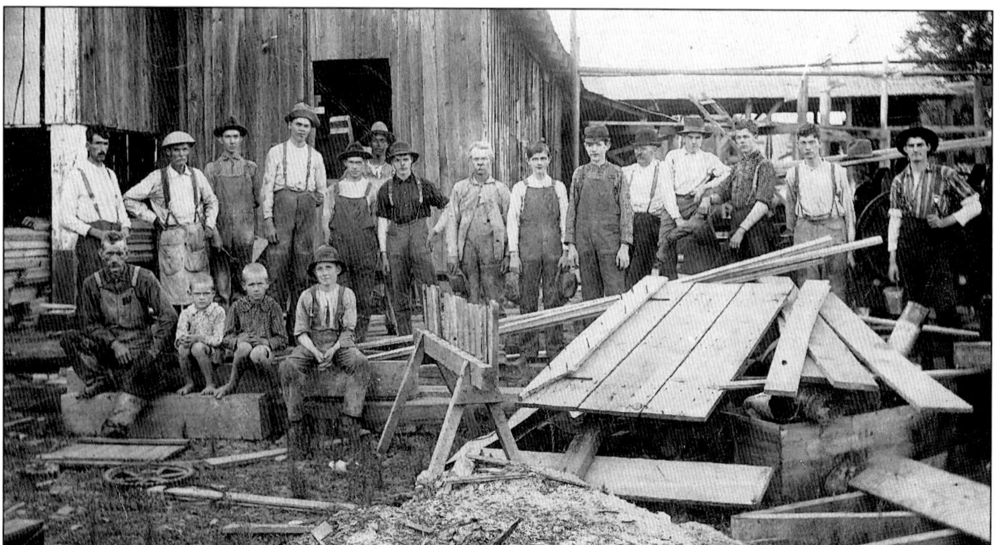

Henley's Studio in Thomasville took this early picture of workmen when Scotch was just beginning. "The Swede" is wearing the strange, round hat, standing second from the left. The fourth man from the left is a Fendley, and the third man from the right is Thomas T. Henley.

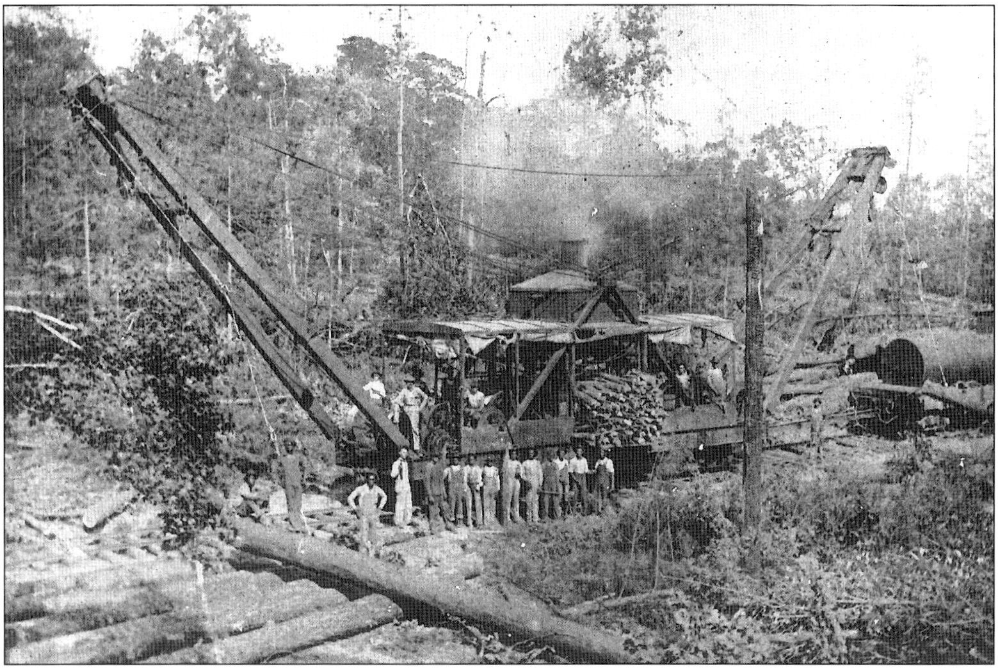

Scotch's first skidder was a single-boom McGiffert skidder. The Clyde skidder with double booms, pictured here, shows one on each end. On the skidder, someone had to fire the boiler, operate the take-up drums and the cable-splicer, and be the foreman of the crew.

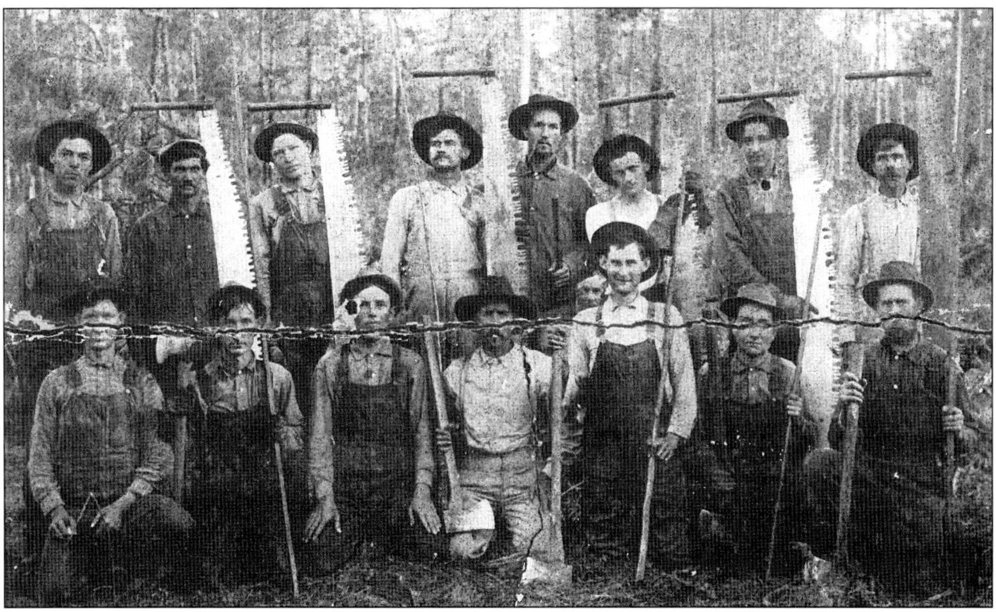

The Scotch Lumber Company saw crew was made up of men from the Chilton area. The picture was taken around 1911 near Smith Cemetery. The crew members are, from left to right, as follows: (front row) Daniel Sanderson, Dovard Philen, Ernest Smith, unidentified, Robert Stifflemire, John Buckalew (peeping from behind), Burke Dortch, and Robert "Bob" Smith; (back row) Carl Smith, Will Philen, Sidney Smith, unidentified, Brad Philen, Claudie Harrison, Enoch Stephens, and William "Billie" Sheffield.

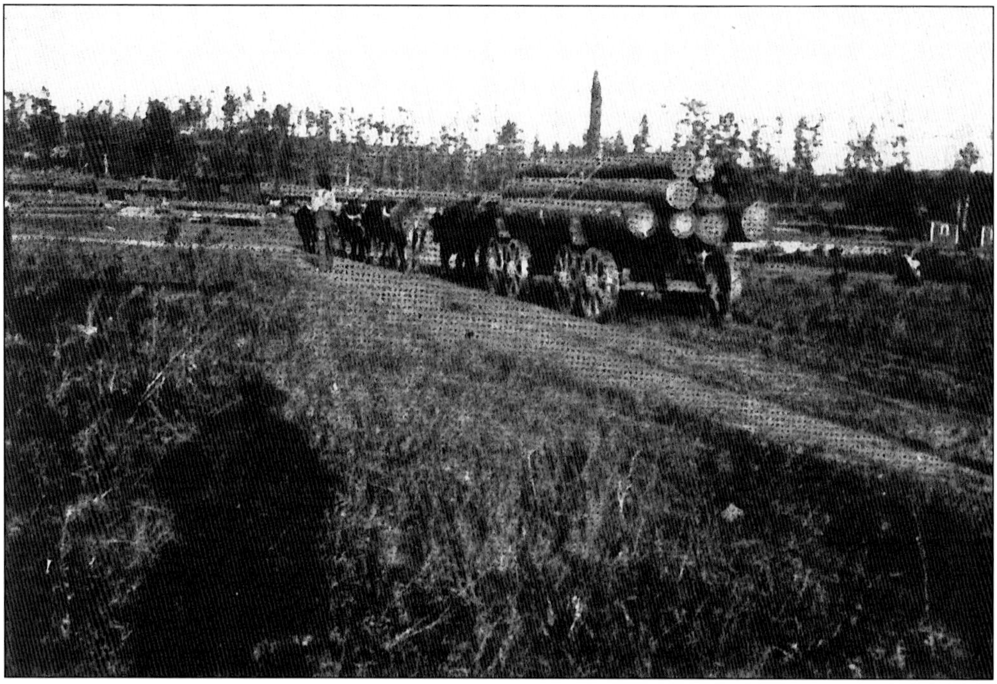

Eight-wheel wagons pulled by oxen, such as this one in the Pritchett Field, carried logs where the tracks or dummy lines did not go.

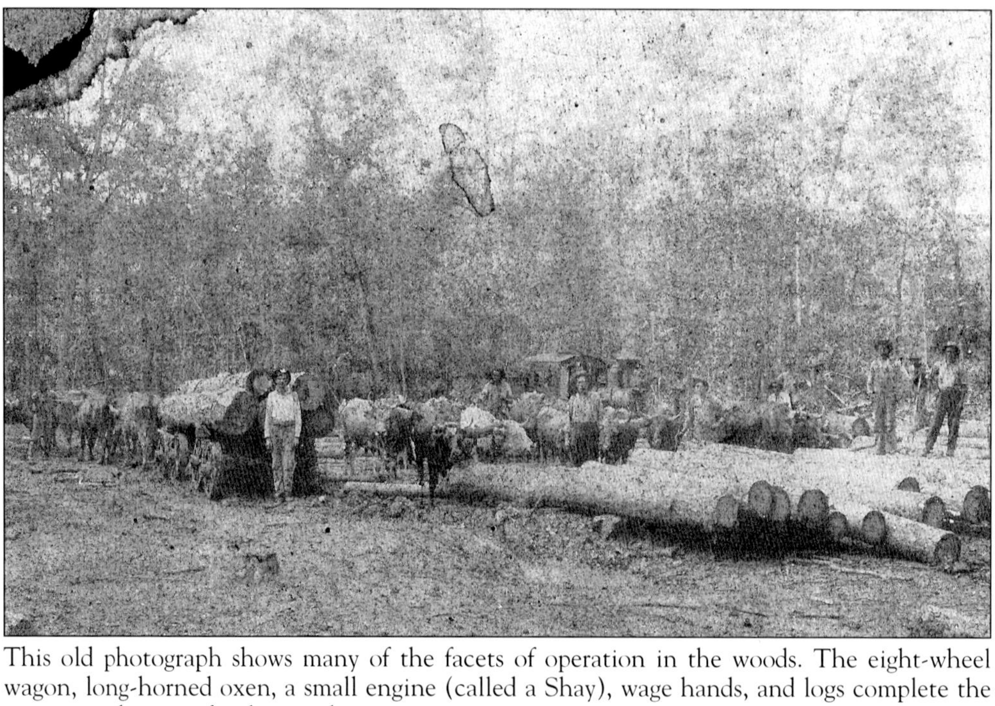

This old photograph shows many of the facets of operation in the woods. The eight-wheel wagon, long-horned oxen, a small engine (called a Shay), wage hands, and logs complete the necessary elements for the woods operation.

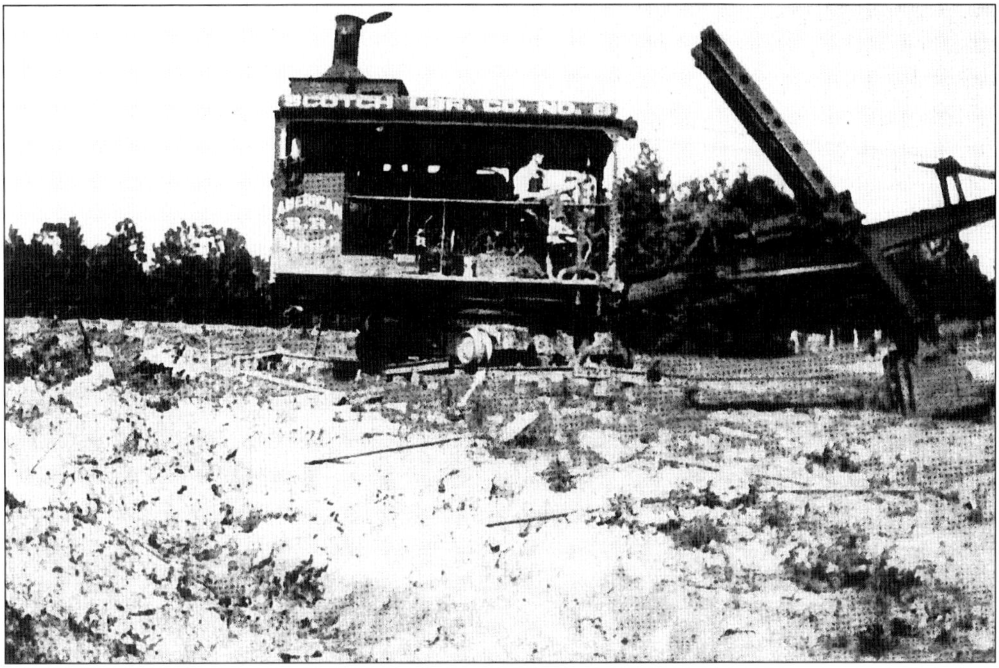

A steam-operated shovel that advanced on tracks as the work was done is pictured here. It dug its way through steep hills and was used by grading crews who preceded the logging crews, to purchase right-of-way, survey the lines, and lay the track. The shovel's purpose was to keep the railroad beds as level as possible.

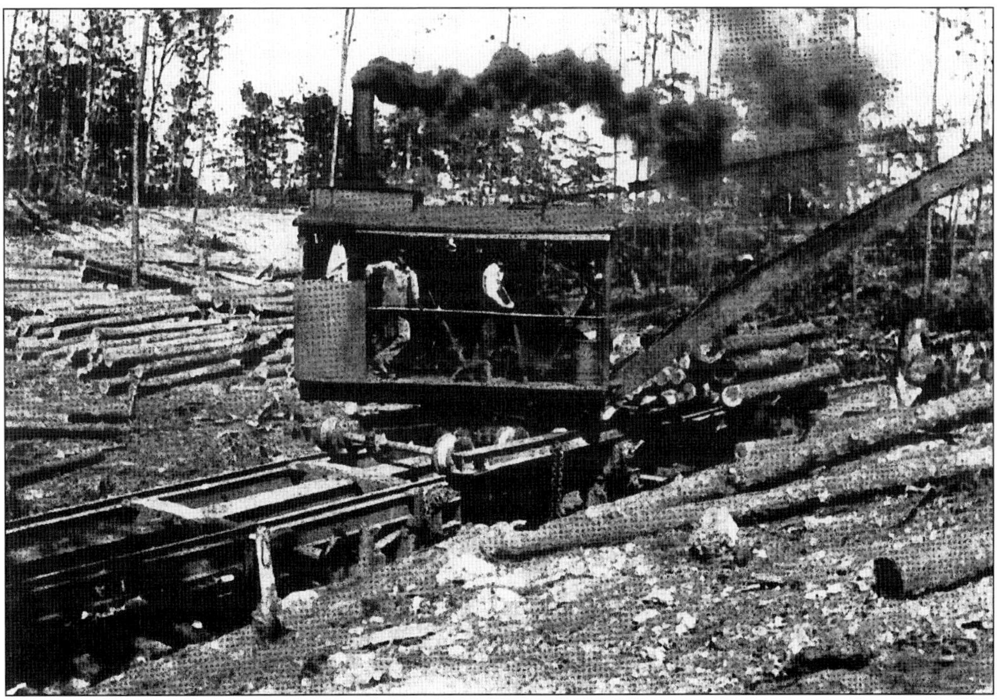

The steam-operated log loader did as its name indicates. Shown here, it boils black smoke into the air while wood is fed into its boiler, producing the powerful steam.

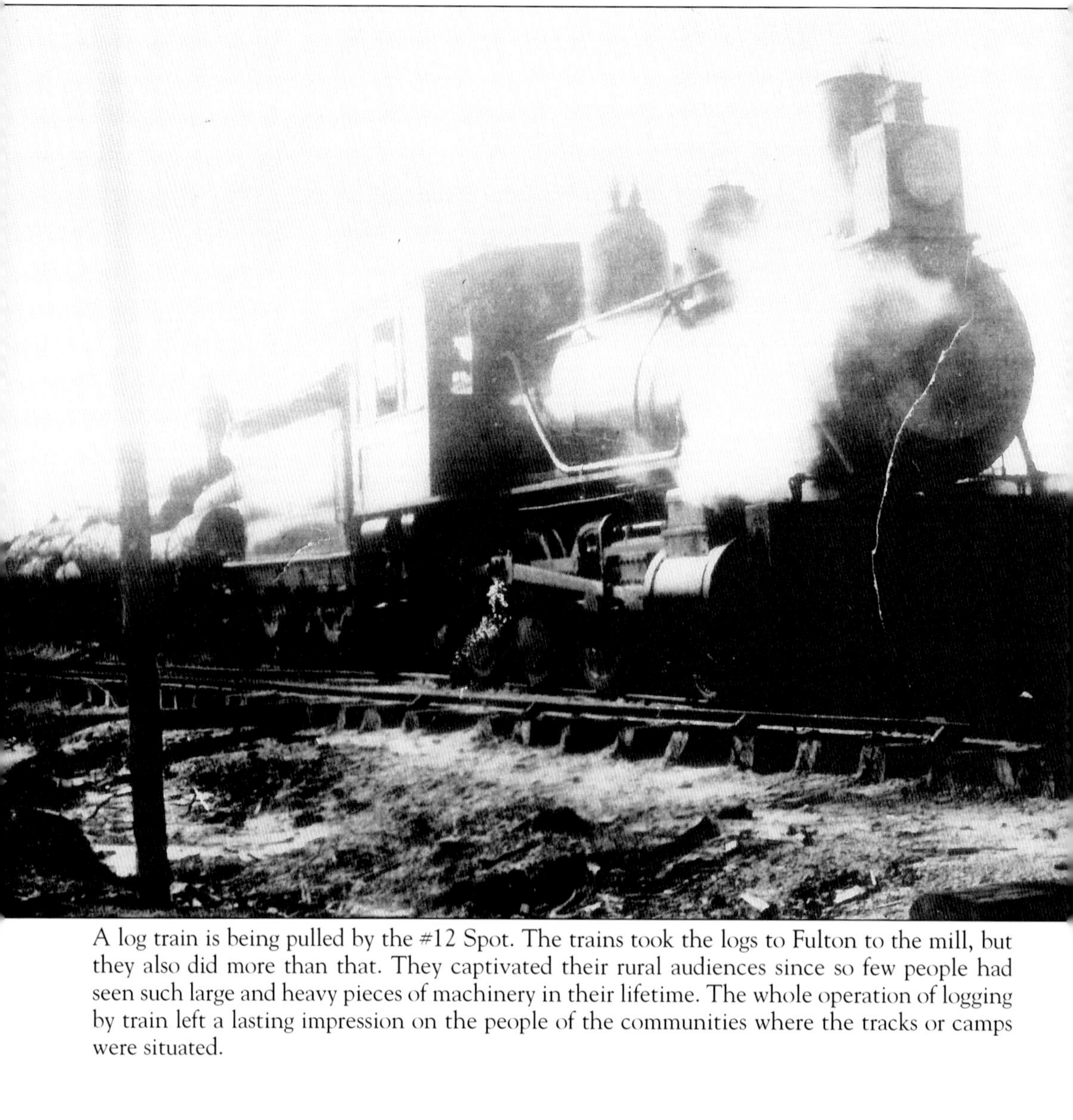

A log train is being pulled by the #12 Spot. The trains took the logs to Fulton to the mill, but they also did more than that. They captivated their rural audiences since so few people had seen such large and heavy pieces of machinery in their lifetime. The whole operation of logging by train left a lasting impression on the people of the communities where the tracks or camps were situated.

Nine

Defenders of Freedom

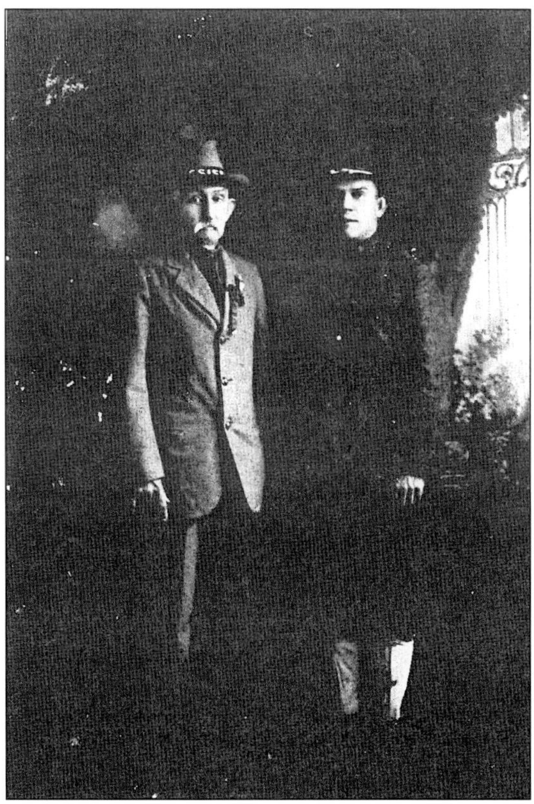

Clay Park was named in honor of W.W. Clay, who came to Thomasville when the tracks were being laid for the railroad. Clay talked the railroad officials into donating the land for the park to the town. Shown here in his Confederate uniform is W.W. Clay and his son, William Dixie Clay, in his WW I uniform. In appreciation for his efforts, the park was named Clay Park in honor of this man. The family lived in a house known as the Leonard Dozier home. This house stood on the lot now occupied by the former United Security Bank. Clay Park is located near what was once the thriving warehouse and office of the railroad.

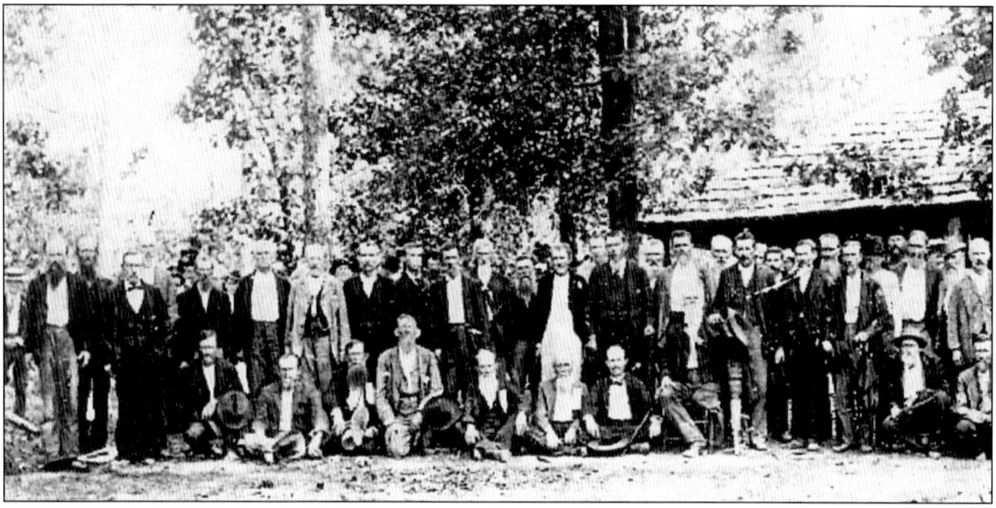

At Old Union Methodist Church and Campground, near McVay, this group of Confederate veterans met in the 1890s. A Confederate reunion for those who had given much for the cause was held and photographed during the activities of the day.

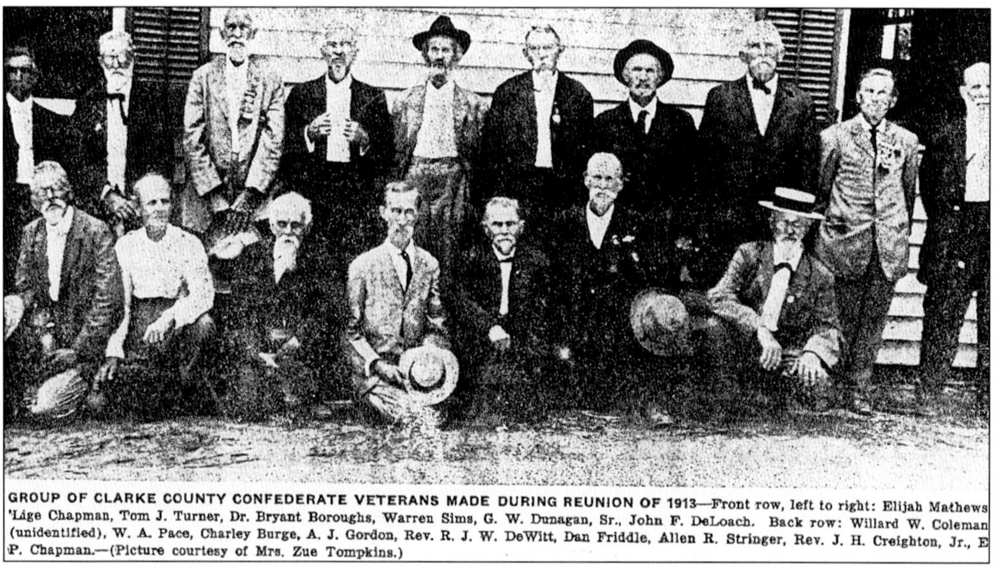

GROUP OF CLARKE COUNTY CONFEDERATE VETERANS MADE DURING REUNION OF 1913—Front row, left to right: Elijah Mathews 'Lige Chapman, Tom J. Turner, Dr. Bryant Boroughs, Warren Sims, G. W. Dunagan, Sr., John F. DeLoach. Back row: Willard W. Coleman (unidentified), W. A. Pace, Charley Burge, A. J. Gordon, Rev. R. J. W. DeWitt, Dan Friddle, Allen R. Stringer, Rev. J. H. Creighton, Jr., E P. Chapman.—(Picture courtesy of Mrs. Zue Tompkins.)

This group of Clarke County Confederate veterans met in 1913. Surely some of the same ones in the above picture are in this one also. They are, from left to right, as follows: (front row) Elijah Mathews, "Lige" Chapman, Tom Turner, Dr. Bryant Boroughs, Warren Sims, G.W. Dunagan Sr., and John F. DeLoach; (back row) Willard W. Coleman, unidentified, W.A. Pace, Charley Burge, A.J. Gordon, Rev. R.J.W. DeWitt, Dan Friddle, Allen R. Stringer, Rev. J.H. Creighton Jr., and E.P. Chapman.

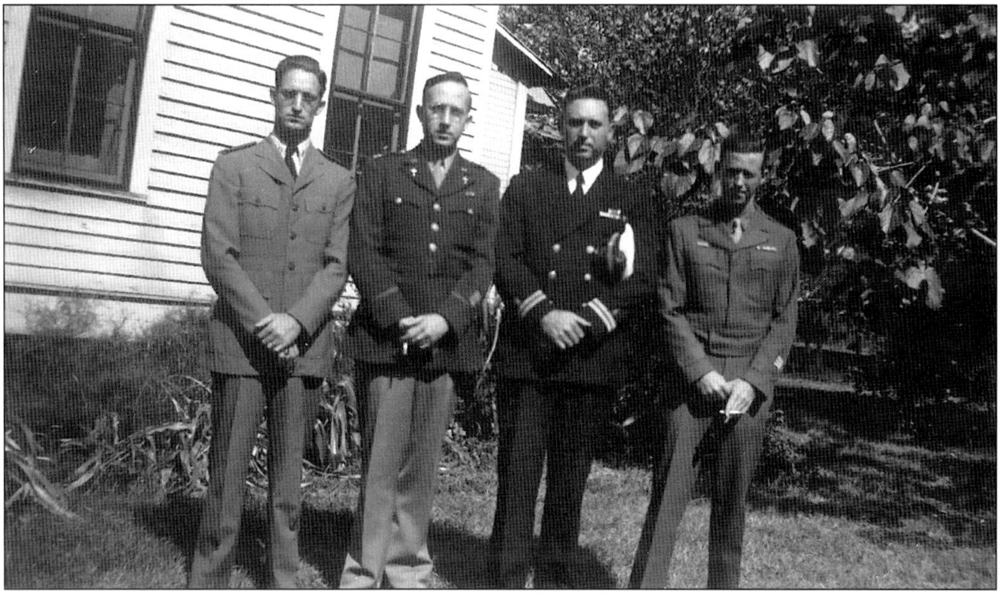

Lamar McLeod and his brothers who served in World War II are pictured here. This photograph is typical of many American families who had more than one young man fighting for freedom.

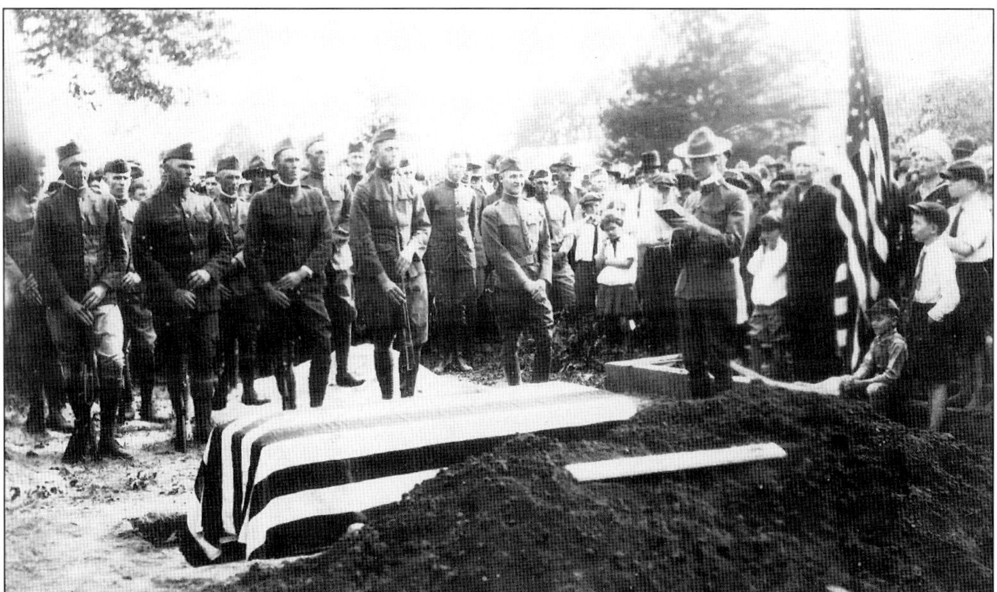

This is a picture of the military funeral in July, sometime around 1918, in the Grove Hill Cemetery for John R. Lavender, who served in WW I.

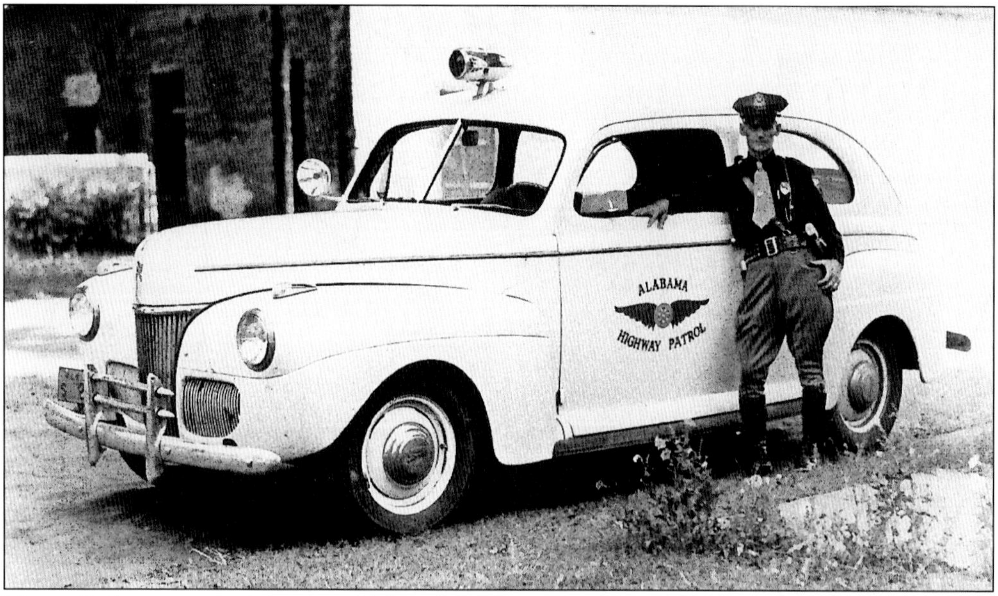

Horrie Faile was one of the first Alabama Highway Patrolmen hired to serve Clarke County. This photograph was taken in 1935.

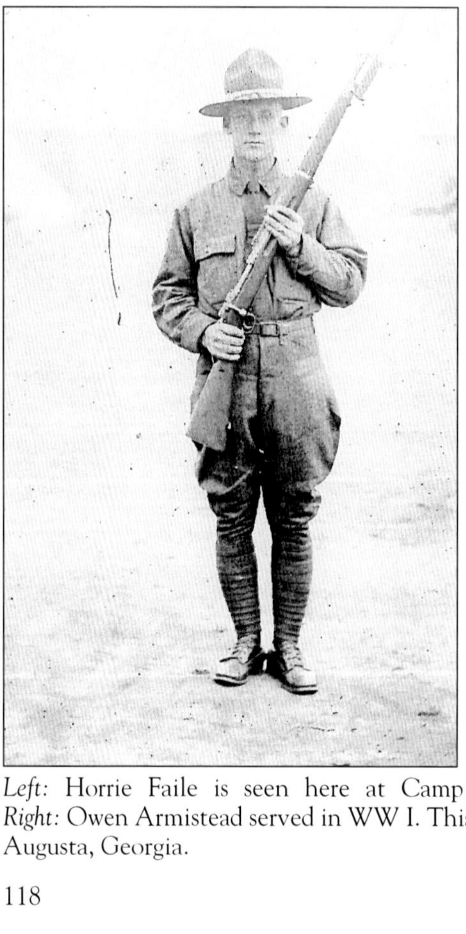

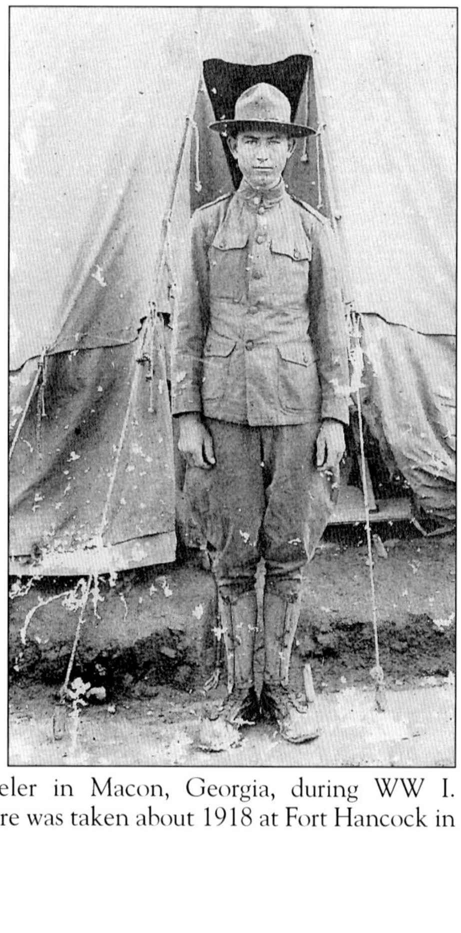

Left: Horrie Faile is seen here at Camp Wheeler in Macon, Georgia, during WW I. *Right:* Owen Armistead served in WW I. This picture was taken about 1918 at Fort Hancock in Augusta, Georgia.

Ten

People at Play

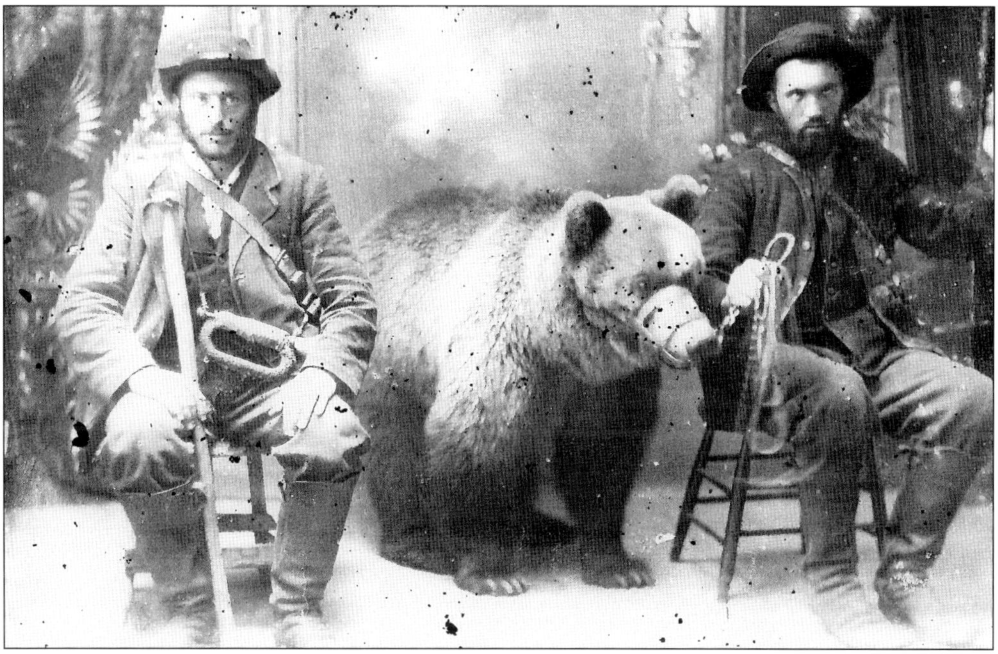

Between 1893 and 1896, two Italians and Jenny, the dancing bear, made their way through Clarke County. Reports of the trio resurfaced when glass negatives of them were discovered in an old building on Main Street in Grove Hill, where a photographer had set up shop in the late 1800s. Both Mr. J.Y. Huggins of Coffeeville and Mrs. Lallie Armistead of Walker Springs reported following the tracks of the bear and his two masters to John R. Bell's Store in McEntyre. Mrs. Armistead said that the two men spent the night with her father, J.W. Brewer, when she was about seven years old. She reported that they left with the bear and went to Campbell, while another story said that they crossed into Monroe County. Both stories agree that the bear killed one of her owners when she smelled freshly killed beef being dressed. After Jenny killed one owner, the other one shot her. The two Italians and the dancing bear, Jenny, created quite a stir in the county.

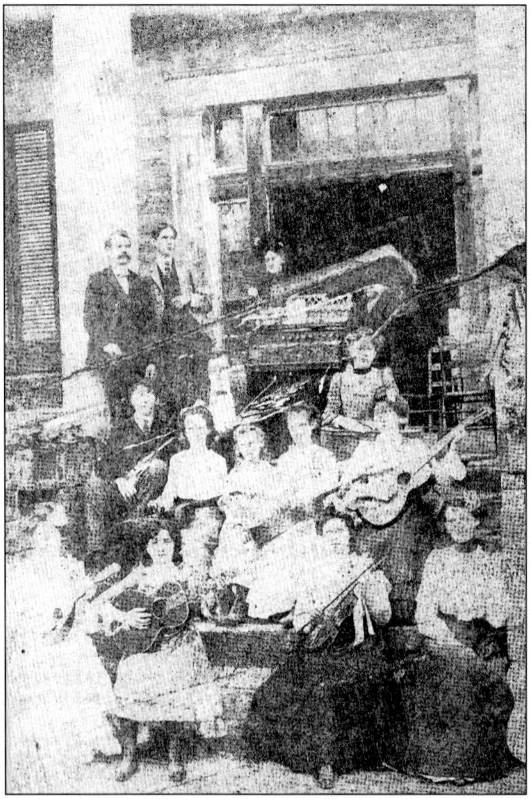

This picture features Saturday afternoon musicians in front of the York Home near the turn of the century, though the exact date of the picture is unknown. People in the picture are Myrtie Coate, Maggie York, Minnie Coate McCoy, Necie White, Cole Robinson, John J. McCoy, Otis Coate, Dalton Robinson, Mamie York, Mr. and Mrs. Bass, musicians from Mississippi, and boarders at the York Home.

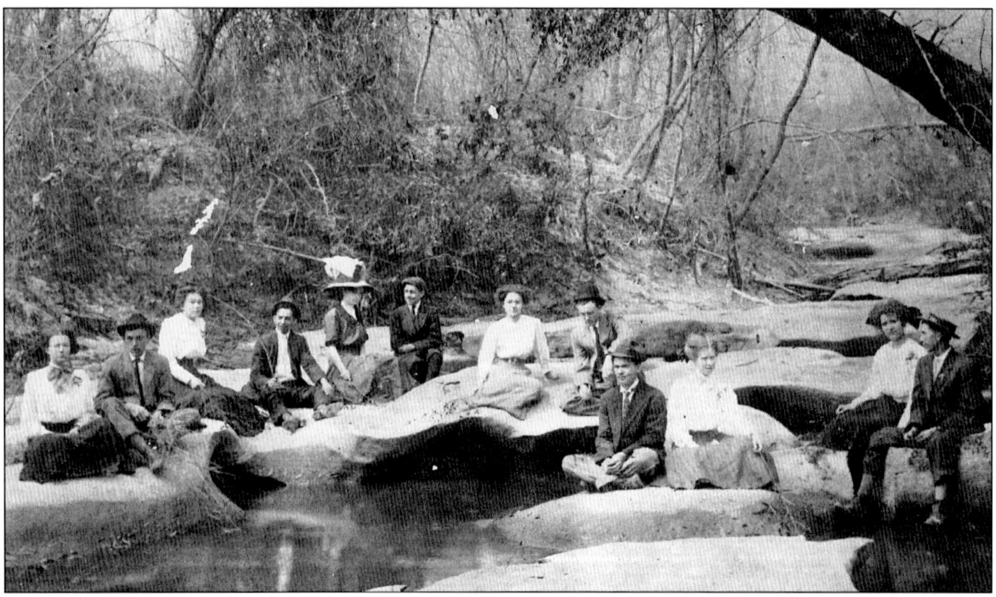

These people are courting on Sunday afternoon on Tallahatta Creek in 1909 at the "Rocks." They are, from left to right, as follows: Essie Armistead, Fincher Williams, Eunice Williams, Will Armistead, Winnie Lee (Griffin) McCorquodale (with big hat), Johnny Todd, unidentified, Herbert Williams, Mabon Pugh, Orrie Mae Armistead, Mae Williams, and Grady Armistead.

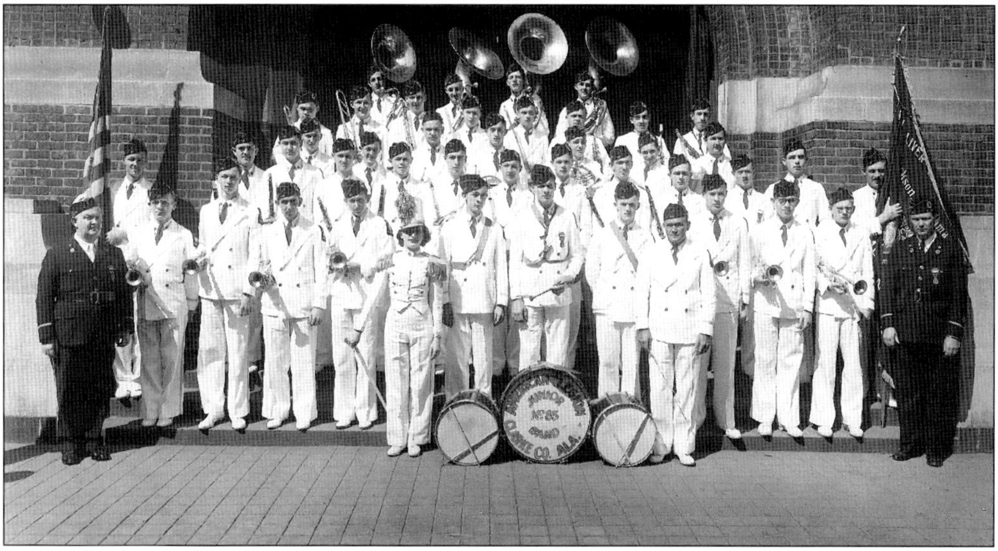

The American Legion Junior Band, No. 85, of Clarke County performed at the National American Legion Convention in 1937 in New York City. Identified here are Hannis Kennedy (third tuba from the left) and Cornell Outlaw (sixth from left, second row from top, on saxophone).

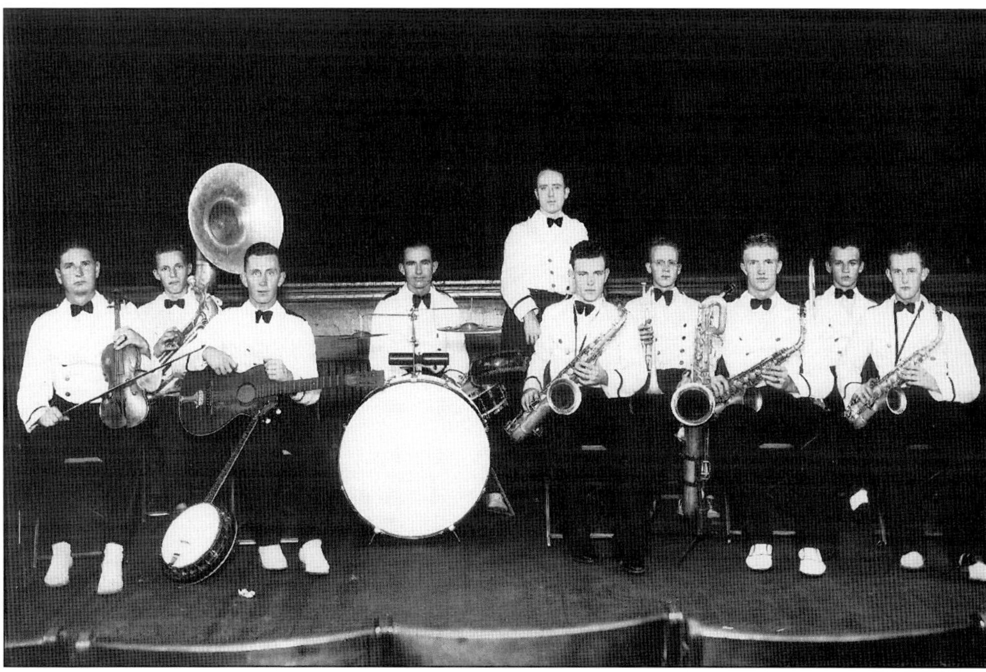

This orchestra—made up of, from left to right, Henri Mayton, Hannis Kennedy, Alton Whatley, Charles Poole, Felix (Red) Feagan, Fielding Kimbrell, Aubrey Feagan, Williams McCurdy, Billy Andrews, and Floyd Tucker—played for many occasions in Clarke County during the 1930s and 1940s. They performed the dance music for the Silver Slipper, north of Thomasville, two or three times a week. The Silver Slipper was a roadhouse typical of those scattered across the country in the 1930s and 1940s.

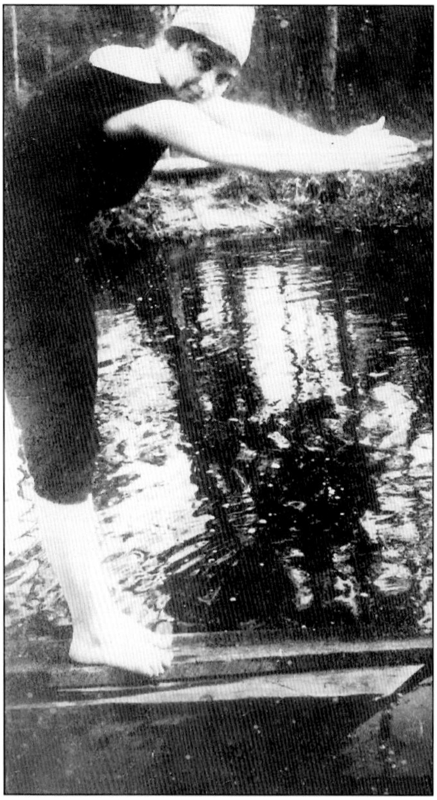

The Gillis Pond, the local swimming hole for Grove Hill, was located out Court Street, going south out of town. What a treat in the days of no air-conditioning!

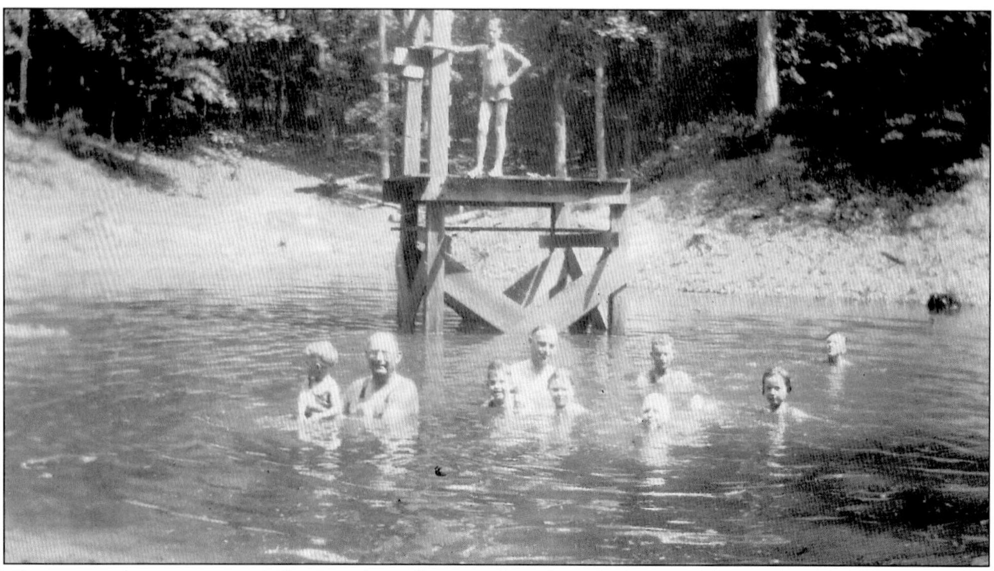

This is another scene at Gillis Pond. A diving tower has been erected to provide even more fun in the water. It is estimated that these photographs were made in the 1930s.

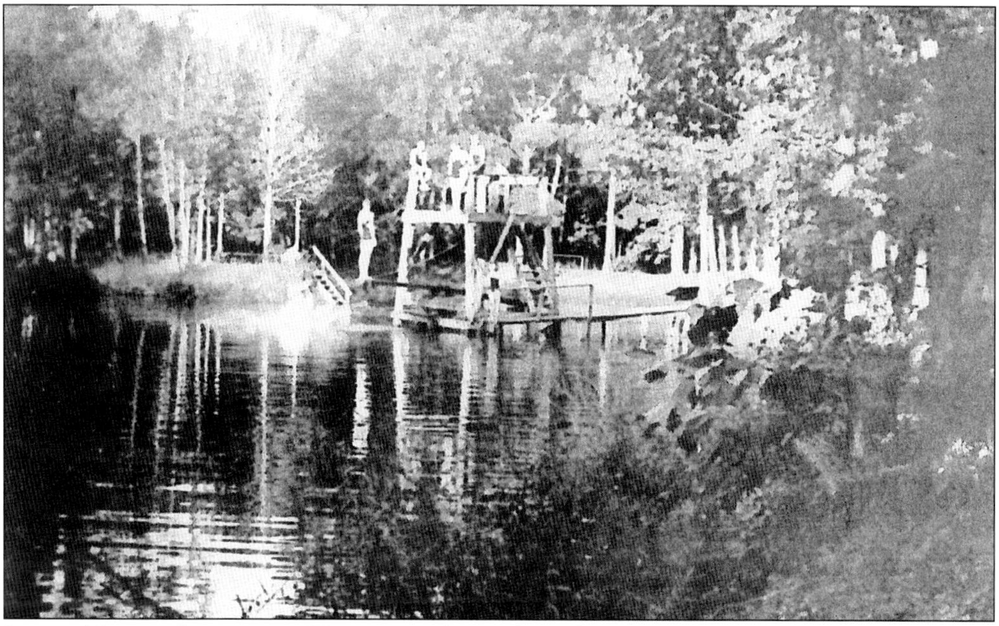

Pictured here is the tower at Warren Pond in Jackson, located where the Vanity Fair Park pool is now. Pond facilities included a concession stand, suit rentals, and two dressing rooms. The cost to swim was 10¢; the cost to rent a suit was also 10¢. The pond was operated by Irby Henley in 1933.

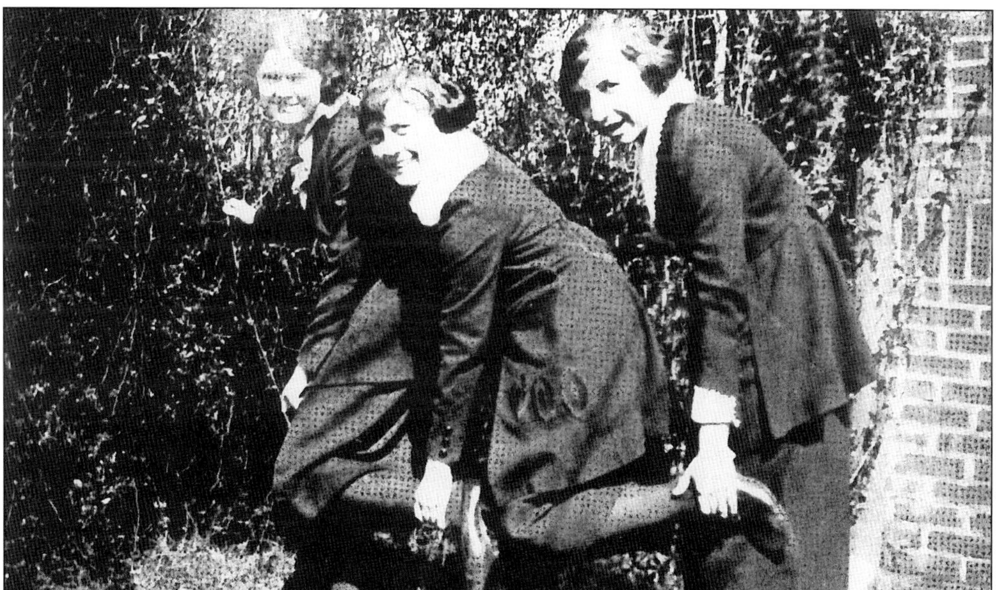

"Flappers" from the 1920s at Judson College are pictured here. The first on the left is identified as Minnie Mae Pugh, beloved historian and genealogist of Clarke County. Much of the material in this book came from her research.

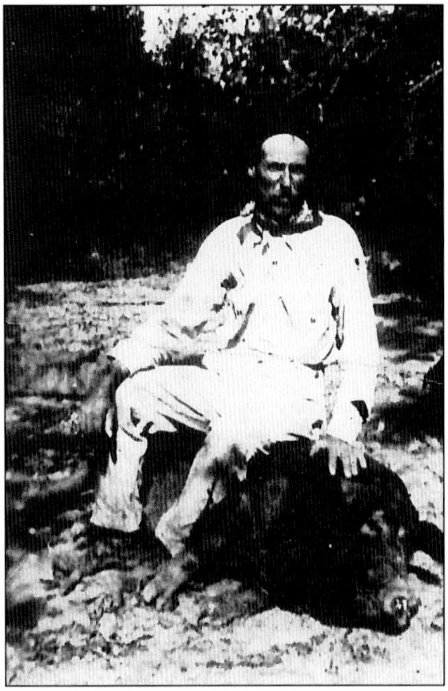

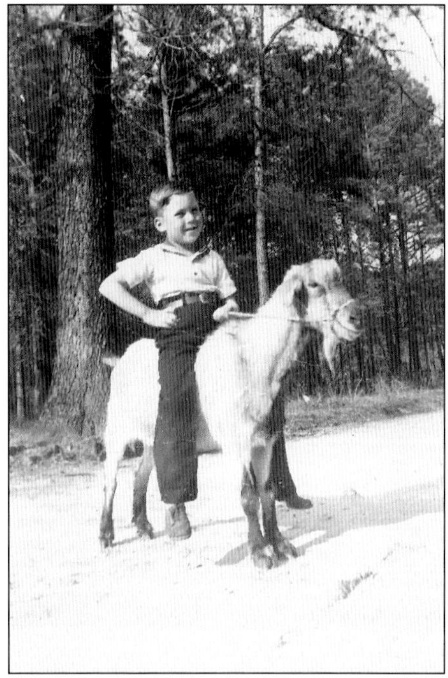

Left: Farmers prided themselves on the large size of the animals they raised for food; however, sometimes a farmer became so attached to an animal that it was hard to do anything except keep it. The man seen here is George Hare.
Right: Who says kids had no way to ride? A very gentle pet, a goat could be a good horse.

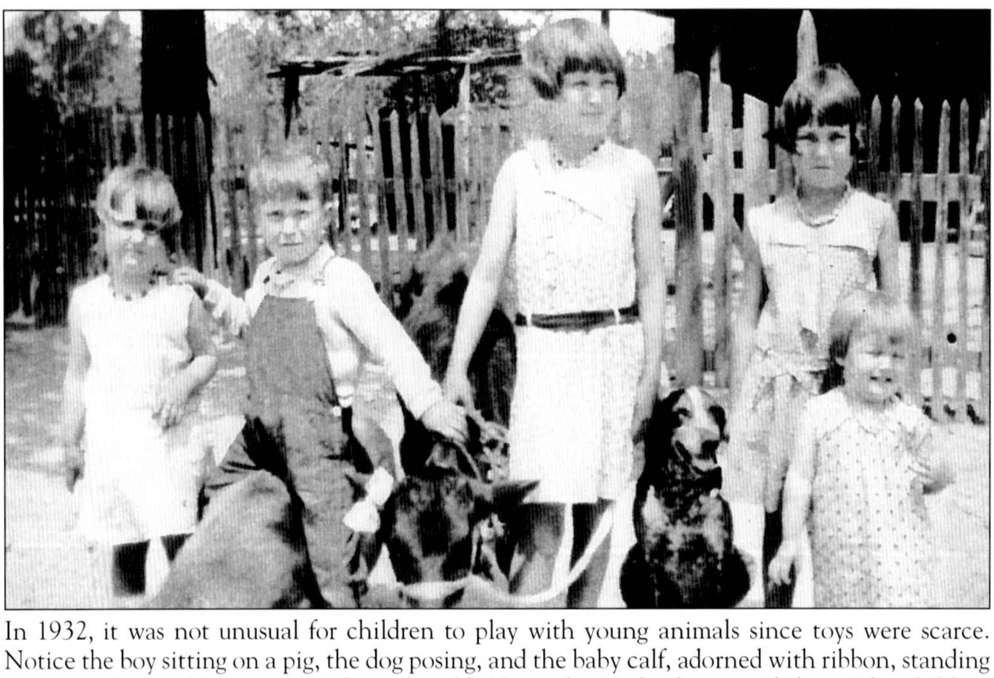

In 1932, it was not unusual for children to play with young animals since toys were scarce. Notice the boy sitting on a pig, the dog posing, and the baby calf, adorned with ribbon, standing quite tamely for this picture made at the old Alexander Pugh place in Chilton. The children are, from left to right, as follows: Marjorie, Leonard, Lillian, Vera, and Katie Pugh.

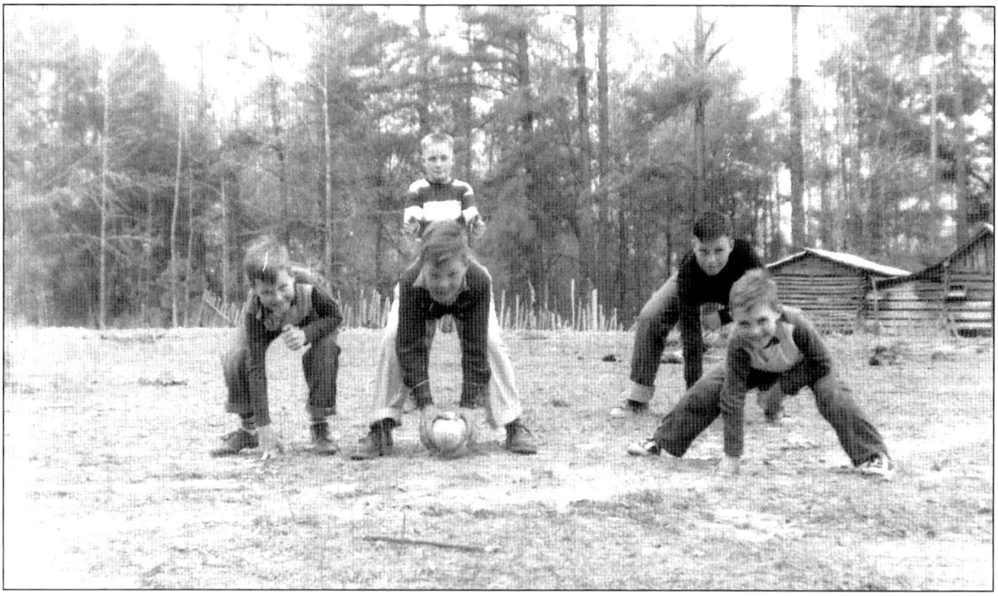

Country boys, a vacant field, and a football make for a great Sunday afternoon's fun. From left to right, Ray, Billy (with ball), Don (behind Billy), Roy, and Wendell (behind Roy) posed for this picture in 1952.

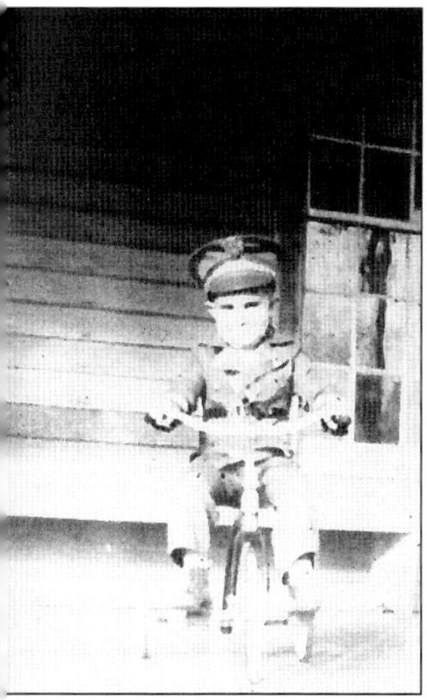

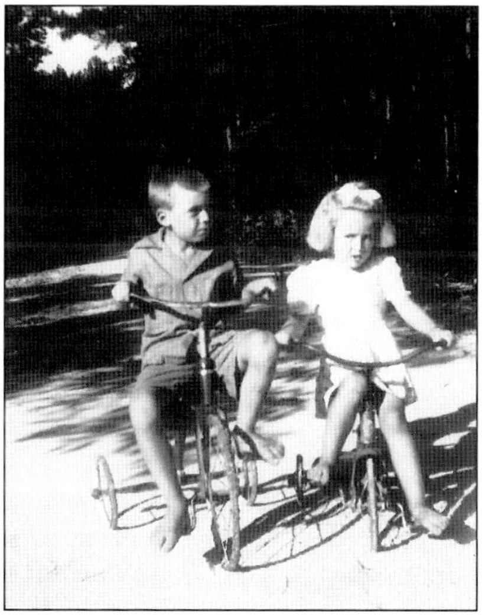

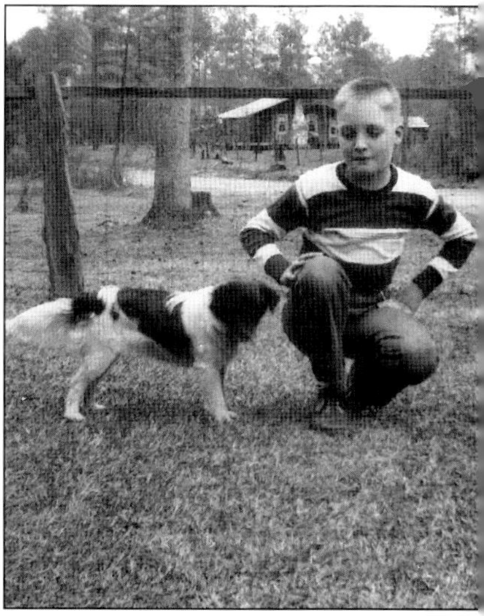

Left: During Christmas 1942, children's clothes and toys had the overtones of the war which was raging in Europe. Mac Huggins is a model soldier.
Center: About 1942, when things were tense and everyone was troubled by the war news, tricycles, summertime, going barefoot, and the wide, dirt road with almost no traffic made life seem normal. Joyce and Melvin are riding in front of Mama and Papa Pugh's house in Chilton.
Right: This picture of the view from Don White's front yard has changed considerably. The Chilton Country Store sits exactly where the boy and dog are romping on the grass. The photograph was taken around 1950 or 1951.

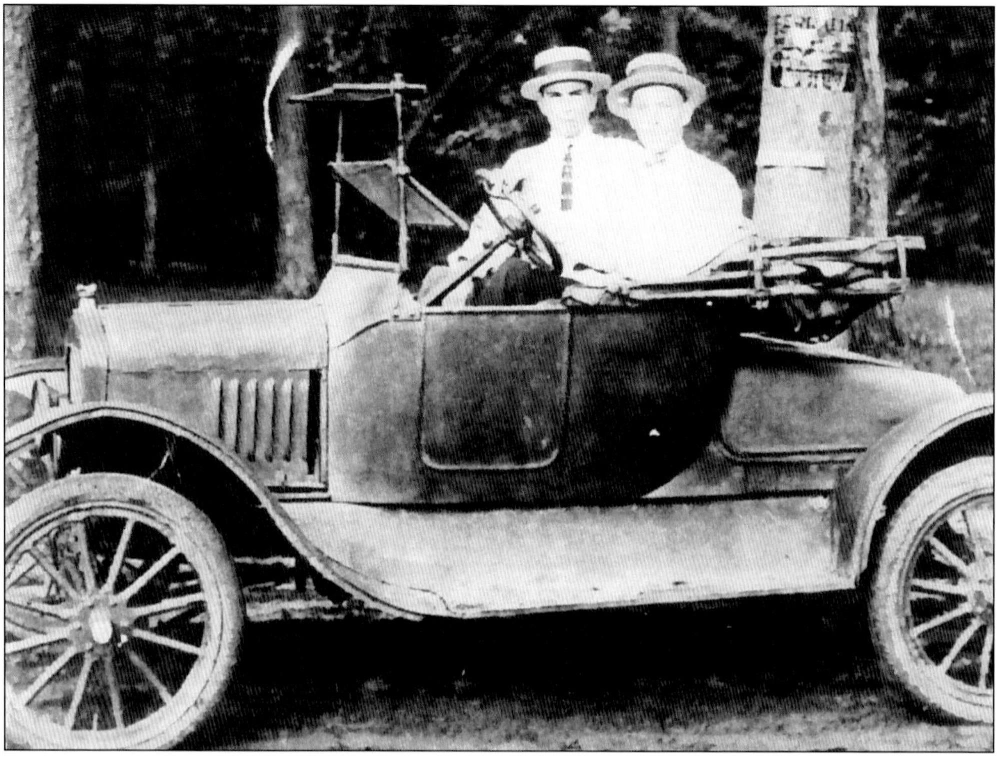

Two good friends stopped long enough for this picture near the entrance to the campgrounds at Dixons Mill in 1925. Johnny Wood and Luther W. Cogle, seen here in the newest car model available, foretell of the interest the Cogle family will have in cars. Bruce Cogle Jr. sponsored sprint and midget racing cars from 1970 to 1979. Cogle owned the Ford dealership in Thomasville for years.

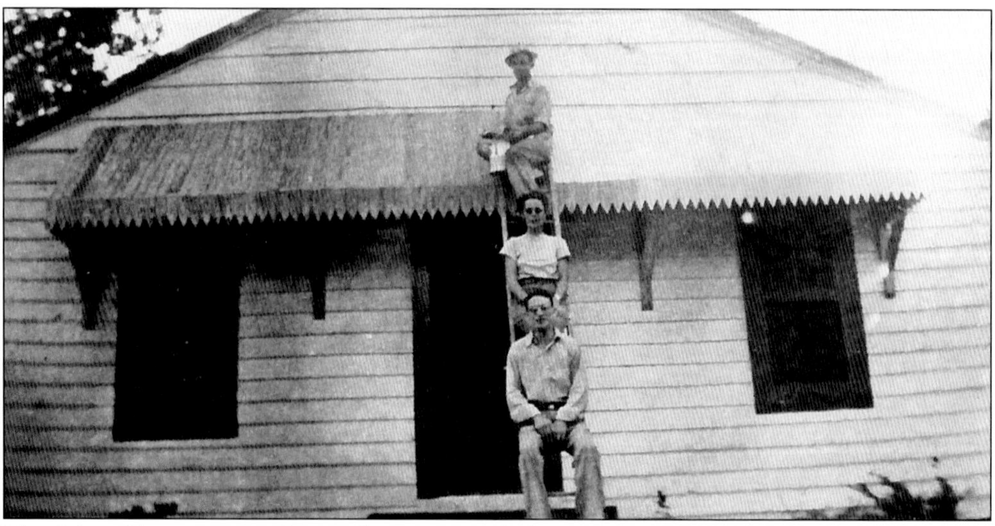

The Silver Slipper, a popular roadhouse, provided recreational entertainment. It was located north of Thomasville on Old Highway 5. Excellent orchestra music provided the type of music that was popular in the Big Band era of the 1930s and 1940s. A Rockola, a kind of jukebox, was inside to provide music when the orchestra was not present for the dancing.

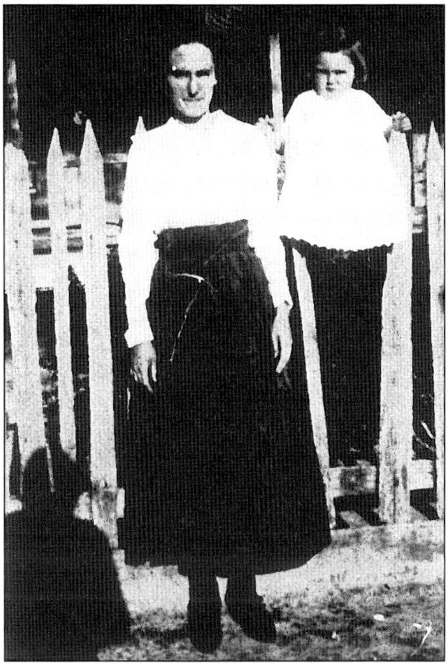

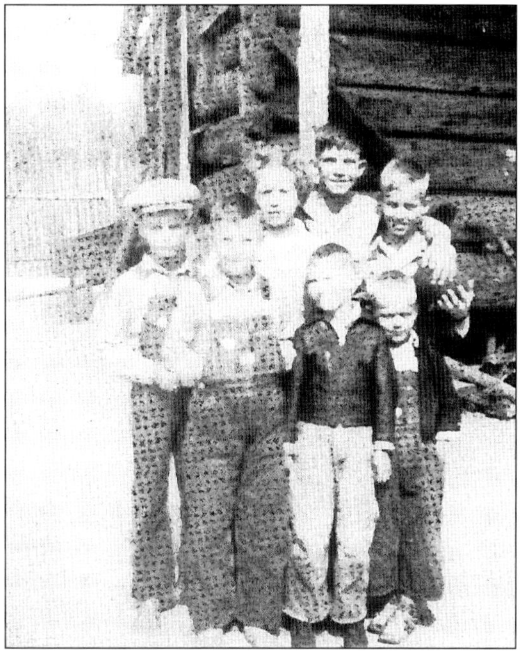

Left: The old, dog-trot house in the background was the George Hare home in Chilton. The palen fence, typical of country dwellings, was the perfect spot for Louise when her mother, Katie Hare Pugh, brought her home to visit. She is seen here with her grandparents, Frances and George Hare, in 1917.
Right: This is the only photograph of the old Ennis White log home in Chilton thought to exist. The "gang" in 1937, when this picture was made, knew little of grass yards. Note the clean, sandy yard in front of the house, which sat to the right of the Charlie White home. Identified here are, from left to right, as follows: (front row) Kimbrough and Freddie Roberts and Billy Gibbs; (back row) Reuben Harrison, Willie Mae White, Elvin White, and Jessie Gray Gibbs.

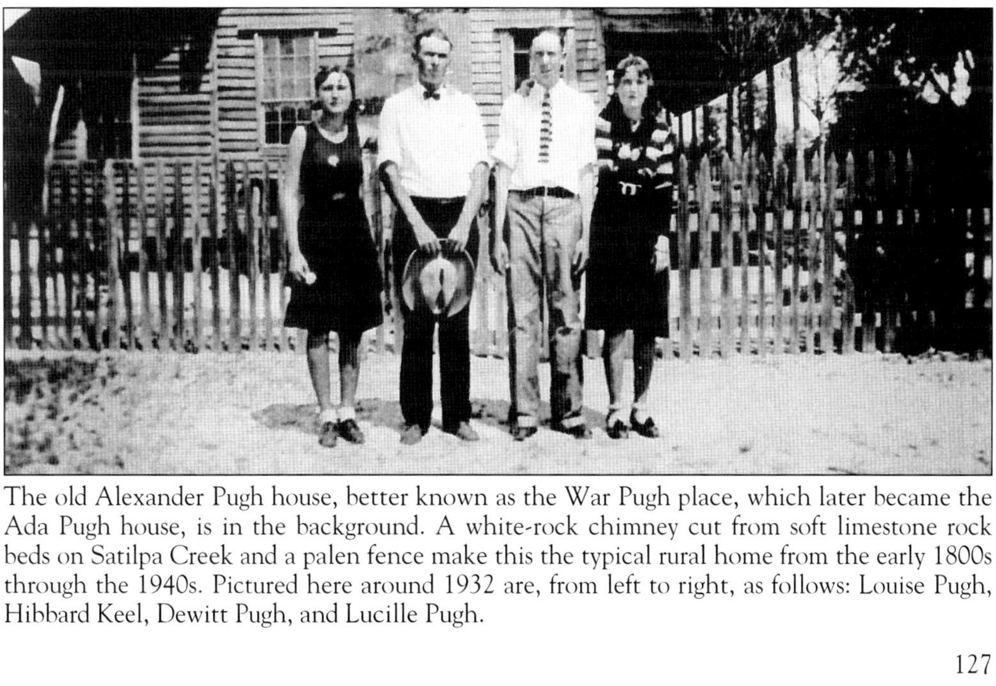

The old Alexander Pugh house, better known as the War Pugh place, which later became the Ada Pugh house, is in the background. A white-rock chimney cut from soft limestone rock beds on Satilpa Creek and a palen fence make this the typical rural home from the early 1800s through the 1940s. Pictured here around 1932 are, from left to right, as follows: Louise Pugh, Hibbard Keel, Dewitt Pugh, and Lucille Pugh.

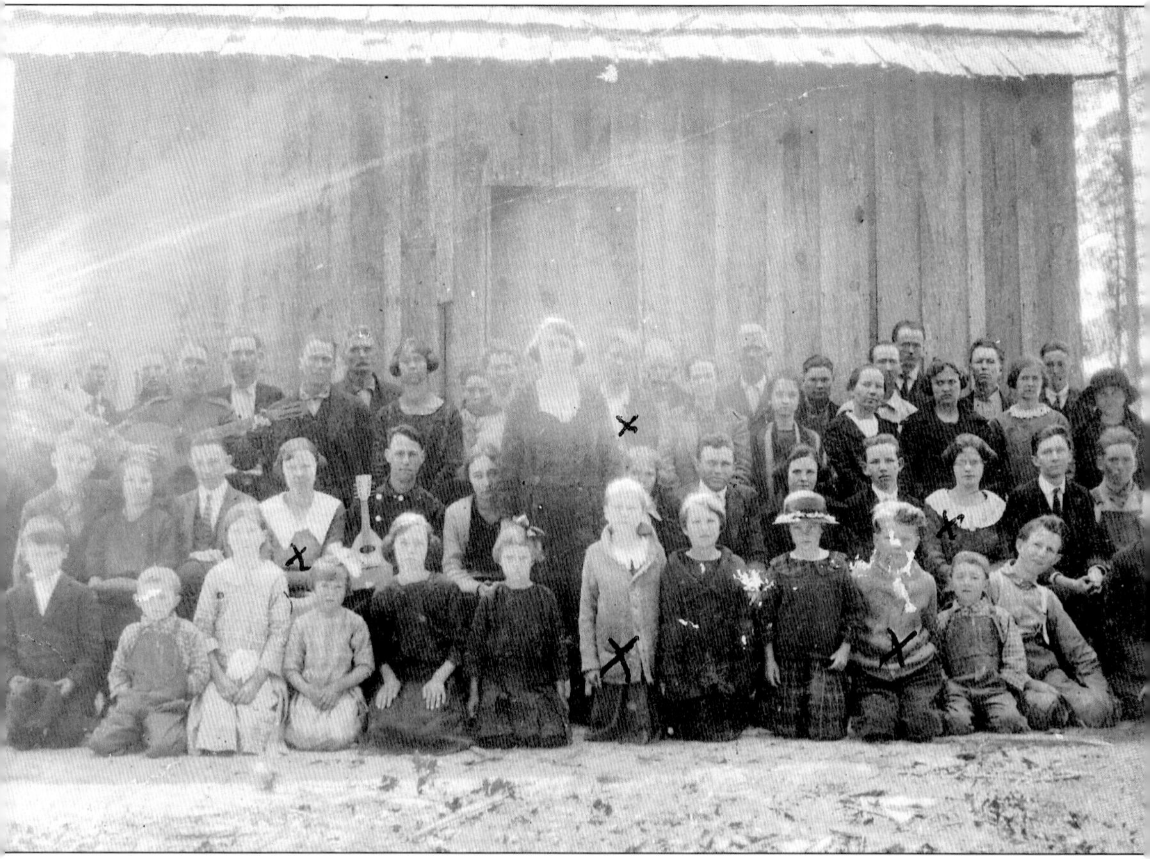

Bedsole School, near Bedsole's Store in the Bedsole community (or more properly called McEntyre or Mitcham Beat), was the scene of a gathering of parents and children. This is the second Bedsole School; the first one, located west of Wes Bedsole's Store, burned down. The third Bedsole School is still standing and was built as close to the one in the picture as was possible. This is a typical example of a country people's gathering for school business, maybe a dance, or even a church service such as a singing. The church and the school were the centers for socializing. The musicians seen here are as follows: Howell Hutto (fiddle), Ed Huggins (mandolin), and Jesse Huggins (guitar). Those seated on the ground include Essie Phillips, Claudie Phillips, Bealie Hutto, Nora Huggins, Lester Morgan, and others not identified.